Culture and Identity

Selected English Writings of

Faiz

Culture and Identity
Selected English Writings of

Faiz

Compiled and Edited by
Sheema Majeed

Introduction by
Muhammad Reza Kazimi

OXFORD
UNIVERSITY PRESS

OXFORD
UNIVERSITY PRESS

No. 38, Sector 15, Korangi Industrial Area, PO Box 8214,
Karachi-74900, Pakistan

Oxford University Press is a department of the University of Oxford.
It furthers the University's objective of excellence in research, scholarship,
and education by publishing worldwide in

Oxford New York

Auckland Cape Town Dar es Salaam Hong Kong Karachi
Kuala Lumpur Madrid Melbourne Mexico City Nairobi
New Delhi Shanghai Taipei Toronto

With offices in

Argentina Austria Brazil Chile Czech Republic France Greece
Guatemala Hungary Italy Japan Poland Portugal Singapore
South Korea Switzerland Turkey Ukraine Vietnam

Oxford is a registered trademark of Oxford University Press
in the UK and in certain other countries

Published in Pakistan by Oxford University Press, Karachi

ISBN 978-0-19-597995-4

Cover Design: K.B. Abro

Third Impression 2011

Typeset in Calisto MT
Printed in Pakistan by
Kagzi Printers, Karachi.
Published by
Ameena Saiyid, Oxford University Press
No. 38, Sector 15, Korangi Industrial Area, PO Box 8214,
Karachi-74900, Pakistan.

CONTENTS

Editor's Note   vii

Introduction   ix

Section I: Autobiographical

1. Faiz by Faiz   3
2. Impact of Prison Life on Imagery   21

Section II: Culture

3. The Quest for Identity in Culture   25
4. Cultural Problems in Underdeveloped Countries   33
5. Problems of Cultural Planning in Asia—With Special Reference to Pakistan   37
6. Cross-Cultural Encounter in East-West Literature— Brief Historical Background   49
7. What is the Role of International Exchange in Cultural Development?   62
8. Problems of National Art and Culture   79
9. What Would You Have?   120
10. Shackles of Colonialism   122

Section III: Art

11. The Concept of Beauty   127
12. The Unicorn and the Dancing Girl   129
13. The World of Sadequain   133

Section IV: Literature

14. The Literary Heritage of Pakistan   137
15. The Legacy of Literature   149
16. Khusrau: Catalyst for Social Change   153

17. Mirza Asadullah Khan Ghalib (1797-1869)   156
18. Mohammad Iqbal   164
19. Iqbal—the Poet   171
20. Iqbal   178
21. Pakistan Modern Urdu Short Stories   184
22. Music Research Cell   186
23. Major Literary Questions   188
24. Moscow Film Festival   194
25. Visit to the Soviet Union   197
26. Homage to Tolstoy   200
27. Writers, Where do you Stand?   203
28. Poetry and Sense   206
29. Thoughts on the Future of *Ghazal*   212

Section V: Social

30. No Holiday from Virtue   219
31. Who was Tabata Sharra?   221
32. The Right to Own Women   225
33. Gentlemen vs. Players   228

Section VI: Political

34. Like a Vesture shalt Thou Change Them   235
35. Disgrace   239
36. Stalin's Peace Offer   241
37. Ghosts of Yesterday   243
38. Borrowed Feet   246
39. Indonesia Week   249
40. Pilgrimage to Washington   250
41. The Servants of the People   254
42. Sindh Hari Report   257

Chronology   259

EDITOR'S NOTE

Faiz Ahmed Faiz is among those persons who cannot be confined to one field. No doubt, he is essentially a poet but his is a multi-dimensional personality. Rather, it will be correct to say that he was a metaphor of his age. In order to observe different dimensions of his age, it is necessary to peer into the personality of Faiz.

This present collection explains and elucidates Faiz's views on different subjects. The purpose of this book is to present some facets of Faiz's personality to his admirers and readers.

Sheema Majeed

INTRODUCTION

Poetry is the most intimate cultural interest of the masses, therefore, most fittingly, poets have come forward to define and interpret their cultures; Amir Khusrau for Medieval India, T.S. Eliot for the English speaking world, and Faiz Ahmed Faiz for Pakistan. Literary criticism, by poets in some measure, turns out to be a justification of their own art, of the foundation of their reputation and the basis of their popularity. Faiz, in his lifetime enjoyed an enviable popularity at home and unprecedented esteem abroad. Faiz was at the pinnacle of fame as an Urdu poet, yet his concern with culture began when he noticed that Urdu was the mother tongue of a tiny minority in Pakistan: 'Hardly any child sulked in Urdu, hardly any mother sang lullabies in Urdu'.[1]

The dominance of Urdu over the indigenous languages of Pakistan was an anomaly which invited a complete reappraisal of Pakistani culture. The languages arraigned against Hindi in India far outnumber the regional languages of Pakistan, but Hindi has not been half as vulnerable, for though Hindi has on occasion been called a provincial language,[2] it has never been called an alien language. In his first foray into this debate, Faiz called history the length, geography the breadth, region, class and language the depth of culture.[3]

It is this third dimension which is most problematic, yet the most vital. For Faiz 'region is the most' authentic storehouse of what is distinctively Pakistani' (p. 45). More telling is Faiz's observation, that 'if the creative potentialities of our regional art and culture are allowed to wilt and die, we shall soon find ourselves with nothing to synthesise' (p. 92). His definition of national culture, thus allows for a synthesis: 'It is an aggregate of regional cultures, plus the unifying bonds of faith and history' (p. 91). Now, whether Urdu is one of the unifying bonds, Faiz does not say.

As distinct from our national culture, Faiz has a definition of culture which is general: 'Culture is the whole way of life, of a given human community' (p. 37). He further clarifies this point by referring to two categories. First comes the cultural *medium* which consists of language, manners, the idioms and the forms of artistic expression. Second comes cultural *substance* which includes value patterns, ideologies and institutionalized ideas. Faiz has two other corresponding terms. External formal aspects and inner ideological aspects. Faiz maintains that both are components of a given social structure. Under another heading, Faiz explains that the external forms of culture, whether social or artistic, are basically an organized expression of its inner ideological content.

Since region is the basic unit of culture, Faiz relegates ideology to an internal content, and does not assign to it the role of a regimenting external. This is also the point where he makes a distinction between art and culture:

> Art, unlike culture, is not the raw material, or the social life, which exists independently of individuals, but a deliberate and superior manufacture created by a body of specialists (p. 82).

Elsewhere, culture itself is considered to be the behaviour of educated and informed sections of society. Nevertheless, Faiz views culture as reflecting mass participation because anything less would not let it realize its potential. In one of the most perceptive remarks ever made about the process of culture, Faiz points out:

> Even though culture cannot transcend the limitations of a given social structure, it can certainly lag behind it. (p. 40)

Among the reasons why a people cannot fulfil their cultural potential he lists the lack of state patronage, which is based on wrong priorities. More money is spent on golf links and ski resorts, the preserve of the plutocrats, than on the dissemination of national culture. Although ideologically Faiz is an opponent of the 'Arts for Arts sake' approach, he is not prepared to put bread ahead of art, arguing that culture, like education, counts as a basic factor in development. On the mundane level, he asserts that art can improve the quality of industrial production (p. 88). On the spiritual level, he defines the role of the artist as being imbued with all-round awareness. Through the medium of his art, he modifies the awareness of his audience:

> And this, in turn, is a measure of the extent he exchanges or modifies reality through his art. (p. 64)

Art, according to this view, can transform perception into substance. Some poetic licence is evident in this conclusion, because Faiz has stated that the purpose and function of the artist was to express the sentiments people felt, but could not articulate. It is through this attribute that artists become the exponents of national culture. Articulation is the province of language, and in our discussion of culture, we come back to language. Coming full circle, we find that Faiz defines the creative role of language quite differently from its cultural role:

> Language is more the colleague of the intellect than of feeling. If we use it to express feeling as in poetry, we must preserve it as an intermediary. (p. 209)

Coming from a lyrical poet, this conclusion is somewhat curious. When we reverse the creative process, we find that thoughts are much easier to analyse than emotions. Pure emotive expression would not require an intermediary; the expression of a novel idea would. Then again, how does one define an intermediary. As language; a simile, a metaphor or an image? If we scrutinise Faiz's own poetry under this rule, we find examples of both types. The first is a quatrain translated by Victor Kiernan:

> Last night your faded memory filled my heart
> Like spring's calm advent in the wilderness
> Like the soft desert footfalls of the breeze,
> Like peace somehow coming to one in sickness.[4]

This quatrain expresses a primary emotion, but the expression is through elaborate similes. In the last line 'somehow' (or in Kiernan's alternative translation 'without cause') is rendered too abstruse to remain a simile. Then there are two other quatrains where feelings defy expression:

> By going far, you are near
> When before, were you so near?
> Now you shall neither come, nor go
> How fused are meeting and parting.[5]

Here we find no similes for meeting or parting, and of course, the overriding sentiment is that of parting. Is the imaginative state an intermediary form of expression? Words are themselves a medium, but since Faiz divides this medium into primary and intermediary, we also have to categorize this medium. Let us now turn to the third and last example from Faiz:

> There is neither sight nor speech, nor word or message
> There is no pretence of satisfaction, and the longing is great
> Hope of the beloved, sight's disposition, the colour of pain
> Today do not ask anything, for my heart is sad.[6]

Let us focus on the third line. The abruptness, the scrambling, makes it abstract. Abstraction appeals in totality, and totality is primary, not intermediary. Moreover, Faiz knows, and who better, that eloquence can be as demanding of intermediaries as primaries. Since Faiz refers to Empson, he knows that ambiguity, in order to be eloquent, cannot be an intermediary construct.

II

After these theoretical musings on language, art and culture, let us view Faiz's practical criticism of the poets who have shaped our identity, Amir Khusrau, Ghalib and Iqbal. Amir Khusrau is briefly touched upon as a catalyst of change during the formative period of Indo-Muslim culture. Ghalib is chosen for being the last poet to represent this culture. Faiz points out that despite his innovations and individuality. Ghalib's greatness lies in representing his age. Faiz clearly states that Ghalib was not a philosopher or even a thinker but finds some depth because he possessed a transcendence of a negative nature; Ghalib's poetry is unified by a single mood, and acquires gravity because it is pervaded by an obtrusive pathos.

Faiz does not deny the status of philosopher to Iqbal, but in *Meezan* he clearly attributes Iqbal's greatness not to the philosophical but the emotional content of his poetry.[7] About all three poets, Faiz arrives at an estimate less effusive than the usual tone of Urdu criticism, but, for a number of reasons, it is on his estimate of Iqbal, that we tend to focus, the main reason being the evident affinities between Iqbal and Faiz. Both hailed from Sialkot, both had the same teacher, Mir Hasan, both were scholars of Arabic, both wrote in English, both served as college lecturers, and once, in Sialkot, Faiz had begun the proceedings of a function presided over by Iqbal, by reciting from the Quran.

Normally, such closeness would result in a subjective even adulatory attitude on the part of Faiz, but though his essays on Iqbal form the bulk of his literary criticism, as well as the core of his literary standards, his approach to Iqbal is, most properly, objective. Faiz freely charts the contradictions and confusions that he discovers in Iqbal's thought, but he explains that these existed because Iqbal authentically reflected the confusions and contradictions of his age. It is on this account that Iqbal deserves to be called the national poet in Pakistan. Here we find Faiz's cultural criticism and Ghalib's criticism converge. Pakistani culture suffers from anomalies and Ghalib was great for representing his age. Faiz resolves what he conceives to be contradictions in Iqbal's thought by explaining them to be the evolutionary steps of Iqbal's political outlook. This is perfectly correct, but what needs emphasis, is that Faiz's critique of Iqbal is equally evolutionary. Charting the course of Iqbal's poetry from his early poems, nature-poems, poems for children, poems projecting Indian nationalism, poems celebrating Pan-Islamism, he concentrates on Iqbal's final humanist stage:

At last he arrived at a theme big enough to fill the whole of his vision, the twin theme of Man's grandeur and his loneliness. (p. 169)

It was the constant complaint of Faiz that Urdu literary critics have concentrated on Iqbal's thought and message and have neglected his art, but when he came to say that Iqbal's theme began to suit his style, he also said that this was the point at which Iqbal's style underwent a change:

> To relieve the severity of his style, he introduced some completely new *devices* unknown to Urdu poetry. First a *very conscious* use of subtle sound patterns based on the Persian classics, second, the use of proper places and personal names, thirdly, by the use of unfamiliar metres and fourthly, by the usage of ancient classical words and expressions, unfamiliar without being ambiguous or obscure (pp. 182). ...I don't think that any poet in Urdu has used the patterns of consonantal and vowel sounds as *deliberately* as Iqbal has done. (p. 176) [Emphasis added].

Again, it is startling that a poet, himself so lyrical and fluent as Faiz, would focus on deliberate, conscious and contrived patterns in Iqbal's poetry. We are startled because, though a thought can be contrived successfully, a style cannot. His criticism becomes vague at this point, since it is not enlightening to be informed that Iqbal, a poet of Persian, derived sound patterns from the Persian classics. What needed to be focused on, was the subtlety he mentions. The use of ancient classical words and expressions would be sufficient to form a rhythm. The devise of using proper nouns, euphonically carrying, but single layered in meaning, would be superfluous. It goes without saying that the spacing of consonants and vowels cannot be consciously planned.

The elements of Iqbal's style which Faiz describes, are evident not as a contrivance but because of an elevation of Iqbal's theme. With all our reservations about Faiz's critique of Iqbal's style, we have to admit that it is in relation to Man's epic struggle in the universe that Faiz makes his most original comments on Iqbal. Man's struggle is great, because it is unending; but then comes the observation which is breathtaking in its impact:

There is very little talk of the hereafter in his poetry. There is no mention of any rewards or punishments in the other world...the hereafter in which there is no action, in which there is no struggle; is entirely irrelevant to his thought. (p. 176)

We can either let this tribute stand by itself, or read it alongside Faiz's contention that the basic state of Iqbal's emotion was impatience. The differences between Iqbal and Faiz ran deeper than their similarities. These begin to seep through where Faiz complains that Iqbal: 'frequently confused the materialist and the capitalist point of view' (p. 179). This brings home the fact that: Iqbal was a philosophical poet, while Faiz was an ideological poet; Iqbal was an epic poet, Faiz was a lyric poet, and more significantly, Iqbal was an exponent of civilization and Faiz was the exponent of culture. Civilization, according to Shireen T. Hunter, being an outward manifestation of culture.[8] One springs from religion, the other from region. The sum total of Faiz's literary encounter with Iqbal was, that far from finding Iqbal's poetry contrived, we find that even the literary criticism of Faiz was inspired, leading him to judgements he could not have intended to deliver. Urdu poetry could not have progressed had Faiz—in his essence—been subservient to Iqbal.

III

As we have said above, the political development of Faiz was also evolutionary. In his *Pakistan Times* editorials he was ready with invective. He called Khizr Hayat Khan 'a name that is synonymous with wilful national betrayal' (p. 243). Yet as Faiz himself recounts, he shocked his patriotic friends both in the 1965 and 1971 wars by poetically siding with the enemy (p. 15). There is nothing in the text of the poems, or in any independent account to reveal the real sentiments of Faiz during those trying times. This shows that the memoirs with which this volume begins, although very brief, are among the most revealing ever written. Also revealing is his account of his 1974 Moscow visit which coincided with India's first nuclear test; Faiz gave his impressions of his Russian hosts, the Indian envoy and the ambassador of Bangladesh:

> The same attitudes were developing in Bangladesh towards India as they previously harboured towards Pakistan, and the communal question was also worrying the Bangladesh Government. (p. 198)

Also in this volume we find the ideological strands of his literary criticism. In his essay 'Writers, Where do you Stand?' he pleads for writers to combat socially purposeless, intellectually superficial and similar traits smacking of mediocrity and hypocrisy. Faiz describes the model writer: 'He is committed to his country and his people'. In line with his ideological stand is the more artistic assessment of Lord Tennyson and Leo Tolstoy. He states frankly that the *Lady of Shallot* is superficial, the result of 'piling up poetical words without any organic connection' (p. 207). On the other hand, Tolstoy's greatest merit was 'divesting war of its aura of myth and legend, by debunking the glorification of its half-crazed heroes'. Tolstoy, he adds 'gave a new methodology of historical evaluation' (p. 202). From Tennyson to Tolstoy, from Khusrau to Iqbal, these essays cover a very wide range. This is natural, as they were written over a lifetime. In these pages, Faiz represents his age in the same fashion as he admires Ghalib and Iqbal for representing theirs. Sheema Majeed has performed a magnificent task by preserving what otherwise would surely have been lost.

Faiz's address at the Mir Anis death centennial, his lecture on the symphonic nature of Iqbal's long poems, the poems he recited during the 1977 crisis, all of which I heard and all of which is lost. None of the writings preserved here were responsible for establishing the reputation of Faiz. They have been retrieved twenty years after his death, yet they constitute an integral part of his personality and his art.

His Urdu essays are short, and some of them seem to end abruptly, but they impress because of his commitment, his confidence and because he probed those aspects of life and letters, which few critics even dared to approach. He was recognized as an important critic, independent of his status as a poet, as early as the 1940s, although his poetic profile even then, was high.

It was Faiz who gave a classical status to the modern western forms of Urdu poetry, and his solitary English poem *The Unicorn and the Dancing Girl* (1961) displays a rare sensitivity to the discordant grooves of time and space:

Who is not even a unicorn
Is not even a legend
For even a legend is memory
And the memory is in time
But the Past is timeless....

This poem also provides an underpinning of human suffering on a different beat than his Urdu lyrics. This poem anticipates as none of his Urdu poems do, the dark and shadowy rhythm of N.M. Rashid's *Hasan the Potter*. Similarly these English essays which provide his critical acumen greater room for expression, constitute the real hinterland of his Urdu poetry. Any one reading this collection, will now find the Urdu poetry of Faiz Ahmed Faiz imbued with added meaning.

Muhammad Reza Kazimi
25 August 2004

NOTES

1. Faiz Ahmed Faiz, *Meezan,* Lahore: Minhas, February 1962, p. 104.
2. For example N.V. Gadgil in Indian Parliament, 13 September 1949, cited in Prem Nath Bazaz, *The History of the Struggle for Freedom in Kashmir,* New Delhi: Kashmir Publishing Co., 1954, p. 348.
3. Faiz, op. cit., p. 95.
4. Victor Kiernan, (Tr. and Ed.) *Poems By Faiz,* Karachi: Oxford University Press, 1973, p. 49.

5. My translation:

دور جا کر قریب ہو جتنے
کب مرے تم قریب تھے اتنے
اب نہ آؤ گے تم نہ جاؤ گے
وصل و ہجراں بہم ہوئے کتنے

نہ دید ہے نہ سخن حرف ہے نہ پیام
کوئی حیلۂ تسکیں نہیں اور آس بہت ہے
امید یار، نظر کا مزاج، درد کا رنگ
تم آج کچھ بھی نہ پوچھو کہ دل اداس بہت ہے

6. Ibid.
7. Faiz, op. cit., p. 256.
8. Shireen T. Hunter, *The Future of Islam and the West*, Westport, Praeger, 1995, p. 8.

Section I
AUTOBIOGRAPHICAL

1

FAIZ BY FAIZ[1]

Thank you very much for inviting me over, I asked Pasha what he wanted me to talk about. He said, 'about yourself and what you have been up to'. In a way, that came as a relief, which means I did not have to prepare a discourse. At the same time, I found it disconcerting for two reasons: firstly, because it is quite some years since I arrived at the age of what Disraeli calls 'the age of anecdotes'; and, secondly, because I have been such a long time in an unconscious frame of time, in living that I would not know, I am not so sure how I can cut a long story short.

I was born in the house of a gentleman who was a nineteenth century adventurer, who had a far more colourful life than I have had. He was born in the house of a landless peasant in a small village, in our Sialkot district. And, according to the story he told us, (which of course had been authenticated by other members of the village) because his father was a landless peasant, so he was employed by the people who had some land to tend their cattle. So he said, 'I used to take the cattle out of the village, and I found there was a school, little distance from the village. I would leave the cattle to graze and attend the school'. Thus, he passed his primary. Then he said 'there is no further education in my village, so I ran away to Lahore'. There he lived in a mosque and he said that 'in the evening I used to go to the railway station and work as a coolie. During the day, I would study. And in every mosque in our days (unfortunately, it is one of the customs which has died out) every mosque served as a house for indigent students, and food was provided by people of the area, and education was provided by the priest in the mosque itself or somebody, and got free education.

When he was living in this mosque, it so happened that an Afghan grandee was counsel to the Government of the Punjab. He used to come and pray in this mosque. He saw this young boy and he rather liked him and he said 'Look, we want an English interpreter for Afghanistan'. This was the time of the grandfather of the ruler of Afghanistan, before Nadir Shah, because after every one or two three years, one dynasty was overthrown and another dynasty came into power. The dynasty which was overthrown in 1924–25 was that of Amanullah Khan, his grandfather was the king at that time. Anyway, this King wanted an English interpreter, because this was the time when the Durand Treaty was being negotiated between the British and the Afghans. So this Afghan diplomat said, 'would you like to go to Afghanistan?' My father said, 'Why not. I have nothing else to do'. The king employed him firstly as interpreter and then he negotiated with the British. Later on, he became his chief secretary then his minister, and so on and so forth. There were a number of tribes which were conquered during his period and every time a tribe's area was taken, the princesses of the vanquished tribe were distributed among the courtiers. So my father got his share of my stepmothers (I don't know how many—three or four).

Anyway, after spending about fifteen years in the service of the king, he got fed up because he was an outsider and naturally all the ministers and grandees of the court were feudal. So they got resentful of this man encroaching on their preserve. He said that he was often denounced as a British spy and every time he was sentenced to death, it was discovered that the charge was false and then he got a promotion. So he thought, 'one day they might carry it (death sentence) out'. So he disguised himself as a beggar and escaped, came to Lahore and was promptly arrested there as an Afghan spy!

There was an Englishwoman, an adventurer like him, who had descended on the court as a doctor. Her name was Dr Hamilton and they became friends. The various bounties that he got from the king, this woman was wise enough to take a part of it and invest it in London. So when he was thrown out, she wrote to him from England and said, 'Come to London'. So he went to London and joined Cambridge University and the king seeing that he had escaped said, 'Well, since you are in London, why don't you become my ambassador?' So he was both a student at Cambridge and then he joined the Bar and did his law degree and at the same time he was an ambassador. In Persian there is a saying, if anyone wants to boast about his father he says 'my father was king', the word for king being, Sultan. Now my father's name was Sultan, so I can say my father was Sultan!

Anyway, after getting his law degree, instead of going back to Afghanistan he landed up in his own town, or rather his own district, which is Sialkot. And when the king found out that he had left, he sent his family to Sialkot—my stepsisters and maybe also a stepmother or two. Now there is a novel about him called 'Daughter' something.[2] It is out of print, but perhaps you can find it in some old library, written by this Englishwoman. So, he came back and started law practice. Once my stepmother died, he married my mother from the next village. My mother and stepsisters were thus more or less the same age; the elder sister was older than she was.

We went to school in Sialkot; I got my first schooling in the mosque, a mosque in our locality. There were two schools in the town, one belonged to the Scotch Mission, and the other belonged to the American Mission. I went to the Scotch Mission because it was near the house. Later on, the American mission packed up. This period—the end of the First World War and the beginning of the 1920s was a period of great upheaval in India. There were various nationalist movements belonging to all the three communities. The Congress movement had both Hindus and Muslims in its leadership, but the rank and file were largely Hindus. There was the Khilafat Movement of the Muslims, the Muslims being romantic people. This was the time after the First World War and the Turks had been defeated and the Ottoman Empire was disintegrating and the Turks were fighting against both the British and the Greek invaders. The Muslims of India, started a movement to see the Caliph, whom they had never seen, never known who was somewhere in Turkey. They could not save him because he was thrown out by Kamal Ataturk, the founder of modern Turkey. The Sikhs started the Akali movement to assume the caretakership of the Sikh shrines. So all the three, the Muslims, the Hindus, and the Sikhs, for a short period of about 6-7 years, made common cause against the British and there was great upheaval all over the country. In our small town Sialkot, great leaders, Mahatma Gandhi and Nehru's father[3] and the leaders of the Sikhs, whenever they came to the town, the whole city was decorated, flower gates were set up and the whole city turned out to welcome them. That is how one imbibed; one got the first whiff of politics during those very eventful years.

At the same time, the October Revolution had taken place. News of that event also filtered down into Sialkot. I heard people talking 'Look, we have heard that in this country called Russia, somebody called Lenin has overthrown the king and he has distributed the wealth of all the people among the workers. Suppose you rob a banker and distribute his wealth, it would be great fun!'

Anyway, that what was going on in our early schooldays. In school, I got inducted into poetry in two ways. Firstly, next to our house was a small bookshop run by a young man who lent books— rented them out at 2 pice a book a week. So I borrowed all the books that he had. All my pocket money was spent on reading these books. I had read all the classics by the time I got into high school. Secondly, in this town, there was already the great name of the great Poet; Iqbal was born in the same town and therefore his poems were recited and sung in the common current. And, thirdly, in a big mansion next to our house which during the day was a primary school where I studied and in the evenings, once a month it became the venue of what we call a *mushaira*.[4] When I was in my last year in school, our headmaster said, 'Look, I am going to have a competition. I will compose five or six couplets from this line and we will send these couplets to the great scholar of the town (who was a teacher of the great poet Iqbal) and he will decide who wins the prize.' I won the prize. The prize was one rupee, which was a fortune in those days.

After finishing my two years at Sialkot, I went to Lahore, to Government College. Now coming from a small town like Sialkot into Lahore was just like going into a foreign country. Because at that time, there was no running water in the town (Sialkot), there was no electricity. Water was brought to the house by water carriers or if they did not come, you had to fetch water from the well. Every locality had its own well, and some of the big houses had their own wells. There was no electricity; we read by kerosene oil lamps which are very interesting, very picturesque lamps. There were no cars in Sialkot. Even the head of the district, the Deputy Commissioner, used to come in a horse driven carriage. And he had a one-horse carriage while my father had two horse carriages.

Anyway, I came to Lahore; here for the first time we saw cars and we saw people in those wonderful dresses and we saw young women going about without veils. And in this college half the teachers were English, unlike our college in Sialkot, and everything was out of this world. At the very first examination that I took in college, my English teacher was an old man called Langhorn, extremely bad-tempered, but a very good teacher. In my first English paper I got a mere 63 marks out of 150. So everybody hung his head and I immediately became a celebrity. The senior scholars, the Muslim scholars, who later on became high civil officials in Pakistan, said: 'Look, start preparing for the Indian Civil Service examination.' I said 'all right'. But at that time instead of preparing for the Indian Civil Service examination, I started gradually becoming a poet. Two or three things determined that. First of all, the trial; before I finished my first degree, my father died and I suddenly discovered that from grandees and rich men of the town, we became paupers. He had left some property—some landed property—but he had left bigger debts than the property. That was one factor that had great impact on myself and my family. Secondly, suddenly came the Great Depression. As a result, the prices of agricultural produce went below rock bottom. The countryside became very impoverished and the little income we had from land also stopped. The Great Depression had a great impact politically and personally, not only on myself, but also on whole communities, particularly of the Muslims. They were mainly an agricultural community and they depended entirely for a living on what the land brought and the land brought hardly anything. So in there was no employment because there were hardly any industries. Whatever industries were there, belonged to non-Muslims

The third avenue of employment was Government service. And there again the Muslims, who were educationally backward, could not really find jobs. So, politically and personally, this was a period of great hardship for the family. On top of it all there was one thing which created the impulse and the motivation for expressing this ordeal into poetry, I fell in love as everybody does at that age—17 or 18, I fell in love with an old playmate of mine, an Afghan girl, whose family had come from Afghanistan at the same time as my father. When we were children, their family left Sialkot and she went into purdah (seclusion) when she was 12 or 13 and I had not seen her since childhood. They settled in a village near what I know as Faisalabad and my sister was married in that town. So I went to this village to see this family and there, one morning, I woke up, I saw a very beautiful girl feeding the parrot. She looked at me and I looked at her and then we promptly fell in love; rather, I did. As was the custom, we sort of secretly held hands, but that's as far as we could go. But the next day she was married off to some rich landlord. She went there the first time as a girl. When she came back, I never met her again. So we lived unhappily ever afterwards— for eight years. By this time, I was doing my education and I think after reciting at my third *mushaira*, I was acknowledged as a writer or as a poet. Then in the town of Lahore, the great writers, my senior writers who were my teachers, well, they adopted me, as one of their protégées, and so I became a poet.

This was the period of the first terrorist movement in the subcontinent. These terrorists had also infiltrated our college and one of the members was a bosom pal of mine, who later on became a great music composer, Khwaja Khurshid Anwar. He was arrested stealing acid from the college laboratory to make a bomb and was sentenced for three years, some of which he served. Then they let him go because his father was a big man. I got to know things through him, he used to leave his illegal literature in my room in the hostel. Sometimes, when I flipped through it, I felt very frightened, because my father was a titled person, acknowledged as one of the well wishers of the British Empire. That is how I got to know terrorism and some of the phraseology of revolutionaries.

That must have rubbed off on me, but I did not take much notice of it.

After three or four years, I finished my degree. I first got a Master's degree in English, then I got a degree in Arabic and then I started teaching and that was the time when I got over this period of great hardship and my brother got a job and the family was slightly better off.

During this period, my colleagues in college, two people who had come back from Oxford had become Marxists, and they introduced me to Marxism. Later on, a whole bunch of young men returned from British universities all belonging to rich or aristocratic families and all communists. Some of them stayed communist, others after dabbling in it for a few years, took on various jobs. Anyway, they came back and they started a literary movement which was called the Progressive Writers Movement. It was not a communist or a Marxist movement as such, although many of the office holders belonged to this group, but it was a sort of realistic movement. Because previously during the classical period and the period afterwards, our poetry and our literature was very largely given up to legends and fanciful tales and romanticizing and poetry of very largely linguistic gymnastics. During this period, a genuine lyrical political poetry was born.

At the same time during the 1930s, the great antifascist movement rose and the literary movements both in Europe and in America turned to literature of social comment. We got directly influenced by the movement and that is how between 1932 and 1935, I got involved in this political-cum-literary movement. Secondly, in trade unions and workers, peasants movements and thirdly, by creating a new style that was an amalgam both of lyricism and of politics, of classicism and modernism and that appealed to the people. When my first book came out in 1941, it was an immediate best-seller. Then came the war. First of all, we did not care much about the war. We thought this was something concerned with the British and the Germans, but in 1941, the Japanese entered the war. On the one hand, the Japanese came to the borders of India and on the other hand, the Nazis and the Fascists, came to the doorsteps of Moscow and Leningrad. We felt it was time to go and join the fight, so we joined the army. I joined the army and I remember my first day when I was produced before the Public Relations Department. He was not a regular soldier; he was really a journalist from the *London Times* (onwards to *London Times*, a very jovial Irishman). He said: 'look, I have your police report. It says you are an advanced communist. Are you?' I said, 'I don't know what retarded communist is.' So he said, 'I do not care, you may even be a Fascist, so long as you do not let us down. You won't let us down?' I said 'No'.

This was the time when on the one hand, the British and the Allies were not having a good time during the war. On the other hand, Mahatma Gandhi had started his 'Quit India' movement and that movement spread like wildfire. So the British had two problems on their hands: recruiting people for the Army and at the same time fighting this great movement against the British Raj.

The brigadier started talking to me about this movement. He said, 'What line do we take on this movement so far as the Indian troops are concerned?' I said, 'We take no line at all.' He said, 'What do you mean?' I said, 'What I mean, the line you take is, you are not fighting for the British, you are not fighting for what we call the salt,[5] but you're fighting for your country, because now your country is in danger because the Japanese are on the brink and the British will walk out after two to three years because they've been fighting here for so long. If the Japanese or the Germans come, that means you will be slaves for a hundred or two hundred years. So we have to defend our land—you are not fighting for the British, you're fighting for India'.

He said, 'My boy, but that's politics, how do we make it acceptable to the army? How do I put it across to the army?' I said, 'Put it across the same way the communists do'. He said, 'What do you mean?' I said, 'We make a cell, a proper kind of cell in every unit of the army and through this cell we teach first the officers what is Fascism, what the Japanese are doing, what the Italians are doing. Then we ask them, because our soldiers are not very literate, so you can only teach them by word of mouth. So first we will teach the teachers, we teach them about Fascism, the Japanese, etc., etc., then they teach the men and we form these groups.' After a great deal of controversy, it went to the Viceroy, it went to the Commander-in-Chief, and it went to the India Office. He said, 'Write it down'. I wrote down the scheme. Finally, it was approved. We started these groups; they were called *Josh* Groups. *Josh* means fervour, enthusiasm, and élan. So these groups were formed. They were very successful and that is how I got my Order of the British Empire.

And through various ways I became a colonel in three years. This was the highest rank you could attain as an Indian at that time. During this period, firstly, I came to know the army; secondly, I came to know the British; and thirdly, I could not write much poetry but I learned journalism, because I was in charge of the entire publicity for the entire Indian Army on all the fronts and I became more or less the Political Commissioner of the Indian Army. The war ended, and then I left the army and I had the option of either going into the Foreign Service or into the Civil Service. 'Well', I said, 'nothing doing'.

That was a time when the movement for Pakistan and the movement of the Indian Congress were at their height. An old friend of mine—big landlord—who was previously the President of the Punjab Congress party, moved over to the Muslim League and he said, 'look to hell with Foreign Service and Civil Service, we want to start a daily in Lahore. You come and edit this paper.' So in January 1947, I came to Lahore and started *The Pakistan Times*. I edited it for four years. At the same time, I became Vice President of the Pakistan Trade Union. At the same time in 1948, after Hiroshima and Nagasaki, the Korean War started. We got an appeal from Stockholm that we should start a peace movement. So we made a peace committee. I was in charge of Trade Unions; I was in charge of *The Pakistan Times*. Those were very, very satisfying days for four years. This is when I first went to Europe, as a workers' delegate to the International Labour Organization. I attended their meetings, first in San Francisco and then twice in Geneva. This was the first time I was introduced to America and Europe.

From 'Pindi Conspiracy' To Beirut

Then at the end of 1950, I met an old friend of mine from the army who had been appointed Chief of General Staff, General Akbar Khan. He had distinguished himself as a soldier in Burma and then, during the fighting in Kashmir. I met him by chance in Murree, where I was holidaying for ten days and he said to me, 'Look, we people in the army, particularly we who fought in Kashmir are very disgruntled because this country is going to the dogs. We have made no constitution for four years, there is so much corruption, there is so much nepotism, no elections are being held ... and there is no hope and we want to do something.' I said, 'Do what?' He said, 'Overthrow the government and we want to have a non-party government and have elections and a constitution...' and this that and the other. I said, 'All right!' He said, 'Well, we want your advice.' I said, 'Well this is an army exercise, I can't give you any advice.' He said, 'Anyway, you come to our meeting and listen to my plan.'

Then, in a very stupid way, I went to his meeting along with two civilian friends and we listened to this plan. The plan was to occupy the Presidential House, occupy the radio station—of course, there was no TV then—and make the President announce that the government was overthrown and a non-party government had been formed and a new constitution would be promulgated in six months and new elections would be held and then there were to be social reforms, etc. This was discussed for about five or six hours and eventually—there were about fourteen or sixteen officers there— eventually, they decided after a good deal of discussion that it was not on, for the simple reason that there was no issue before the country on which you could mobilize the people and, secondly, suppose the thing was discovered before it went off. Besides, it was too risky. So it was decided that nothing should be done.

However, somebody got cold feet—this was the first Pakistani government under the Prime Ministership of Liaquat Ali Khan. They got really jittery and by this time, I had forgotten all about it. Nothing had happened, you see, nothing was going to be done. Suddenly, one fine morning at about four o'clock, I found my house surrounded by soldiers. Somebody came up and said, 'Come along'. I said, 'What has happened?' He said, 'You are under arrest'. I said, 'What for?' He said, 'I do not know what for, but this comes from the Governor-General himself.' I said, 'We have not done any thing, we do not know what it is all about'. We discovered later. For four months, I was in solitary confinement; I do not know what had happened until after four months. A special Act was passed by the Constituent Assembly; it was called the Rawalpindi Conspiracy Act. Then we were brought to trial, a secret trial under this Act, which was passed only for this particular case. The conspiracy law from the British days was bad enough, you did not have to do anything, if it was proved that two people had agreed to break the law, it became a conspiracy, and if a third person deposed that he had witnessed these two people agreeing, that was enough. No power to act was necessary; this was all that was necessary under the British law. The government thought that this was not good enough, so they made a special Act abolishing whatever safeguards were open to the Defence, and in this Act, there was really no escape from conviction. It was a long trial lasting for about a year and a half—the game of defence. Finally, we were all sentenced to various terms of imprisonment according to rank: the general got ten years, the brigadier got seven years, a colonel got six years. We, as civilians, had the lowest sentences—we got four years.

This was the period of my imprisonment, which was, in some ways, very productive because I had no amusements. I had plenty of time to read and one felt angry all the time because one knew one was innocent. So during these four years, I wrote two books of poetry. My first book had come out in 1941 and sold out immediately. These two books came out—one while I was still in prison, the second, when I came out of prison. When you have been in prison for four years and you have been in solitary confinement, it naturally adds to your market value a great deal. So when I came out, I found myself an even greater celebrity than before. I went back to my newspapers, another three or four years I worked for the same papers, continued with the Peace Movement. The trade union movement in the meantime had been destroyed because all the Left organizations had been banned. This lasted for three to four years, and then came the first Martial Law and the first Army government and that was the first march to prison without any charge. The funny thing was that the government at that time—the Martial Law Government—rounded up everyone whose name appeared on police files from 1920 onwards!

So in the prison we found people ninety years old, eighty years old, many of them were off their nut, some had died of tuberculosis or something. After four or five months, we had a wonderful judge—everyone who applied for habeas corpus was let out. This was the time when I spent a month and a half in the Lahore Fort, the famous urban concentration place. After four or five months, I was released. So I thought I will go back to my newspapers. Three days after I was released, I went to my office and I found the place was surrounded with police. I said, 'What happened?' They said, 'It has been taken over.' All these newspapers had been confiscated, they had all been taken over by the Military government and that was the end of my journalism. I said, 'What do I do now?' After a short period, since I had friends in high places because of poetry, they said, 'What about doing some culture.' I said, 'Very good.' So I founded the Arts Council in Lahore, and even this was in a broken down old building, not the very impressive thing that you see today, the place caught on—exhibitions and concerts and plays, and so on and so forth.

We had funds for three or four years. I fell sick after three or four years of running this place. I had my first heart attack, and during my heart attack, I got the news that I had been given the International Lenin Prize. Somebody phoned me from the newspaper office, 'You have been given the Lenin Prize.' I said, 'Shut up!' I said, 'Look, I am sick and you are joking.' He said, 'No, no, this is no joke it is on our teleprinter. It said you and Picasso and this that and the other person.'

So when I got over my sickness, I was invited to Moscow to get my prize and also to get my treatment. From Moscow I went to London, spent two years in London, came back. Instead of coming to Lahore, we stayed in Karachi for eight years, because the Haroon family, (your present Minister of the Interior Mahmood Haroon's family) knew me. His sister was a friend of mine who was a doctor and she said, 'Look, we have a charitable Foundation. There is a school, there is a hospital, there is an orphanage and if you have nothing better to do, why don't you take over the Foundation and administer the funds, because my sons have no time, they are busy in their business and their politics,' I went and looked at the place. It was right in the slums and this was the centre of the drug peddlers, the camel drivers, the fishermen, and cut-throats. I said, 'Very nice very picturesque.' We made the school into a college, we set up a technical institute, we had a public hall, and we organized the orphanage.

So for eight years I returned to teaching and administration and then came back. In between there were two wars, the 1965 war with India and the 1971 war in Bangladesh. These two were difficult periods for me because I was under a great deal of pressure to write war songs, but I said, 'Look here, I am not writing any war songs!' They said, 'Well, why not? It is your patriotic duty.' I said, 'Look, firstly, because I consider these wars to be a very wanton waste of precious lives and secondly, because I know that Pakistan is not going to get anything out of either this war or that war. I am not going to write any war songs.' But I did write poems about both wars. In the first war, I wrote two poems, one was called 'Black-out' and the theme was that it is autumn with the lights—physical lights—which have gone out, the light of reason has gone out, the light of love has gone out, and all the lights in the hearts of people have gone out. And the second poem was an elegy for a fallen soldier and his mother mourning for her son. This infuriated my patriotic friends even more.

During the second war in Bangladesh, I wrote more than three or poems. One was 'The Festival of Bloodshed' and the second one was 'The Dust of Hatred in My Eyes' written from the point of view of Bangladesh. Well that naturally infuriated these people even more. So for a few days, I was obliged to go underground in Sindh and not to stay with the wrath of my patriotic friends. And then the war was over. Pakistan was dismembered.

Because of the elections, the military government was overthrown, and the Bhutto government—People's Party—came into power. I had known him (Bhutto) from the old days, first when he was foreign minister, then when he was leader of the opposition. So he sent for me, he said, 'What about joining us?' I said, 'And do what?' He said, 'Look, you have been doing this cultural business, now you do it on the national scale.' So I founded the National Council of the Arts, this PNCA that is here. I formed this and then I formed another institution with the humble name 'Folk Arts', which is now National Institute of Folk Heritage. I did this for about four years until the government changed. At the same time, I was writing, I wrote another three books; I wrote two or three books on prose, two or three books of poetry. By this time, I had been translated into English and French, Russian, all sorts of languages. And then, that government was overthrown and the present (Zia-ul-Haq) regime came in. They did not bother me, but so far as the cultural work was concerned, it was not precisely as it was before. Also, I thought I'd better do something else.

Now during this period, things had happened outside. The organization for which I had been contributing had taken shape—it was an organization of African and Asian writers called the Afro-Asian Writers Association. I had been working for them, attending their meetings and so on. Now they had their headquarters in Cairo from where they produced a magazine called *Lotus*. After the Camp David Agreement, the Arabs insisted that the office be moved from Cairo, shifted somewhere else. The Chief Editor of this magazine was also the Secretary General. He was shot in Cyprus. So there was nobody else to look after this magazine and no place for a new office. It was decided to set up a new office in Beirut and I was invited to take over this magazine. So I took over this magazine in Beirut worked for this organization for four years. And then, of course, we were thrown out.

I managed to slip through the blockade a month after the city was surrounded and then I came back here. And immediately I fell sick again after twenty years and well that is the end of the story.

I am sorry I have taken so long, but I could not make it any shorter! Now, the lady asked me whether I would recite some poems. I told her, 'I'll tell you a story.' The story is that when I joined the army, for sometime I was posted here in Rawalpindi, which was then the Headquarters of the Northern Command. Here in the garrison at the Northern Headquarters, I was the only Indian officer—the rest were all British. We had a party by one of the British officers. And a dear old lady said, 'I hear that you are a poet.' I said, 'Yes, I plead guilty to that.' She said, 'How nice! We hope that we'll listen to some poetry after dinner.' I said, 'I'm sorry, I write in Urdu, my language.' She said, 'Then why don't you write in English?' I said, 'Why should I write in English?' She said, 'isn't it so much easier?'

I am sorry, I do not have my English translations and there are—there is more than one English translation, but I think Pasha has been reading out somethings to you. Sorry I took so long, if there is anything else...

Question from audience: You mentioned falling in love, but you did not mention Alys. (Laughter from audience).

Faiz: That is right, I forgot! Well, you see, as I told you, that love lasted for seven or eight years. When I started teaching, one of my colleagues, whom I told you had come from Oxford and was a Marxist—so was his wife. He was also a very good writer. One day she asked me, 'Why are you looking so crestfallen? What's wrong?' I said, 'Well, look...' She said, 'You're in love and suffering from insomnia.' I said, 'to hell with it!' She said, 'You read this book!' So she gave me two or three books. She said, 'What is this small sorrow of yours? Look at the masses of India, they are hungry and they are suffering. What are your sufferings compared to theirs?' Then I stopped this love thing and began to think of bigger things. That is when I wrote my first poem, 'Don't Ask for More Love'. My colleague, the principal of this college I was working with, he had brought with him from England an Englishwoman as his wife and after two or three years, her sister came to see her on a visit to Amritsar, where I was teaching and I met this young lady and we became friends. Then came the War, so she could not go back. In fact, I had also booked my seat to join Cambridge, and so I could not go either. So we became friends and got married, that is where Alys comes in.

Question: Can I ask another personal question? Pasha did give Urdu translations of your poems. Many of them were based in Beirut. In that time, you were talking about, were you living in Beirut, or were you just... (Faiz interrupts)

Faiz: No, no I was living there all the time.

Question: And were you politically involved in Beirut?

Faiz: I was, indeed, yes! You had to be, if you were part of the suffering of the place and of the people.

Question: Were you attached to a faction?

Faiz: No, no particular faction, but mainly I was working with the Palestinians, who were the people who had been driven out of their homes, people who were suffering through no fault of their own. It was very strange that—actually somebody explained it to me why the Israelis who had suffered so much under the Nazis, how they became so brutalized, as far as the Palestinians were concerned. And then, someone explained to me, that if you go through a brutalizing experience, it is a type of suffering that makes you almost lose your compassion and your humanistic instinct. Then you become equally cruel like those people who made you suffer, you become a sadist like them, and that is why as far as the Palestinians are concerned, the Israelis have lost all their compassion. Anyway, that was one of the reasons I got involved with the suffering parties, as normally one does. It is very easy to join the winners, but it is very unproductive, it is much more productive to join the losing side, as far as creativity is concerned.

NOTES

1. On 7 March 1984, just eight months before he died, Faiz Ahmed Faiz was invited to talk to the Asia Study Group in Islamabad. This slightly edited version of the transcript—he spoke extempore—was published for the first time on the occasion of his birth anniversary on 13 February.

2. *The Vizier's Daughter* by Dr Hamilton, published by John Murray.
3. Motilal Nehru.
4. A symposium or gathering of poets where they are invited to recite their poems.
5. The tradition 'you're fighting for your salt' means where your money comes from.

2

IMPACT OF PRISON LIFE ON IMAGERY[1]

From the tangled staircase of evening stars step by step the night
descends

Or

These in the prison courtyard busy embroidering flowered patterns
on the hem of the evening sky.

Or

Lotuses of stars falling from the hand of the moon, floated and
sank, blossomed and withered.

These images were not conjured up by imagination, nor
reconstructed by memory and recalled in tranquillity. They are, on
the other hand, fragments of direct perceptual experience translated
into words. To some extent this is true of all poetic imagery which
is a compound of imprints of sensory stimuli and the feeling they
invoke.

The normal life of 'one who has been long in city pent', however,
is too crowded with the non-sensory or extra-sensory stimuli of
daily living that clog the receiving end of the sensory nerves and
befog the retina of the mind. It is only in rare moments that the
mind can seize 'the fatal beauty' of some visual phenomena and
discover the excitement of 'splendour in the grass'.

In prison, particularly in prison par excellence which I have
experienced twice, namely, solitary confinement, the mind has

nothing to feed on except its sensory impressions and its pain. The minutiae of external phenomena are matched by the sharply etched detail of their reflection in the mind. This process together with its emotive element facilitates the transliteration of the visual into the verbal. The experience, as I have already written somewhere else, is akin to the experience of falling in love again—it suffuses the world around with a similar aura of wonder and beauty, it brings to every perceptual image a peculiar sensuousness of feeling and a transparency of form.

NOTE

1. *Viewpoint*, Lahore, 12 February 1981.

Section II
CULTURE

3

THE QUEST FOR IDENTITY IN CULTURE[1]

Faith holds me back and apostasy pulls me forward.
I have the Ka'ba behind me and facing me the Church.

Thus wrote the nineteenth century poet Ghalib, symbolically enunciating the predicament of the Muslim intelligentsia of his period, the period which witnessed the final extinction of the feudal Mughal empire and the formal establishment of British suzerainty over the subcontinent.

In a more generalised way, the twentieth century poet and thinker of the subcontinent Iqbal postulated the same predicament in prose:

> The spirit of man in his forward movement is restrained by forces which seem to be working in the opposite direction. This is only another way of saying that life moves with the weight of its own past on its back, and that in any view of social change the value and the function of the forces of conservatism cannot be lost sight of.
>
> – *The Reconstruction of Religious Thought in Islam*, p. 166.

In a way, the people of the region which is present-day Pakistan have been called upon to resolve this conflict oftener and more grievously than their conferrers in South Asia.

In its thousands of years of history, this region has seldom been, and then only for brief periods, the centre of any great empire. For the most part, it has served as a buffer zone between rival imperialisms, and this is a continuing factor and an important one in its cultural history. Being a peripheral rather than the central limb in imperial anatomies, it was at the same time more receptive to the influences which suited the psyche of its people and more resistant to what was either repugnant or irrelevant to its own identity.

Every dominative group sought dis-identification of its subjects from their old subjective and behavioural patterns and tried to impose upon them a new identity through its own specific system of inducements and deterrents. But this process remained largely confined to the classes directly dependent on the bureaucratic apparatus of the rulers or the aspirants to this status, and its penetration into the imperial hinterlands was necessarily limited. Conversely, this also softened its clash with the traditional and the time-honoured.

During the first five centuries or so, the new arrivals were largely concentrated in more or less autonomous kingdoms and principalities in the Indus region, and the process of integration and assimilation between the foreign and the indigenous was fairly fast and largely painless. This is partly because the native population, being virtual outcasts from the point of view of Brahmanic hierarchy in the Gangetic lands, were more easily susceptible to the ideological and cultural mores of the newcomers who largely reciprocated the same acceptability, and partly because the nexus of the Hindu political, religious and economic power lay far beyond its borders. It is possible, therefore, that in this region except in the very initial stages no acute crisis of identity arose.

With the establishment and consolidation of the Turkish Muslim Sultanate in Delhi in the thirteenth century, both the locale and the characters on the central cultural stage shifted and changed. The new ruling bureaucracy and its country-wide retinues now found themselves in a minority in a comparatively developed and hostile land, and began their quest for various formulae of self-preservative adjustment to their new social and cultural environment.

This period coincided with the destruction of the Abbasid empire at the hands of the Mongols and, thus, effectively dismantled what was left of a centralised political and theocratic authority in the Muslim world, thus reinforcing centrifugal and nationalistic upsurges in all Muslim lands. And at the same time it brought the frontiers of the newly established Delhi empire within reach of the Central Asian hordes.

Dual Challenge

Faced with this dual challenge from the alien majority within and the alien invader without, the imperial court in Delhi alternated between two broad formulae of social and cultural polity. These are best represented by their two most eloquent advocates at the court of Delhi. In his *Fatwa-i-Jahandari* (the Code of Kingship), Ziauddin Barani (1284–1355) opined that 'the sheet anchor of virtue and goodness' was noble blood and birth, which obviously meant aristocratic Turkish blood, that Islam's authority could not prevail as long as 'the rulers allow the infidels to keep their temples, adorn their idols and make merry during their festivals' and that 'heretics, philosophers and all others who demonstrate ill-will against the religion of Islam should be kept in suppression and destitution'.

As against this, Amir Khusrau (1252–1325) sang praises of Hind, 'the land of my birth, my refuge and my motherland'. He held that 'a beggar with some skill was better than a worthless prince', 'that to adore false idols with true love is pure faith' but 'to worship true God without love, was nothing but dust and ashes'—that to die of love was far more virtuous than 'to kill an infidel in battle'.

Thus, one school stood for social elitism, racial exclusiveness, doctrinaire religion, political absolutism, and total alienation from their new homeland and its culture. The other school propagated social egalitarianism, humanistic mysticism, racial and national integration and total identification with the land. The latter school naturally found ready acceptance in the borderlands, which is present-day Pakistan, because the bulk of population were in any case, converts indigenous to the land. The latter view kept oscillating among the central imperial domains according to the inclinations of the Emperor or the exigencies of the State. And, thus, two cognate, interpenetrating, but nevertheless distinct, cultural streams took shape in the two regions—the elitist, court and classical culture on the one hand and the 'populist', folk and earth-bound culture on the other.

Cleavages

In the arts, the former found expression in classical Persian and Urdu literatures, mainly lyrical or panegyric, in classical music, palatial architecture, miniature painting and ornate decorative arts. The latter produced great folk classics, heroic or mystical, in the Pushto of Khushal Khattak (1613–1691) and Rahman Baba (?–1706), the Sindhi of Shah Latif (1690–1757) and Sachal Sarmast (1739–1826), the Punjabi of Waris Shah (1722–?) and Bulleh Shah (1688–1728), the wealth of folklore in song and legend and a great variety of purely localized architecture, and folk crafts. In periods of crisis, this cleavage, vertical between the 'segregationists,' and the 'integrationists', the native and the 'foreign'-oriented, and horizontal among the different ethnic and linguistic regions, became even sharper.

Thus, even after centuries of sojourn in this land the Delhi poet Altaf Hussain Hali, while lamenting the downfall of the Muslim Mughal empire, writes in one of his better-known poems:

> Farewell O' Hind, land of paradise
> We have lived here long enough as your
> foreign guests.
>
> – *Shikwa-i-Hind* (Complaint against Hind)

And as another extreme, the founders of the first Western-oriented Muslim College in Aligarh proclaimed that 'the British rule in India is the most wonderful phenomenon the world has ever seen'. Neither of these voices found an echo in the rural hinterlands of Pakistan. Their hearts and minds were differently attuned.

The land which comprises present-day Pakistan and its people represents an outstanding study of a historical process, wherein there has been great richness of cultural and political development together with an equally great poverty of social transformation. It is precisely this feature which gives rise to a traditional structure in which there is at once a continuity going back to thousands of years and with it the organic super-imposition of many different layers of tradition. The latter while occurring in specific segments of society have interacted over the whole of it.

Perhaps, as stated earlier, the traditions of the earliest known period of history also survive today in certain segments of our society in modified but easily identifiable form. Not only do the traditions of the nomadic-tribal democracy of the Aryan invaders survive in the hilly areas of the Punjab, but also the traditions of the pre-Aryan slave and serf society in the southern areas of the Punjab and in northern Sindh. The tribal traditions of the Pathans and those of the Baloch go back even more unchangingly into the hoary past despite their ethnic differences.

What is of great interest here is the historical process through which these traditions have passed, leading to the present-day situation which is extremely complex and difficult to unravel.

Not Clear-Cut

While there are different cultural and social groups in Pakistan, the Baloch, the Pathans, the Sindhi and the Punjabi, as in many other parts of the world, the demarcation is not clear-cut. And yet the mainstreams of social and cultural tradition are clearly identifiable. Each of these, therefore, is capable of a separate historical survey. We will limit ourselves here to those broad conclusions which emerge as significant and general features on an all-Pakistan basis, while omitting the separate cultural development of its constituent communities.

Cultural traditions may be classified into two categories, the categories of 'cultural medium' and of 'cultural substance'. By 'cultural medium' we mean language, manners, the idiom of living and the forms of artistic expression. By 'cultural substance' we mean value patterns, ideologies and institutionalised ideas underpinning collective purposes and motivation of people. Questions relating to cultural medium have only recently become

significant in the context of the political and economic struggle on
class and regional issues in the contemporary situation. In the
context of the traditional past, the questions of cultural medium do
not seem to have given rise to any significant issues except those
mentioned earlier. For the present study our focus will be mainly
on the real areas of cultural substance while considering the past.

In the absence of fundamental changes in the social and
economic order, the human struggle seems to have occurred on the
plane of the toiling masses—in the tempo and dimension of
centuries—on the elementary issues of justice, humanism and its
basic expressions of integrity, love, brotherhood and peace. This has
been a recurring struggle and a recurring theme. Even long periods
of stagnation and oppression have failed to destroy either the
human spirit or its living theme and its periodic expression among
the masses. Inexorably, it has re-asserted itself and has always
discovered an appropriate practical social expression—not only in
the face of powerful odds, but even in the absence of the inspiration
and dynamics of a social revolution with which this country has
not yet been blessed by history.

There is no lack of evidence of the mass collectivities successfully
asserting themselves as human beings, even when they could not
possibly replace an oppressive social order with a radically different
one. If there is one thematic thread which runs through the history
of our cultural substance, it is the refusal of our people to
permanently accept injustice.

In Pakistan's history, it is this process that has mattered most to
the people, irrespective of age and time, and perhaps this might
provide one worthwhile basis for the interpretation and
reconstruction of our multi-layered tradition and an essential clue
to our history.

It only needs to be emphasised that not only foreign historians
but our own historians of recent times, in one way or another, failed
to establish this underlying truth of our cultural tradition. There is
a mountain of misinterpretation which our future historians
confront and a tremendous misrepresentation of our people which
has to be cleared up. It has been fashionable to highlight the
'passive', 'negative' and even 'collaborationist' traits of our people.

And it has been the pre-occupation of many academic studies to discover evidence in support of these propositions from our history and a study of our culture. So much so that one of the heaviest crosses that our people bear today is the disdain of their own intelligentsia. In the process of its own alienation, the intelligentsia today, or at least some of them, have come to accept somewhat apologetically the social and political behavioural patterns of the minority power-groups as typical of the mass generality.

The latter could have been correctly understood only through a methodical analysis of their cultural substance as expressed in each different period of their history concretely, through their great spokesmen and leaders, the poets, the spiritual mentors, the traditional heroes and heroines and the clearly identifiable congregate of values and ideas to which they not only subscribed almost unanimously, but also supported in practice. This is borne out by the fact that even in the absence of any powerful socio-economic convulsions, the people of the area did occasionally succeed not only in overthrowing their oppressors but also the superstructures that went with them.

Impact of Imperialism

Before independence, the only radical change which occurred in our economic and social structure was under the impact of British imperialism. While we all agree about the essentially oppressive character of imperialism, the final evaluation of its role in our history is yet to be made. Whether it was a necessary surgery upon an over-ripe society to introduce the developmental process of the industrial age or whether imperialism was a wholly counter-revolutionary event in our history, remains to be decided. The significance of this question today lies in the crystallization of our attitude towards the post-imperialist period, and consequently the discovery of our present identity and its relationship to our future.

Without saying so in so many words, the consensus seems to be that imperialism, for all its evils, was a necessary and even useful stage in our historical development. Important conclusions flow from this position. On the basis of hindsight, however, one is driven to the conclusion that the imperialist interlude was perhaps a wholly reactionary event in our history, unnecessary for our future development as an industrial society. There is at least a hypothetical probability that the industrial age having first come to Europe would have sooner rather than later caught up with the subcontinent, through increased commercial intercourse, if we had succeeded in warding off imperialism.

In such an event, we would have gone through a rapid phase of bourgeois development, which, apart from bringing national and cultural relief to our people, would also have smoothened the path much more surely and effectively for a post-bourgeois socialist transformation of our society. We certainly would not have been saddled, as at present with the peculiar features and problems of the 'Third World' situation.

The present crisis of identity arises not only as a corollary to the colonial period of our history, but also as a result of our continuing failure sufficiently to reject it and as a consequence of mistaken perception of it as a mixed blessing.

It would appear, therefore, that as of present, in the field of culture as in other fields, the body of tradition and history alone cannot supply a true and tangible picture of our identity. There is certainly no lack of the necessary ingredients which go to produce such a national identity, both in history and tradition. But our ambivalence towards imitative colonial cultural and behavioural patterns, mistakenly termed modernist, preclude the possibility of the aforesaid ingredients falling into place to produce any definite identity.

Perhaps, it is only in the negation of this state, the so-called Third World state, that the emergence of a definite social identity of our people lies on the basis of which alone they can fit rationally into the community of nations.

NOTE

1. *Viewpoint*, Lahore, 20 February 1976.

4

CULTURAL PROBLEMS IN UNDERDEVELOPED COUNTRIES

Culture, in human societies, has two main aspects; an external, formal aspect and an inner, ideological aspect. The external forms of culture, social or artistic, are merely an organized expression of its inner ideological aspect, and both are an inherent component of a given social structure. They are changed or modified when this structure is changed or modified and because of this organic link they also help and influence such changes in their parent organism. Cultural problems, therefore, cannot be studied or understood or solved in isolation from social problems, i.e. problems of political and economic relationships. The cultural problems of the underdeveloped countries, therefore, have to be understood and solved in the light of the larger perspective, in the context of underlying social problems.

What, then, are the basic cultural problems of the underdeveloped countries? What is their origin, and what stands in the way of their solution?

Very broadly speaking, these problems are primarily the problems of arrested growth; they originate primarily from long years of imperialist-colonialist domination and the remnants of a backward, outmoded social structure. This should not require much elaboration. European Imperialism caught up with the countries of Asia, Africa or Latin America between the sixteenth and nineteenth centuries. Some of them were fairly developed feudal societies with ancient traditions of advanced feudal culture. Others had yet to progress beyond primitive pastoral tribalism. Social and cultural development of them all was frozen at the point of their political subjugation and remained frozen until the coming of political independence. The culture of these ancient feudal societies, in spite of much technical and intellectual excellence, was restricted to a small privileged class and rarely intermingled with the parallel unsophisticated folk culture of the general masses. Primitive tribal culture, in spite of its childlike beauty, had little intellectual content. Both feudal and tribal societies living contagiously in the same homelands were constantly engaged in tribal, racial, and religious or other feuds with their tribal and feudal rivals. Colonialist-Imperialist domination accentuated this dual fragmentation, the vertical division among different tribal and national groups, the horizontal division among different classes within the same tribal or national group. This is the basic ground structure, social and cultural, bequeathed to the newly liberated countries by their former overlords.

One basic cultural problem which faces many of these countries, therefore, is the problem of cultural integration. Vertical integration which means providing a common ideological and national basis for a multiplicity of national cultural patterns and horizontal integration which means educating and elevating the entire body of their peoples to the same cultural and intellectual level. This means that the qualitative political change from colonialism to independence must be followed by a similar qualitative change in the social structure left behind by colonialism.

Imperialist domination of Asian, African, and Latin American countries was not and could not be merely a passive process of pure political supremacy. It was and it had to be an active process of social and cultural deprivation. It tried to weaken and destroy whatever was good, progressive, and forward-looking in the old feudal or pre-feudal structures, by way of arts, skills, customs, manners, dignity, human values, and mental enlightenment. It tried to sustain and perpetuate whatever was bad, reactionary and backward looking; ignorance, superstition, servility, and class exploitation. What was handed back to the newly liberated countries, therefore, was not the social structure which it took over but the perverted and emasculated remnants of this structure. And it superimposed on these remnants cheap, spurious, second-hand imitations of its own capitalist cultural patterns by way of language, custom, manners, art forms, and ideological values.

This poses a number of cultural problems for the underdeveloped countries. First, the problem of salvaging from the debris of their shattered national cultures these elements which are basic to national identity, which can be adjusted and adapted to the needs of a more advanced social structure, which help to strengthen and promote progressive social values and attitudes. Second, to reject and discard those elements which were basic to a backward and outmoded social structure, which are either irrelevant or repugnant to the more advanced system of social relationship, which hinder the progress of more rational enlightened and humane values and attitudes. Third, to accept and assimilate from imported foreign and western cultures those elements which can help to elevate national culture to higher technical; aesthetic and scientific standards, and fourth, to repudiate those elements which are deliberately aimed at promoting degeneracy, decadence, and social reaction.

These problems, then, are the problems of new cultural adaptation, assimilation, and emancipation. And these, again, cannot be solved through cultural means alone without drastic social (i.e. political, economic, and ideological) reorientations.

In addition to the above, the coming of political independence has also brought some new problems to underdeveloped countries. First, the problem of chauvinist revivalism, second, the problem of neo-colonialist cultural penetration.

The reactionary social sections in these countries; capitalist, feudal or pre-feudal, and their conscious or ignorant allies insist that it is not only the good and valuable elements of cultural and social tradition which should be revived and revitalized but also the bad and worthless elements which must be revived and perpetuated. It is not only the bad and worthless elements of modern Western culture which must be discarded and repudiated but also the useful and progressive elements. This attitude has given rise to a number of Asian and African countries. The aims of all these movements are primarily political, i.e. to hamper the rise of rational social awareness and thus to confirm the exploiting classes in their interests and privileges.

Simultaneously, the neo-colonialist powers, primarily the United States, are trying to fill the cultural vacuum confronting every underdeveloped country with a deluge of cultural, or more correctly anti-cultural trash in the form of debased films, books, magazines, music, dances, fashions which glorify and extol crime, violence, cynicism, perversion and profligacy. These exports invariably accompany the monetary or goods exports by way of American Aid and their aim is also primarily political, i.e. to hinder the growth of national and social awareness among the underdeveloped countries and thus perpetuate their political and intellectual dependence. The solution of these two problems, therefore, is also primarily political, i.e. to replace reactionary native and foreign influences by progressive influences. And in this task the more enlightened and more socially aware sections of a community—writers, artists, and intellectuals have an important role to play.

To sum up: The major cultural problems of underdeveloped countries arrested growth, uneven distribution, internal contradictions, imitativeness, etc. are primarily social problems; problems related to the organization, values, and practices of a backward social structure. These problems can be effectively solved only when the political revolution of national liberation is followed by a social revolution to complete national independence.

5

PROBLEMS OF CULTURAL PLANNING IN ASIA—WITH SPECIAL REFERENCE TO PAKISTAN

The vast land mass known as Asia encompasses numerous countries and peoples and the cultural patterns specific to different lands do not easily yield to broad generalisations. Thus, we have in Asia a number of Socialist States where cultural planning obviously takes on a completely different orientation from other countries operating under a different socio-political organisation. Then there are countries which have escaped direct foreign colonialist domination or occupation and where the continuity of cultural traditions was not radically subverted by foreign influences. Lastly, there is a group to which my country—Pakistan—belongs who have been only recently liberated after a prolonged era of subjugation. This paper is mainly relevant to the cultural problems of the last group, although some of these problems may be shared in some measure by the other groups as well because dominative western influences have been operative there as well at some stage of their political history.

Culture in the broader sense is commonly defined today as the whole way of life of a given human community. In a more restricted sense it comprises finished or stylized expression of this way of life in various forms of creative and artistic expression. For purposes of convenience these two inter-related aspects may be discussed separately.

In the broader sense, culture in human societies has two main aspects: an external formal aspect and an inner ideological one. The external forms of culture, social or artistic, are basically an organised expression of its inner ideological content. Both are integral components of a given social structure. They are changed or modified as this structure changes and because of this organic link they also promote and influence such changes in their parent organism. Cultural problems, therefore, cannot be studied or understood or solved in isolation from social problems, i.e. problems of political and economic relationships. The cultural problems of Asian countries, too, have to be understood and their solutions found in the light of this larger perspective—in the context of their underlying social problems.

Very broadly speaking, these problems are primarily the problems of arrested growth: they originate primarily from long years of foreign domination and the remnants of a backward, outmoded social structure. This should not require much elaboration. Industrialised or economically powerful Western countries caught up with various Asian lands between the sixteenth and nineteenth centuries. Some among these were fairly developed feudal societies with ancient traditions of advanced feudal culture. Others had yet to progress beyond primitive pastoral tribalism. The social and cultural development of them all was frozen at the point of their political subjugation and remained so until the advent of political independence. The culture of these ancient feudal societies, in spite of much technical and intellectual excellence, was restricted to a small privileged class which rarely intermingled with the parallel unsophisticated folk culture of the general masses. Primitive tribal culture, in spite of its child-like beauty, had little intellectual content. Both feudal and tribal societies living contiguously in the same homelands were constantly engaged in tribal, racial, religious or other feuds with their tribal and feudal rivals. Foreign colonialist domination accentuated this dual fragmentation, i.e. the division among different tribal and national groups on the one hand and the division among different classes within the same tribal or national group on the other.

One basic cultural problem which faces many of these countries, therefore, is the problem of cultural integration. Vertical integration which means providing a common ideological and national basis for a multiplicity of national cultural patterns and a horizontal integration which involves educating and elevating the entire body of the people to the same cultural and intellectual level. Thus, the qualitative political change from colonialism to independence was required to be followed by a similar qualitative change in the social structure left behind by the colonialist era.

Alien imperialist domination of Asian countries was not merely a passive process of pure political supremacy. It was also an active process of social and cultural subversion. It tried on the one hand to kill or destroy whatever was good, progressive, and forward looking in the old feudal or pre-feudal structures by way of arts, skills, customs, manners, humanist values or mental enlightenment. It tried to sustain and perpetuate, on the other, whatever was unwholesome, reactionary, or backward looking; ignorance, superstition, servility, and class-exploitation. What was handed back to the newly liberated countries, therefore, was not the original social structure taken over at the point of their subjugation but the perverted and emasculated remnants of this structure. Superimposed on these remnants were cheap, spurious and second-hand imitations of western cultural patterns by way of language, customs, manners, art forms, and ideological values.

This poses a number of other basic cultural problems for these countries. First, the problem of salvaging from the debris of their shattered national cultures those elements which are basic to national identity, which can be adjusted and adapted to the needs of a more advanced social structure, and which can help to strengthen and promote progressive social values and attitudes. Second, to reject and discard those elements which were relevant to a backward and out-moded social structure, which are either irrelevant or repugnant to a more advanced system of social relationships and which hinder the progress of more rational, enlightened human values and attitudes. Third, to accept and assimilate from imported foreign and western cultures those elements which can help to elevate national culture to higher technical aesthetic and intellectual standards. Fourth, to repudiate those elements among these imports which are deliberately aimed at promoting degeneracy, decadence, and social reaction. Roughly speaking, these problems may be termed problems of new cultural adaptation, assimilation, emancipation, and purification.

In addition to the above, political independence has also given rise to certain new attitudes, subjective as well as social, which also require rectification and reorientation, e.g. the craze for chauvinistic revivalism and the craze for indiscriminate modernism. Thus, certain social groups insist that it is not only the good and valuable element of traditional, cultural and social practice which should be revived and revitalised but also the bad and worthless elements. Conversely, not only the bad and worthless elements of modern western culture must be discarded and repudiated but the useful and progressive elements as well. The baby must be thrown out with the bath water. The motivation of these schools is primarily not cultural but political, i.e. to hamper the progress of rational social awareness and to confirm the exploiting classes in their interests and privileges. Secondly, political and commercial entrepreneurs from the more advanced western countries have sought to fill the cultural vacuum confronting newly liberated countries with a deluge of cultural, or more correctly, anti-cultural trash in the form of debased literature, magazines, music, dances, fashion, etc. which extol and glorify crimes, violence, cynicism, perversion, and profligacy. A good deal of this trash has been indiscriminately accepted by certain other sections of these communities under the mistaken notion of modernism.

From this point of view some of the major cultural problems of Asian countries, e.g. arrested growth, uneven distribution, internal contradictions, imitativeness, etc. are primarily social problems related to the organisation, value, judgements, and social practices of a backward social structure. Their solution, therefore, lies outside the domain of a purely cultural endeavour and falls within the domain of political and socio-economic reforms

Notwithstanding what has been said above, it should also be borne in mind that while national culture cannot transcend the limitations of a given social structure it can certainly lag behind it.

In other words, while cultural activities cannot go beyond the progressive potentialities of a particular society it can certainly fall short of what is both possible and desirable within the limitations of this society. It can accept or reject attitudes, it can adopt or ignore measures in the cultural field which are conducive to social progress and intellectual enlightenment within its own social framework. This is particularly true of those forms of human culture which are amenable to deliberate planning and conscious promotional effort, e.g. creative skills and the body of the arts. It is in this context that I would like to speak about the situation in my own country and the problems and solutions that have been, or are being faced and attempted.

In May 1968, the then Government of Pakistan set up a Committee under the chairmanship of the writer of this paper to investigate and report on these problems and what follows are some of the conclusions arrived at by this Committee.

While discussing certain national attitudes inimical to the promotion and development of art and culture it was observed:

There is a school of thinking which holds that all cultural activity in general and the performing arts in particular are immoral and anti-religious. The anti-culture, anti-art attitudes fostered by this school mainly derive from the following factors:

(i) Prolonged colonial subjection subverted the native cultural patterns of our old society and the imperialist rulers sought to replace them by their own cultural imports. Everything 'native' by way of culture and the arts was held up to contempt and ridicule and their western counterparts held up as the only models fit for imitation. The resultant disruption of national life and impoverishment of all the national arts robbed large sections of our people, particularly the influential section called 'the Civil Lines', of all love, respect and understanding of their national arts.

(ii) During the declining years of the Mughal Empire in the subcontinent, as elsewhere in similar historical conditions, the arts were reduced to become handmaids of dissolute courts and instruments of their decadent pleasures. This was particularly true of music and dancing which were encouraged to become the monopoly of a socially and morally unacceptable class. After the downfall of the Mughals, the moral indignation evoked by these decadent practices and the social prejudices attaching to the class of 'singing girls' were detached from the social conditions which gave them birth and transferred, in the popular mind, to the arts themselves.

(iii) Since Independence these anti-art attitudes inherited from the past have been seized upon by certain factions in the country for topical political ends. They first sought to equate all culture with music and dancing and then to equate all music and dance with the lewd vulgarizations of these arts by inept professionals. From these premises, it was easy to proceed to the conclusion, as has often been done, that all art is immoral, hence anti-religious, hence ideologically unacceptable. Any ideological objection that can be brought against any art, however, must relate to some particular form and content of a particular art and not to the art as such. This obvious platitude is deliberately ignored because the basic motivation of this school is neither moral nor religious but socio-political. This motivation seeks to promote attitudes hostile to all agencies of sensitive feeling and enlightened thought, including scientific research and artistic creation.

(iv) The generally negative public and official attitudes towards nation's art and culture have opened the gates for a resolute cultural invasion by Western commercial and political agencies. Thus, in the last few years many corrupt and perverted versions of Western culture focused on sex, violence, and profligacy have provided the staple cultural fare for the sophisticated Pakistani boy and girl and the main outlet for his or her natural craving for self-expression.

(v) A second fairly influential point in the country is that culture and the arts, even though they may not be morally undesirable or ideologically reprehensible, are still something of a luxury which only the rich countries can afford. Developing countries, like Pakistan, must put first things first and devote all their resources to material developments, i.e. agriculture and industry, and let the harp and the fiddle wait until better days come round—just as a poor man would put his daily bread before the pleasures of art.

We are unable to agree with this point of view.

In a developing society, where the paucity of funds hinders all development, education constitutes personal capital and hence counts as a basic factor in development. Similarly, culture which represents the awareness of a society of its values, aims, and aspirations provides an important incentive for a national development. Any development efforts which ignore the emotional and spiritual aid provided by a nation's awareness of its own goals and aspirations are bound to engender antagonistic contradictions between the people and the agencies responsible for such development. Cultural activity in a developing nation is in many ways a form of socio-political activity and it is only through this activity that a people's full participation in nation-building efforts can be ensured.

Secondly, the arts are as much a factor in the material process of production as is education. Just as an investment in national education has a direct bearing on national productivity through creating superior skills, an investment in the arts has a direct role in improving the standards and qualities of many forms of industrial production by superior fashioning and designing.

Thirdly, in the world of today, advertising and public relationing are no longer regarded as a luxury but an important change on industrial revenues. Nations do their advertising and public relationing through cultural exchange, i.e. exchanges of art products and performances.

Culture and National Identity

Before the inception of Pakistan there was, understandably, no such entity as a Pakistani nation. Politically the people of present day Pakistan (leaving aside some minority groups) were part of the Indian Muslim Community. Ethnically and geographically they were called after the areas they inhabited, i.e. Bengalis, Punjabis, Sindhis, Balochis, Pathans, etc. Understandably, therefore, the culture of the new Pakistani nation when it emerged was not a finished, ready-made unified entity. The differences in social development among different regions of the country, differences of climate and geographical habitat, ethnic and historical factors and administrative divisions enforced by foreign rulers, all combined to make the culture of the people of the present-day Pakistan a composite of diversified patterns. Nevertheless, these people in all parts of Pakistan shared a common historical experience as well as those common ethical and cultural mores which originated from the religion they professed. It was this common religion and the sum total of these values and their expression in social life which made the Muslims of the subcontinent emerge as a separate and distinct cultural entity over a long period of history.

There is considerable difference of opinion on how precisely this culture should be defined. There appears to be some agreement, however, that the culture of the people of Pakistan includes everything which has been integrated into the bloodstream of the social and historical life of our people. This conglomeration is principally composed of (a) the religion of Islam which provides the ethical and ideological basis for the people's way of life, (b) the indigenous cultures of different linguistic regions inherited from their own specific cultural past, and (c) elements of Western culture absorbed since the days of British occupation. Added to the above are the distinctive cultures of minority groups who form a part of the Pakistan nation.

This raises some debatable issues, e.g. the issues of regional cultures. The basic and characteristic vocabulary of our people's culture, i.e. language, dress, customs, architecture, music, folk arts, etc. has naturally been better preserved in our villages and the countryside of various regions than in big towns where dominative foreign influences have introduced a cosmopolitanism composed of many elements and characteristics which are not exclusively national. The growth of these folk cultures was arrested at various levels of development with the disintegration of feudal societies, the withdrawal of feudal patronage, and the concentration of power, wealth and educational and cultural facilities in the big towns. A reversal of this process of stagnation, therefore, and a revival of these regional cultures-the most authentic storehouse of what is distinctively Pakistani—seems obviously called for.

This raises two issues: first, whether such a revival would promote centrifugal tendencies of narrow regionalism and militate against the goals of national integration; secondly, whether such a revival and the development of regional cultures would yield to some sort of a synthesis on the national plane.

The consensus of the opinions may be summarised as follows:

(a) In as much as all regional cultures are an organic part of the totality of our national culture, love for the past does not preclude and, in fact, predicates love for the whole. The confusion of thought which continues to plague this subject stems from one basic fallacy which seeks to counterpoise national and regional cultures as antagonistic rivals and thus postulates that one can or would develop only at the expense of the other. This fallacy can be dispelled by a clear understanding of the obvious fact that just as the country is a geographical union of its constituent regions and the nation is a political union of the people inhabiting these regions, similarly, national culture is an aggregate of these regional cultures plus the unifying bonds of faith and history.

(b) A genuine synthesis of diverse forms of regional cultures into national patterns cannot be brought about by any forcible impositions through administrative means. It can only evolve through a gradual accumulation of affinities and a gradual assimilation of 'sympathetic elements into a new compound.' This is possible only if 'diversity' is not

misinterpreted as disunity and the natural process of the
growth of diverse elements is not perverted or stifled by an
impatience for immediate results.

Culture and Traditions

The problem of national identity also relates to the classical
tradition of the arts. And this presents a different set of problems.

(a) Since this tradition, particularly in arts like music and
    dancing, is much older than the Muslim era, it contains
    many ingredients unrelated to Muslim social traditions.
(b) Since the Indo-Muslim civilization was not confined to the
    areas which now form Pakistan, it contains many ingredients
    which transcend our boundaries and cannot be deemed
    exclusively Pakistan.

Should this tradition, then, be owned and accepted wholesale or
should it be recast into a mould nearer to the heart of a present-day
Pakistani citizen? There is considerable difference of opinion over
this issue. One school holds that to establish a completely different
national and ideological identity it is necessary to discard all these
ingredients, and if this is not possible with regard to a particular
artistic tradition, it were best to do away with this tradition
altogether. The opposite view is that by maligning a tradition
evolved by Muslim society in the days of their greatest glory, a
tradition which represents their main contribution to the cultural
history of this subcontinent, we really malign our own history; that
we are not justified in taking exception to what our ancestors, in
whom we take pride, not only took no exception to but actively
sponsored and patronized.

As for territorial limits, it should be obvious that some of the
most basic components of our cultural heritage originated and
evolved in areas beyond the present geographical boundaries of
Pakistan. These include the Urdu language and literature and the

whole body of Arabic, Iranian, Central Asian, and various other influences which have been integrated into our cultural tradition.

Lastly, there is the problem of re-evaluating our cultural and artistic tradition in the light of contemporary experience, the adjustment of 'continuities from the past' with 'the demands of the present'.

Western societies, after nearly two hundred years of scientific, industrial, and technological advancement, mainly at the expense of the peoples they dominated, have introduced to the world techniques, methodologies, tools, materials, and modes of production unknown before. These advances, in their turn, have induced new habits of thought and cultural expression, thus modifying or eliminating various traditional elements in social or cultural life. In developing and newly liberated countries, like Pakistan, this process has just begun. And along with it have emerged the horns of a dilemma—of tradition vs. modernism.

This dilemma has generated three tendencies—one of blind imitativeness of our own past in the name of tradition, the other of blind imitativeness of everything Western in the name of modernism, the third of a tasteless hodgepodge of the two in order to have the best of both worlds.

We are of the opinion that all these attitudes are incorrect, that:

(a) The continuity of tradition does not mean its perpetuation in toto. For instance, the place of our traditional arms, the sword and the spear, is no longer in the battlefield but in the museum. Nevertheless, they should be preserved, loved, and respected as a part of our heritage.

(b) The acquisition of scientific, technological, industrial, and intellectual knowledge from the West does not necessitate a negation of our own historic personality.

Therefore

(c) Those elements of our traditional culture which were only relevant to another set of conditions in the past and have outlived their utility cannot and should not be artificially perpetuated merely on the grounds of sentiment. The sentiment of love and respect alone should be enough.

(d) The application of new techniques in the arts, experimentation with new forms of expression, utilization of new materials, popularization of new artistic concepts should not be discouraged merely because they have originated in the West, provided the artist retains his identity as a member of his own community.

(e) A living and dynamic culture is one which provides conditions for maximum contribution by national talent for the aesthetic and intellectual enrichment of the community at the highest level of contemporary attainment. Our endeavour should be to create the most favourable conditions for this maximum contribution at appropriate levels.

6

CROSS-CULTURAL ENCOUNTER IN EAST-WEST LITERATURE—BRIEF HISTORICAL BACKGROUND

'The classical configuration of the meeting of cultures is that of East and West.' This formulation is certainly relevant in the present day context but in the context of literary history, it calls for a number of qualifications. In Eastern literatures, particularly those pertaining to West, Central and South Asia, the most incisive and the most significant cultural encounters were intra-Asian rather than East-Western. Beginning with the Aryan invasion into the land of the Indus, where I come from, the entire cultural and literary map of these regions is criss-crossed with an unending series of major and minor encounters, Arab-Persian, Indo-Persian, Indo-Arab, Turko-Persian, Turko-Mongol, Indo-Turkish, etc. etc., to mention just a few of the more recent ones. And the more enduring ones among these left in their wake great new languages and great new literatures: Sanskrit and the body of Indian regional languages, Neo-Persian which is now classical Persian, Turkish and its various cognates—again just to mention a few, nearer home to me. Concomitantly and inevitably, these encounters led to a great deal of promiscuous cross-fertilization in myth and legend, thought and belief, story and song. Nevertheless, it would be correct to say that the origins, products and causations of this multi-lingual and multi-national heritage have been researched with such care and industry by eminent Orientalists of both East and West, that even though a scholar's work like a woman's is never done, and even though some gaps have yet to be mapped in, by and large the major points of identification have been accounted for.

The East-West encounter, on the other hand, is a comparatively recent pre-occupation. And the very first problem we are confronted with is the identification and the genesis of the East-West concept itself. Rudyard Kipling, who really started the 'East is East' and 'West is West' racket in our times, hastened to add to his much-quoted lines:

> But there is neither East nor West, nor breed nor birth
> When two strong men stand face to face even though they
> come from the ends of the earth.

This rejoinder, however, went almost unheard, and it was the concept of East and West as mutually exclusive entities that anchored itself in prevalent thought. Normally, one would begin an examination of this concept from the beginning, if one could find a beginning. But strictly speaking there is not any. We know that for many millennia, but how many we do not know, in this vast land mass which is now Europe and Asia, there was no East or West, Europe or Asia. Climatic, ecological and other natural factors spewed forth great tidal waves of multi-directional human migrations; North, South, East, and West, and human habitations arose wherever a certain wave spent itself out. We can certainly get some idea of the subjective affinities, ethnic consanguinities or spatio-temporal continuities of these primeval peoples from the stones and sticks they left behind, but this material is hardly relevant to the study of literature. All that we have to go by are the relics of human speech embedded in what is rather loosely termed the Indo-European group of languages (why Indo?). But that is a much later development.

When we come to recorded history we are on surer ground but the ground is riddled with its own enigmas. Among the very first that we come across is the period when the West (or the known part of it) literally was the East and the East was West in the form of Hellenized Asia Minor and Romanized Egypt. It is understandable that this synthesis must have come about because the processes of integrative acculturation, on both sides, must have been greatly helped by the absence of codified religions and the interchangeability of pagan gods, on the one hand and on the other, by institutionalised slavery which knew no boundaries. And yet these Western cultural structures were raised on the ruins of highly articulate Eastern civilizations—Pharonic, Mesopotamian, and Levantine, and it is hardly conceivable that there was no 'literary transaction' between the old and the new. Purely academically, therefore, whatever fragmentary material of this period we have may well deserve a closer look, from this point of view, by specialists in the field.

Would it be correct to assume, then, that the East-West concept, at least in the ancient sense, first became a fact of life and subsequently a fact of literature about 500 years before the Christian era, with the rise of two great and contiguous empires; Persian Empire in the East and Greco-Roman Empire in the West. At any rate, it is during this period that, after primeval migrations, the first major mass contact between Eastern and Western peoples took place with Alexander's incursion into Asian lands. This encounter coloured the cultural and literary blood streams of both sides for centuries to come. The short-lived Satrapies that Alexander left behind in Asia, even though subsequently sucked up into the native soil, yet bequeathed to their temporary abode, particularly in the area which is now Pakistan and its environs, a comprehensive cultural idiom which goes by the name of Gandhara civilization. It is in the field of literature and letters, however, that the Macedonian warrior has left his most enduring imprint. What motivated the medieval romancers in the West and Persian epic poets in the East to resurrect Alexander, not in history but in legend, nearly a thousand years after his death? What were the channels of their interchange, and the reasons for Alexander's acceptability as a hero on both sides? We know that contemporary Greek records are too scanty to provide enough body for a worthwhile legend, and the stories built around the figure of Alexander originate with later Roman chroniclers, notably Plutarch. We also know that Alexander did marry some Asian princesses and that his expeditionary force had as many, if not more, Parthians, Bactrians, and Indians in its ranks, as his native Greeks. For the rest, one can only hypothesize that when first the Arabs and later the Turks overran the Persian empire in the East and snuffed out the glory of Rome and Byzantium in the West, both the Persians and their Western contemporaries went looking for a hero to salvage their humbled pride. And they both picked on Alexander. One can add to this another factor which had then become operative in the East-West scene; the religious confrontation between Western Christianity and Eastern Islam. The legendary figure of Alexander, therefore, first emerges as a prototype of all subsequent heroes of medieval romance: young, handsome, brave, and invincible, ruthless in battle, magnanimous in victory. And second, as a common protagonist of both Eastern and Western national and religious causes. Thus the Persian poet Firdausi, in his great tenth century epic *Shahnameh* (The Book of Kings), makes him a stepbrother to the luckless Darius, and in the *Sikander Nama* (Book of Alexander the Great) which followed, later Persian poets converted him to Islam and even sent him on a pilgrimage to Mecca. Religious commentators went a step further and identified him with 'Zulqarnain' 'The Two-horned One' mentioned in the Holy Koran, who stemmed the onslaught of Gog and Magog. The Western romancers, on their part, made him their protagonist against the Turkish infidels and his dragon-slaying exploit was enough to confuse him with the equally legendary St. George. These are, however, rather large surmises and this unique encounter may be well worth more detailed examination.

In the next major East-West encounter in history—the Crusades, the East-West concept, at least in the Western mind, gradually took on a more defined image. In the earlier stages, this image is largely romantic and benign. Thus, in Geoffrey Chaucer's *Knight's Tale* we find

The grete emetreus, the kyng of inde,
(The great Emetreus, a king of Ind,)

His crispe heer lyk rynges was yronne,
(His crisp hair all in bright ringlets was run,)

And that was yelow, and glytered as the sonne.
(Yellow as gold and gleaming as the sun.)

His nose was heigh, his eyen bright citryn,
(His nose was high, his eyes a bright citrine,)

His lippes rounde, his colour was sangwyn;
(His lips were full, his colouring sanguine.)

And then in the *Squire's Tale* the noble king of Tartary, Cambinskan, and the knight who brought him presents from 'the kyng of arabe and of inde' are sketched in equally attractive colours. By the time we come to the Elizabethan period, however, while Inde and Arabe still retain some of their mystery and allure, the ruddy faced, golden haired eastern character is replaced by the blackamoore and the blacker 'Turkish dog' ('same to you, Christian dog,' the Turk might have retorted but he didn't, partly because to a Muslim Christ is a prophet of God and Christians are 'People of the Book' and partly because the influence of Arab geographers and scientists had made the general body of Muslim writers more scientific minded). The Norman conquest which brought the *Song of Roland* to English shores, and the stories of Richard the Lion-hearted and Saladin in its train, the obliteration of the territorial gains made by the early Crusaders, the expansion of the Ottoman empire under Soleyman the Magnificent, and the total eclipse of the Byzantine civilization, all combined to enfocus the English literary mind on the Turk with obsessive racial and religious hostility. There is hardly an Elizabethan playwright worth the name, Thomas Kyd, Robert Greene, Christopher Marlowe, Francis Beaumont and John Fletcher and the great Shakespeare, who has not at least one play dealing with Eastern characters. And the villain is almost always a Turk both because of his religion and because of his colour. He even enters religious hymns and devotional literature:

Preserve us Lord by the deare word,
From Turk and Pope, defend us Lord.

or

As from the Turk so shield us Lord
From force of Popish power.[1]

And in their hostility against the Turks the Elizabethans provide
the Christians with some strong bedfellows, e.g., Marlowe's
Tamburlaine or Shakespeare's *Othello*. Marlowe's *Tamburlaine* was
'a noble Tartarian' conqueror who laid waste the Ottoman empire,
and attacked Bajazet just when the Turkish army was besieging
Constantinople after their victory at Nicopolis. He was 'a scourge
and wrath of God' for the Turks but was a deliverer of the Christian
powers. Marlowe was obviously unaware that Timur was very much
a Muslim. Similarly, Shakespeare's enigmatic Othello, who 'smote
the circumcised dog' in Rhodes, has become, for unaccountable
reasons, both a Christian and an Italian military hero. Albeit he is
acutely conscious both of his colour and of his cultural deficiency.
'Rude am I in my speech' he admits, and Desdemona is in love
with 'what she feared to look at.' This colour bar is henceforth
an established literary motif and, as for rudeness of speech,
Shakespeare has also a contrary objection; the oriental is pompous
and verbose in expression.

> Here is a silly stately style indeed!
> The Turk, that two and fifty kingdoms hath,
> Writes not so tedious a style as this.
>> – King Henry VI, Part I, Act iv, Scene vii

It may be mentioned here in passing that in earlier centuries,
when Moorish Spain was the main centre of learning in the West,
the urbane Moor, unlike the overbearing Turk, had a completely
different image. Thus, we find a Father Aberus lamenting in the
ninth century:

> All Christian youths, fair of face, eloquent in speech, conspicuous
> in apparel and bearing, learned in gentle science, perfected in Arabic
> rhetoric—these people spend their days in ardently studying Arabic
> books. Gathered together for the purposes of profound wisdom they
> yet spend themselves in voluptuous praise of pagan literature—ignoring
> the beauties of ecclesiastic truth and despising the whole church streams

whose source is so pure. Oh, for shame! The Christian young clerks do not know their own language so that in the whole College of Christ perhaps one in a thousand may be found who can write a decent letter to a brother. And an innumerable crowd of these dandies explain most subtly their Arabic preciosity of diction which lends material decoration to the end of their verse with monorhyme.

This, however, was a passing phase. What endured for a much longer time was a basic romantic pattern with a virtuous Christian knight or king as hero overcoming innumerable enemies, winning among other victories an oriental princess or two who embrace Christianity, an orgiastic oriental court with a bloodthirsty and cruel king and a horde of Muslim pagans who were almost always shown as idol-worshippers.

In Eastern literatures, on the other hand, apart from the solitary exception of Alexander, hardly any Western character puts in an appearance. Having digested Western philosophy, science, and other scholastic and critical methodologies through Greek and Latin sources, the Mid-Eastern scholar or writer had little use for the upstart European languages or literatures. It was nearly three centuries later that the Muslim Indian writer, having read the Christian version of the Crusades, and particularly the novels of Walter Scott, tried to get his own back by reversing the roles of the heroes of romance. Now it was the Muslim prince or warrior, Moor or Turk, who won all the battles and it was the Christian princess who fell for his charms and embraced Islam. But that is a separate story.

By the end of the seventeenth century the political map of the old world had radically changed and the literary and intellectual landscape of the western world changed accordingly. The Moorish kingdoms in Spain had been drowned in blood. The Ottoman empire was rapidly disintegrating. Western maritime power had driven the Turkish fleets and the Barbary Corsairs off the seas. British seamen and travellers were beginning to find access to distant lands they had only known in their dreams. The Turk was no longer a scourge of Christendom. The post-Renaissance humanist and scientific values, by themselves traceable to earlier

East-West cross-cultural encounters, were fast taking over from the old theological mental fixations. The age of reason had dawned.

The English writer and the English reader now began to think of foreign lands and Eastern peoples as essentially the same as their own, with good kings and bad kings, heroes and villains, sages and philosophers. Even Lord Byron, who had good reasons to dislike the Turks, the former masters of his beloved Greece, was singularly free from racial and religious prejudice in his compositions on Eastern themes like *The Bride of Abydos*, *The Corsair*, etc. Sir Walter Scott's revival of the Crusade theme, in spite of its pronounced pro-Christian slant, yet maintains that 'a man is a man for a' that.'

However, it is with the English translation of Galland's French version of the *Arabian Nights* (1704–1712) that the brutal Turk and the blackamoore finally disappear from the English literary canvas. The new Eastern scene now unrolled for the Western reader is a glittering medley of Persian, Arab, Indian, and Far-Eastern lands and characters, romantic, mysterious, highly sophisticated and ravishingly colourful. With the publication of Thomas Moore's *Lalla Rookh: An Oriental Romance* (1817), and the story of Rustam and Sohrab, together with a resume of other tales from Firdausi's *Shahnameh*, written around the same time by an obscure James Atkinson of East India Company, followed by Edward Fitzgerald's *Rubáiyát of Omar Khayyám* and other translations by the first noted Orientalist, Sir William Jones (1746–1794), a number of eminent English poets, Robert Southey, William Collins, Matthew Arnold, turned to Persian odes and pastorals for inspiration. By the turn of the century, Persian literature had even travelled to the new world through the same channels. Thus, we find a Professor of Columbia University writing in his introduction to a volume of translations from Persian literature,

> Persian poetry with its love of life and this worldliness, with its wealth of imagery and its appeal to that which is human in all men, is much more readily comprehended by us than is the poetry of all the rest of the Orient. And, therefore, Goethe, Platen, Ruckert, Von Schack, Fitzgerald and Arnold have been able to re-sing their masterpieces so as to delight and instruct our own days.[2]

All this notwithstanding, it is during the same period that the modern East-West concept takes shape both in the social and in the literary western mind. During the many epochs of early theocratic, and the later more worldly, feudalisms, the basic subjective and behavioural patterns, the norms of value judgement and the mores of character evaluation, were common to both the near East and the near West in spite of bitter mutual antagonisms. Physical prowess, moral rectitude, conviviality in company, fidelity to one's faith and friends—these were the common attributes of a hero who was almost always a Prince or a warrior. The rabble did not count. By the mid-eighteenth century, however, the West, at any rate the West we are talking about, was fast being transformed into a rising mercantile and later industrial power, while the East was littered with the remains of static feudal civilizations. As a result, in Western communities new social class configurations and new subjective and behavioural patterns took birth which had no counterpart in Eastern societies. Inevitably, the two drifted steadily apart until Kipling's East became East and West became West.

II.

We can now briefly survey the encounter more relevant to where I come from—the Anglo-Indian come together. As mentioned earlier, right up to the Elizabethan period the land of Inde was something too mysterious and far away and its people too unfamiliar to provide any material for live literary delineation except as myth and legend. India was neither a rival nor a conqueror nor a subject. John Dryden's *Aureng-Zebe* (1675) is perhaps the first full-length play in the English language dealing with a contemporary Indian theme. Even though the historical facts are greatly garbled and there are the usual intrigues, feuds, and blood-letting associated with Eastern courts, yet there is some attempt at verisimilitude and some description of typical Indian customs. Almost all through the eighteenth century, however, the Persian tale was very much the vogue in English literature and it is only towards the end of this century and the beginning of the next, when the East India Company began swallowing up one Indian territory after another, and its factors, 'writers' as they were called, became regular go-betweens of East and West, that Anglo-Indian themes took hold of the English reader and writer. Walter Scott's *Surgeon's Daughter* (1827), Philip Meadows Taylor's *Confessions of a Thug* (1839), and *Tipoo Sultan: A Tale of the Mysore War* (1840), first set the trend. But this was primarily the age of the journalist, the essayist and the pamphleteer, and it is in their pages that the subject of India finds its most impassioned expression. The general attitude of the British writer and intellectual at this time is one of intense sympathy for the exploited Indian and equally intense indignation against the misdoings of the gold-digging 'Nabobs'—the high-handed functionaries of the East Indian Company. Thus, Dr Samuel Johnson says about Clive: 'a man who acquired his fortune by such crimes that his consciousness of them compelled him to cut his own throat'.[3] Burkes' indictment of Warren Hastings is of course well known. And even after the upheaval in 1857, what the British call the Mutiny and the people of India and Pakistan call the Great War of Independence, when the emotional climate had changed, we find Ruskin saying, 'Every mutiny, every danger, every terror occurring under or paralyzing our Indian legislation arises directly out of our material desire to live on the loot of India.'[4]

John Ruskin, however, is an exception. After 1857, first the emotional shock and later the new relationship between the rulers and ruled engendered a completely different attitude on which Rudyard Kipling finally set the seal. The romance of India was over. It was now the land not of seers and sages but of jungles, tigers, cobras, cholera, and sepoys, 'the white-man's grave.' And the lowly Indian once admired for his wisdom, honesty and so forth, now became a nigger, a pig, a coward, and a cheat. The Englishman, on the other hand, who during the days of the East India Company was fond of imitating native ways, smoked the *hookah* (Indian pipe) and even composed Urdu poetry, was now the Sahib, the master, the bearer of the *White Man's Burden* (1899). The only Indian for whom Kipling has any sympathy was either 'the noble savage' a la' Othello, the Pathan, or the childlike primitive, the Bheel, or the faithful servant and sepoy. This period came to an end with E.M. Foster's *Passage to India*, perhaps the first and last sensitive study of Anglo-Indian characters and their relationships during colonial times.

Now let us have a look at the other side of the coin. In 1799, when the British East India Company had secured their foothold on the Indian soil, they established their first school of oriental learning in Calcutta, which was elevated to a higher status in the following year, with the foundation of what came to be known as the Fort William College. This institution had a two-fold purpose. First, to educate native students in their own languages, literatures, and traditional disciplines and second, to provide reading material for Company's own hands in order to familiarise them with local languages, particularly Urdu or Hindustani, the major spoken language of Northern India. For this second objective Hindustani writers and scholars were set to work to compile readable storybooks in prose. The Urdu language had a rich heritage of poetry but almost the only prose works known were religious or devotional books and tracts either translated or compiled from original sacred texts in Arabic. The legends, romances, and other works of fiction, nearly fifty in number, produced under the auspices of Fort William, are among the first literary prose works known to Urdu language. That they came into being not for the pleasure of the native reader but for the utilization of a foreign establishment must be a unique phenomenon in literary history. In 1835, the Indian Governor General's Council resolved on the propagation of European literature and science in State-sponsored institutions and thus the foundations of a real cross-cultural encounter were laid.

In 1837, Persian was discontinued as the official language of the Indian Dominions and different States or provinces were authorized to conduct business, education and official, in regional languages, thus giving a fillip to the development of regional literatures. A similar incentive was provided for the study of English language and literature in 1844, when English education was given a premium of preference for entry into government jobs.

It is in the Delhi College, however, founded in 1825, that Urdu literature was really exposed to the English literary influence and the modern movement in our literature was born. Again, strangely enough, while the English mind after events of 1857 was sorely estranged with India and the Indians, a reverse stream was flowing in the Indian mind. Some modus vivendi with the new rulers and their civilization had become a political and social compulsion. This is spelled by a noted Delhi scholar and essayist, Maulvi Zakaullah, in the following words,

> When a nation is dominated by another, the former's honour and prestige increase in the degree to which it can assimilate the civilization, knowledge, and ability of the rulers and its degradation is accentuated by its opposition to the same.

And thus Sir Syed Ahmad Khan, the founder of the Aligarh University and the leader of the Muslim Reformist movement,

> When the Turks sit among neighbouring French or British peoples they look like brothers and we hope they will become more and more civilized. So we want the Indian Muslims also to give up their prejudices and false notions and advance towards culture and civilization.

Naturally there were strong anti-attitudes also, both in life and literature, but by and large, and the second half of the nineteenth century was the period of close imitative reproduction of western literary models in both poetry and prose. In poetry, the traditional *Ghazal*[5] form was supplemented by thematic poems on scenic, moral or social themes after Robert Southey, William Wordsworth or Alfred Tennyson. In fiction, two parallel schools took the field. First, the school of the historical or picaresque romance where, as said before, the Muslim hero took over from the Christian one. In this, both Walter Scott and Miguel de Cervantes played their part. And the second, the contemporary social and moral tale, after Daniel Defoe's *The Family Instructor* and the moralists of early English fiction. Completely new ground was broken in the essay, biography, literary criticism, and drama. Samuel Johnson, Richard Steele, Joseph Addison, Thomas Carlyle, Mathew Arnold, and of course Shakespeare, provided ready-made models. This period too came to an end in the twenties when the new generation of Western education intellectuals shed these swaddling clothes and embarked on creative endeavours of their own.

By the thirties, the rise of anti-colonial movements all over the East and the emergence of their sympathizers in the Western intelligentsia, the clash of new ideologies and the opening up of other literary horizons besides the British, a new series of encounters began. Their cross-cultural repercussions in the last half-century or so are about as chequered as the many patterns of similar encounters in the previous centuries. In the twenties the English aesthetics, the French romantics and symbolists, the German philosophers, and in the thirties the Russian realists, the English and American realists fertilized a number of new literary movements in various Indian languages. This period, however, deserves a separate study on its own, which I hope some scholars may be tempted to take up who are better equipped and qualified in contemporary methodologies than I am.

NOTES

1. 'Select poetry, chiefly devotional of the Reign of Queen Elizabeth'—The Parker Society—Part II cxi.
2. Gottheil, Richard J.H. (Introduction), Persian Literature Vol. I: World's Greatest Literature. New York, P.F. Collier & Son, 1900.
3. Boswell's Life-Hills edition, Vol. III.
4. Lecture on Sir Herbert Edwardes.
5. A type of lyrical ode with a string of self-contained couplets.

7

WHAT IS THE ROLE OF INTERNATIONAL EXCHANGE IN CULTURAL DEVELOPMENT?

Communication and the means of communication have always played an important part in the development of human societies. A society voluntarily or forcibly cut off from such communication invariably ceases to grow. This is true of the primitive and aboriginal peoples in our midst whose social and cultural growth was stunted by their seclusion in inaccessible bush or swamp or desert. This is true of some ancient civilizations which withered and died when they shut off the light and air of progressive influences of their times. This is also true in varying degrees of the underdeveloped countries of today who were curtained off from each other and the rest of the world by the dominant colonial powers.

International exchange means the restoration of these vital links of communication among various humanities. In the cultural field this means the opening of all doors on the best in thought and feeling and art and inventiveness that these communities have achieved at the peak of their development. It means intimate and first-hand acquaintance with the forms, techniques, content and methodology of various cultures which means a close and first-hand acquaintance with various peoples.

International exchange thus is of particular importance to all those peoples, the culturally underdeveloped peoples, who have only recently embarked on their exploration for higher forms of social and cultural living. It provides for their study, pathways, landmarks, goals and attainments of their more advanced contemporaries. In the development of their own national culture this pooling together of richer experience and achievement naturally plays a positive and creative role.

But international cultural exchange is not important for the underdeveloped countries alone. It is also important for the advanced and developed societies. This is because the culture of every national group is rooted in its own soil, has grown up with its own people and has its own unique characteristics. And in these characteristics there are elements of value which can inspire and instruct and benefit even those who may have attained a much higher level of cultural development. For instance, the advanced art and music of Western Europe have been considerably influenced during the last century by the art and music of primitive Africa. Thus, every true national culture has much to learn and much to teach, and both of these processes are essential to the cultural development of all peoples. The scope and effectiveness of these processes depend on the scope and extensiveness of international exchange.

It is, however, necessary to make two reservations. First, it is necessary to distinguish between the genuine, serious and valuable manifestations of a people's culture created by its own gifted and conscientious cultural exponents and its corrupt, vulgar and worthless specimens manufactured by hacks and lackeys.

Second, it is necessary to distinguish between the forms, techniques, and skills manifested in a national culture which are largely contributed by its gifted and conscientious artists and its social and ideological content which is largely determined by the nature of its social structure and the class dominating this structure. International exchange can be truly beneficial only if it correctly discriminates between culture and trash, between form and content, between what is totally progressive and what is basically reactionary.

Let us begin with the assumption that a creative artist, whatever else he may or may not be, is not an obscure artist, a charlatan, a hypocrite or a coward. Let us assume that he will not sell whatever measure of truth is revealed to him for a mass of pottage. For his truth is both himself and his art which reflects his trend. We are not talking here of personal ethics in the artist but of the ethics of his art. For essentially the fundamentals of all these aesthetics are inalienable from ethical values.

An artist believes in three concentric circles of being; namely, his own self, the national community to which he belongs, and the contemporary mankind of the age in which he lives. And in three dimensions of time; the past, the present, and the future. And these three circles and these three dimensions are the totality of reality as it exists for him at a particular time, the totality of truth. The measure of this truth reflected in his art will be the measure of his awareness of the totality of this reality. The extent to which he reflects this awareness in his art is a measure of the extent to which he modifies the awareness of his audience. And this in its turn is a measure of the extent to which he exchanges or modifies reality through his art. For an awareness is an awareness of relationships, and any modification in this awareness changes one's relationship to reality, through a difference of attitude.

A creative artist, then, has perspective to experience and apprehend the past, the present, and the future himself, his people, and his times and then to value it and expand what he has experienced and apprehended.

What should be the experience in this context of an artist today in Asia and Africa. First, the past; not only the immediate past of servility and degradation under imperialist and colonialist operation, although this past is the most relevant to his present, but also the remote past; of blood and mould, of happy songs and mournful laments, of much beauty and much agreement, of much nobility, and much degradation. Then, the present; the present of much hope and much despair and much fulfilment and much frustration, of much freedom and much talent, of great expectations and great disillusionment, and finally, the future. The future which will be mirrored according to the dimensions on the globe of his vision. A globe which may be small and mean as mould it after his own puny self or much ignore mould it after the magnitude of the tightness of the universe. The same with the other three circles. A notice may well be imprisoned within the confine of his own self, trying to leave off the agony of his own disaster entrails and without other venturing forth into the world without to such existence. Or he may travel up to the boundaries of the experience of his own community and much of it would be spurious and vain if I said it from the world-wide interplays of social forces responsible for them. Or he might mention further and gaze at the totality of contemporary existence to enable him to merge his personal travel into the collective agony of his people and their agony into the clash of global forces of darkness and light of justice and injustice of freedom and that aggrandizement. It is only in the last case that he will take to a sense of the transcendent of his time a sense of the total reality and the total truth of the time in which he lives. A reality and a truth which are constantly in evolution, which change as the universe changes; the only universe that we know which is the universe of man.

In the immediate past, the most important impact of imperialist and colonialist organization on the artist or the intellectual in African-Asian countries was to alienate him as drastically as possible, both from himself and from his fellows by giving him a language, a vocabulary, an idiom, and a universe of experience which they did not share, and from himself because of his sense of guilt and remorse that his cry was a cry in the wilderness. That his experience was only relevant to himself and his art merely an exercise in futility. He therefore set about solving riddles of forms, seeking satisfaction from petty exercises and words and sounds and lines and planes, justifying and rationalizing his petty under-geniuses by half understood and half baked dogma of whatever decadence crazed Western theorists used to propagate, and refusing, come to terms either with the truth within himself or the reality without. He became an alien not to his people but also to the time.

Developing societies of Asia today demand of their artists that this allusion should end, that their artists should talk to them in their own language, that he should hide and seek, laugh and weep, sing and mourn in unison with them all.

That he should denounce the injustice with the tyrannies, past and present, that they have been subject to, that he should share with them the sorrows that they have been heir to and the happinesses they have so far waited for in vain. That his muse should be their muse; muse in the press of the Russian poet, Nekrssov, of sorrow, as well as the muse of Pope of fulfilment.

II.

Ladies and gentlemen, I would begin from where we left off yesterday. Yesterday we talked about the general concepts concerning culture and cultural heritage.

We then talked about one aspect of this question; namely, what, concretely, is the heritage in the field of culture that we Pakistanis can lay claim to.

To understand that, first of all you have to look at your geography, as I said yesterday. West Pakistan, as you can see from the map, because of its geographical location and because of the location of the last routes as well as the sea routes from this area, has been constantly in touch with whatever civilization has risen not only in Asia but also in the continents which are near Asia, namely, Africa and Europe. As you see from the map, you have three systems of routes leading out and leading into West Pakistan. There is one system which centres around the Khyber. This leads through Afghanistan to Northern Iran, on the one hand, and on the other hand, through Afghanistan to Central Asia; what we call the Oxus region. Then from Northern Iran it leads onwards—through Mesopotamia—to Turkey; to Southern Europe. This is the first system of routes through which various cultural influences travelled into and out of what is now called West Pakistan.

The second system is in Balochistan—passes in Balochistan which lead to Southern Iran; and through Southern Iran to the coastal regions of the Persian Gulf; and also northward again, to Mesopotamia—onward to Southern Europe.

These then are the two land system. And there is the third maritime sea route—along the Persian Gulf; termination of the Makran Coast—number 1 and number 2—the Delta of the Sindh River. Both of them in ancient times contained a number of very important ports and there was considerable trade as well as cultural exchange through this maritime route up the Persian Gulf, right to what made at that time great centres of civilization and what is now that land which is now carved up between Lebanon, Syria, and Iraq, where the great ancient Sumerian, Syrian, and Babylonian cultures arose. The same sea route also led along the Southern coast of the Arabian Peninsula, up the Red Sea, to Egypt.

This was one of the main factors why this particular area has been enriched by so many cultural influences from outside.

If you look at East Pakistan, you will find, on the other hand, that it is bounded on the north by mountains (well, incidentally, there was no East Pakistan as you know it in old times). What is now East Pakistan was a part of a big land mass; it was one unit: Bengal, Assam, and what is now Nepal and Eastern Bihar. This was at one time one homogeneous unit which later broke up into these units which we see today. This area served as an outlet—not as an inlet—of cultures, through which the cultural influences which took rise on the subcontinent and travelled onward to South East Asia; to Indonesia, to Malaysia, to Burma, to Cambodia, and northwards to China.

So, this West Pakistan served as the inlet, and what is now East Pakistan served as an outlet of cultural influences.

Again, from the beginning, not of recorded history, but of known history, all that we can say of what went on before 5,000 years ago is that there must have been, during the Stone Age, some settlements of which the only proof that we have are some stone implements, of which the oldest have been found in the Swan Valley around Rawalpindi, and are dated 5,000 years BC. But the first human settlements that we know of probably were found in the foothills of Balochistan. This is the earliest trace of human settlements in this area that we know of. And we know from the archaeological remnants in this area that there must have been small village communities, small settled communities in these foothills, who used chiselled stone instruments, who were able to fashion ornaments of bronze and copper, and who also produced fairly artistic pottery which was both hand-made as well as wheel-turned, which was glazed and dyed and which carried some crude geometrical and semi-realistic images. The time of these settlements is supposed to be between 4,000 to 5,000 BC, i.e., 6,000 years ago—roughly 7,000 years.

Then, at some stage in history—we do not know when—these tribes, because they had acquired a greater mastery over their means of production, because they were able to cultivate land, because they had probably attained a great many herds, they felt ready to venture down from their hilly settlements where they lived in obviously secluded areas. They probably combined into bigger tribes and ventured down to this great valley of the Sindh River.

Incidentally, probably you are aware that it is in this area which is now West Pakistan that the name 'Indian' or 'Hind' originated after the Indus River or the Hind River. Anyway, some time in history—I think it could not have been one movement; probably many movements—these combined communities came down from the hills and took a very adventurous course to settle in the Indus Valley. They must have been attracted because of the very fertile soil on both sides of the river, because the river could serve as an arterial trade route, because through the river goods could be transported, because through the river trade could be carried on.

And so they founded the first urban civilization in this subcontinent which is the Indus Valley Civilization. The earliest trace of this, as you have read in books, is in Kot Diji, about 15 miles from Khairpur, 25 miles east of Mohenjo Daro, which is the earliest and, in some way, primitive form of urban settlement. It has stone-fortified walls; it has fairly elaborate houses and it gives proof of an urban settlement.

But it took another thousand years before this civilization really matured into these great cities of Mohenjo Daro and Harappa. And I think that really was the beginning of what we might call the cultural history of this area.

What is the contribution of this civilization to cultural history? Mainly three things: firstly, planned cities. If you have been to these places or if you have seen their maps, you will find that these cities give proof of very elaborate and very careful planning for the needs of a settled civic community. What are these needs? Sanitation, defence, traffic, food, and commerce. Then you find in these cities all these needs have been very carefully catered for. There is underground drainage for sanitation; there are roads for traffic—and these roads, as you can see, are very carefully planned. The town itself is made on the grid system. It has a series of regular blocks—rectangular blocks—it is not just a conglomeration of houses, as in Karachi or in some of your modern towns. On the other hand, it has a series of carefully distributed and geometrically designed blocks of houses, intersected by roads, and in each city, for defence, there is what you might call—what the Greeks used to call the Acropolis, i.e., a high fort or fortress inside which are located the public buildings, the administrative buildings and sometimes the granary or the food store. And there are elaborate arrangements for the granary. This is the first contribution to the concept of town planning and the concept of administering to the needs of a community as a whole.

The second contribution is the use of material which for the first time was elaborate, particularly the use of baked bricks and the use of mud-basics. It is the perfection of this art of brick baking on which this whole history of architecture of the area are based.

Thirdly, there are the minor arts: art of engraving, of stone carving, and use of very fine instruments in order to chisel metal.

So they produced the first, so far as we know, specimens of what is conventionally called art. First, they did not know any painting, and they did not know sculpture, which came later. But they did produce in that period chiselling of stone and casting of clay, moulding of metal and, as I said, the baking and fashioning of bricks. And it is on these arts that the cultural history of the rest of the subcontinent in the subsequent period is based.

Then, we do now know that this civilization, as I said, which took about 1,000 years to perfect itself, disappeared. It left behind these great monuments in Harappa and Mohenjo Daro, and in various other sites of lesser importance—slightly outside Pakistan—but in contiguous areas in what is now India.

We do not know what happened; why this civilization decayed. The theory held until recently was that there was some sudden calamity; it might have been an earthquake or an invasion; it might have been an epidemic or a plague. But the theory until recently held was that there was some sudden calamity which destroyed these great cities of Mohenjo Daro and Harappa—something in the line of the calamity which overtook the famous city of Pompeii in

Italy. People are now more inclined to believe that it was not a sudden calamity but there must have been natural causes for the degeneration of this civilization because when they settled here they occupied only narrow strips of land on both sides of the Indus and could not really penetrate through the thick forests. As you know, Sindh was not a forest then. On the other hand, it was a series of forests and swamps. They had only occupied a thin strip of land on both sides of the river. Probably this area had been deforested. They had cut down the forests. There might have been changes of climate. There may have been floods in the rivers; there might have been erosion of land; there might have been a lack of vigilance on the part of the community to fight the epidemics, to fight the wild animals, to fight the floods, to fight the material forces of which they had taken control for a short time but had not been to such an extent as to bring these elements of nature totally into some discipline.

And gradually, as they became ease loving, as they became less adventurous and became less enthusiastic, the forces of nature overcame whatever they had achieved during a thousand years of their own efforts, and the civilization decayed and was destroyed.

Now the point of this period is about 2,500 BC that this civilization declined; and then there is a gap of nearly 1,000 years—until we come to the Aryan invasion in 1,500 BC. What happened in these 1,000 years we know very little of except that in Harappa we do find trace of inferior settlements and inferior civilization superimposed on the original planned cities of the Indus civilization. Maybe people lost touch with the advanced art in those times and probably relapsed into their savage or uncivilized state again, and this must have tempted the Aryans from beyond the border to invade them and occupy their land. So, around 1,500 BC the Aryans came and founded another civilization. But the centre of this civilization was not in this area which is now in West Pakistan but in much to the East, in the plains of the Ganges where they cut down forests, founded cities—cities like Benaras and Patliputra and Hastinapur, and so on. There they founded their great cities and there the great Hindu legends of Ram and Krishna arose.

Then, from the Gangetic Plains this civilization, founded by the successors to the Aryan invaders, namely the Brahmanic civilization, travelled both to the west, in what is now called West Pakistan, and to the east, to what is now called East Pakistan. But there are very few traces of this particular period; this Brahmanic or what you might call the Hindu period. There are hardly any traces of this period today and probably the contribution of this particular civilization was not very great.

The next period of civilization—the next great period—begins around 500 BC, that is, after another 1,000 years. This is perhaps the richest and most fruitful period—culturally speaking—of this particular area.

Now it begins with the conquest of the Punjab by the Persians. The Persians annexed the Punjab area up to what you might call the lower Frontier Province around 500 BC, and then began for another 1,000 years a very rich cultural period because the Persians brought to this land, firstly, the use of iron, which was not known here. The use of iron produced much more elaborate tools and instruments of production; not only weapons but things like ploughs, agricultural tools, tools for manufacturing other things, and through these tools, naturally, there was a great deal of increase in production. The second important thing which they brought was coinage. That again was a great cultural contribution because through coinage it was possible to facilitate trade and to increase commerce, and through commerce, of course, there was a great exchange of goods, both cultural as well as functional. The third thing that they brought was the use of stone for masonry and architecture; and fourthly, of course, they brought their own arts for which they were famous; the arts of sculpture, the art of painting, and the small minor arts like ornamentation, and these arts superimposed on the roots of the indigenous crafts which had been left behind by the Indus Civilization. This process, the process of the Persian craftsmen, of Persian artists, of Persian men of culture coming to these parts and imparting their skills to local craftsmen, was greatly accentuated in the fourth century, when Alexander overran Iran and laid waste a good part of this land. During that period, naturally, there was a great exodus, there was a great migration of Persian craftsmen, of Persian artists, of Persian traders, and of Persian Noblemen from Iran into what is now West Pakistan. So, as you know, the penetration of Alexander into these areas also brought together with these émigrés or migrants or refugee Persians, it also brought the Greeks and the Greek influence, the Greek artists and Greek craftsmen because after Alexander left, for some time there were Greek settlements in this country which remained up to the sixth century AD. So two great new influences came: the Persian and the Greek, and the Greek influence was later supplemented by the Romans when, during the reign of Augustus, which is about 100 AD, the Romans founded some settlements in this area. The main influence, however, during this period, is the rise of Buddhism. As you know, the period of Buddhism, about 500 BC, is more or less the same period as the period of classical Greece, and these two great cultural movements more or less arose at the same time—the Buddhist movement and the classical Greek movement. It was the influence of this particular movement, that is, the Buddhist movement which found expression, as we shall see later on, in one of the great stores of culture which is collectively called Gandhara Art, to which we shall come a little later. I forgot to mention one thing that during this Hindu period a great social change took place as opposed to the period of Indus civilization. In the Indus civilization period, as I said before, the entire community is obviously organized as one unit, although there seem to be classes because there were rich houses and the poor houses, but all utilities and amenities were common. During the Hindu period there is a class system; the caste system, and from then on you find that all culture is divided into two classes—the classical culture or the feudal culture, or the court culture or the culture of the rich, on the one hand, and the folk culture or culture of the people, on the other hand, and this division has remained from that day to this. The so-called classical culture, feudal culture or court culture of this period—of the period both before and after Buddhism—was largely either religious or feudal; namely, it was based on motives which were drawn either from mythology, from religious legends or from various manifestations of particular beliefs. It gave rise to what is collectively called a body of Hindu iconography; iconography means the building of idols and images. So, as I was saying, the Buddhist civilization attained its zenith during the reign of the Mauryan Emperor, Ashoka, whose period is about 356 BC or the middle of the third century. It was during this period that Taxila became the regional seat of government, the regional seat of the Mauryan empire, and became one of the biggest centres of Buddhist learning. At the same time, because of the very close contact with Iran during this period, three great cities arose on the trade route between what is now West Pakistan and Central Asia and some of these cities on this side of the border, of our side of the border were Muskishat(?) which is now Charsadda, Peshiparu which is now Peshawar and, of course, Taxila. So, during this period that I am talking about, this early Buddhist period, three things arose. Firstly, the rise of Taxila as the seat of government; secondly, the rise of cities on the trade route, and thirdly, the importation of classical cultural influences from Persia and Greece and later on from Rome. The main contribution of this period culturally is firstly in architecture because it was during this period that through Persian influence masonry architecture and stone architecture was introduced into this subcontinent. Secondly, great contribution was made in the art of sculpture, and that was again through Persian influence that the sculpture in Iran, unlike the relief, unlike the carving which was previously known, the life size sculpture, the human portraiture was introduced. All these influences; the Persian, the Greek, and the Roman influence; all these were finally synthesized in what we now call Gandhara Art, which had its zenith during the period of the Kushans who were of Central Chinese origin. We do not know exactly where they came from but their origins were somewhere in China, and it was the great King Kanishka whose period is first century AD, that the great cities of Gandhara arose, the cities of Taxila and around. It was during this period that Buddha became a deified god. It was this deification of Buddha which gave rise to the art of body sculpture that we call Gandhara Art because this art; this culture is mainly centred around the life of Buddha and the portraiture of Buddha. And apart from Buddha himself and his image, around Buddha are centred what are called Bodhistavas, who are human figures, patterns of art, who it was supposed would some day tend to become Buddha themselves. So this period saw in sculpture the introduction of human portraiture; it saw a new sophistication brought from classical Greece and from classical Rome. It saw the use of ornamentation, the use of larger than life-size sculptures. Of course, sculpture was known before but unlike the Hindu sculpture of central India or eastern India where there was no attempt made to chisel human features, there was no attempt made to ornament or to decorate the human figure—it was squat and heavy and unadorned—this great body of sculpture which has remained from that time until the present, one of the great marvels of the human hand, this block sculpture, this realistic and ornamental body of sculpture that was produced and, at the same time, apart from sculpture, because when the Buddhist religion became rather elaborate other things, other arts, minor arts also developed greatly. For instance, apart from ornaments which were always known there were religious ritual utensils and incense burners, and a new influence was also introduced in the process of metallurgy itself. New alloys were produced; it was in this period that brass was produced. It was in this period that by an alloy of tin and steel they produced a new more plastic material for casting and moulding of vessels. That is, so far as West Pakistan is concerned. As I said, this period can be divided into two: pre-Ashoka and post-Ashoka. In the pre-Ashoka period, the predominant influence is Persian and in the post-Ashoka period, the predominant influence is Roman and Greek through sculpture.

What was going on in East Pakistan at that time? Unfortunately, because of climatic factors, nothing much has come down to us today, so far as East Pakistan is concerned, of these ancient civilizations. The only traces we have, the earliest traces we have are of the period of Ashoka, but they are so fragmentary that no theory can be built on it and the earliest civilization that we come to know of—although we know that it must have been, being contemporary because the Mauryan empire extended up to East Pakistan—we can only assume that the civilization and the cultural life of that period must have been very similar but unfortunately we have no direct specimens of what the people in that region produced in those centuries. The earliest sizeable remnants of civilized living belong to the seventh and eighth centuries, under the Paras and Deva kings of East Pakistan, and we do have these very elaborate monasteries in…and Mainamati, which again is a proof of very sophisticated organized cultural communities. It was probably the last period of the Buddhist civilization before it was finally destroyed, and it is, therefore, the most ornamental, the most sophisticated period. If you ever go to Bahawalpur and contrast these monasteries there, with the stupas in Taxila, you can find that the civilization had already become decadent because there is far greater emphasis on ornamentation, on rather elaborate luxurious structures than on pure composition or on pure functional uses of these buildings. And you probably know in East Pakistan the rise of Buddhism was finally checked and then destroyed by the Deva kings who tried to bring back Hinduism, tried to re-impose Hinduism, and there was a great deal of persecution of the Buddhists in those days. As a result, when the Muslims came they were welcomed, at least in East Pakistan, as liberators from the oppression of the Brahmins imported from India into East Pakistan. Perhaps you know that some of the gods depicted both in clay figures as well as on wooden tablets depict the Muslim warrior with his beard, as a god, as an avtar who had come to deliver the Buddhists from the oppression of the Brahmins. Anyway, that comes to a later period. But now we have come practically to the Muslim period because in the sixth century the Gandhara period which lasted roughly from the fifth century BC that we are talking about, until about the fifth century AD, when the Huns came and destroyed this civilization altogether. During this period, as we have seen, there are these great contributions in sculpture, architecture, and in the minor arts. I forgot that there is one more contribution which the Persians made and that was the introduction of a new script they brought with them; the Arabic script. The Indus script, as you know, has not been deciphered. That has been lost. And it was through the Persians that the art of reading and writing was reintroduced into this subcontinent through the Arabic script which was adopted and, to a certain extent, modified and because the Karacid(?) script, of which you see the specimens in the Frontier

Province, which is the script of Ashoka, which you see on the inscriptions of stone in North West Frontier Province. So there was the script, there was coinage, there was the use of iron, there was the use of stone, there was a new type of architecture, the use of columns, the use of halls, and the use of sculpture. This is the main contribution and it came from these various sources that I have mentioned. This finally reached perfection during the period of Kanishka and then was destroyed when the Huns came in the sixth century BC and after that the next great cultural period began with the invasion of the Muslims in 711 AD, but I think we have had enough for one day.

So, as I said, there are two great periods of Indus civilization then there is a gap and then what you might call the Gandhara civilization or the Buddhist civilization. These are the two main civilizations, although the second civilization is really not one civilization but a combination or synthesis of a large number of influences which found expression in various arts, and then the third great period begins with the invasion of the Muslims. I am sorry, I should have been more brief but, as I told you before, I am no expert. Probably the experts were going to talk to you later on. I hope to be corrected of any errors I might have made. Is there anything that anybody would like to ask?

After heartfelt thanks to our generous host, I would like to address myself to the question which has been repeatedly posed during our discussions and answered in various ways. The question is, who are we—we the writers, poets and artists, and what can be contributed, if anything, to avert the mortal calamities threatening mankind? If the same question were put to us, say, in London, by another person, it would probably be less politely worded and might read, 'who the hell do you think you are and what the hell do you think you can do about the things around you?' My answer is, and would be, 'we are the offspring, in direct line of descent, of the magicians, the sorcerers and music makers of old.' In times gone by, these ancient ancestors of ours could make the rain come down with their incantations and with their songs; they could make the deserts bloom. And they not only implicitly believed that they held these powers, their community believed it too. This is because they found, for the hopes and fears of their people, for their dreams and longings, words and music that the people could not find for themselves. And by bending their collective will to a desired end, they would some times make the dreams come true.

In subsequent times, with the rise of kings and captains, blood-soaked warriors and professional priests, the rise of moneychangers, scribes and 'pharisees' in the biblical language, much of this power was lost. But the magic and its appeal and the hunger for it have remained. In our part of the world, through long centuries of various feudal empires, the magician of old became the poet-mystic or the mystic-poet, the forerunner of the modern humanist who defied both emperor and priests to articulate the ills and afflictions of his fellow beings, to expose the injustices of their masters and their masters' collaborations; who taught them to believe in and fight for justice, beauty, goodness, and truth irrespective of personal loss or gain. And legends ascribe to them the same supernatural powers that the ancient magicians were supposed to wield. In many places it is a custom even to this day that if a person is looking for an omen to foretell his fortune in love, or whatever his problem, he looks for it in an ancient Persian classic—the poetic work of Rumi, Hafiz or Saadi. The first verse touched by his finger on the first page he opens is supposed to predict his future.

So that is who we are, the inheritors of this magic and the power of this magic, in big ways or small, depending on the intensity of the love our hearts possess, on the anguish we share with an anguished world, on the measure of our strength to defy what is evil and to uphold what is good. And never was the power of this magic more devoutly to be wished than in the world of today, when so many powerful agencies are at work to deny the validity of all ethical human values, to obliterate all refinements of human feeling so laboriously acquired over the centuries, by extolling cynicism, insensitivity, and brutishness as the hallmark of a he-man and woman. And thus as a writer, even though I run no state and command no power, I am entitled to feel that I am my brother's keeper and my brother is the whole of mankind. And this is the relevance to me of Peace, of Helsinki, of detente, and the elimination of the nuclear menace.

But out of this vast brotherhood the nearest and dearest to me are the insulted, the humiliated, the homeless, the disinherited, the poor, the hungry and sick at heart. And this is the relevance to me of Palestine, of South Africa, Zimbabwe, of Chile, of my own people and people like me. The point has already been made by various speakers that the peace we want for them is not merely the absence of war; for that would be no more than a continuation of their present misery and humiliation. The peace we want for them is a peace which brings them happiness and justice and dignity; a peace which might have to be fought for and won.

But the hope for this peace and the possibility are relevant only in the context of life and its continuation in the future. The arsenal of nuclear weapons can put an end to both. Hence, the primary importance of world peace. So I shall end with a fragment of a poem written in the early years of the world peace movement:

What do you want,
Life or death,
Existence or extinction?
Speak, proclaim your decision.
Life or death,
Existence or extinction.
The Universe today hangs
By one word on your lips:
Life or death.

8

PROBLEMS OF NATIONAL ART AND CULTURE[1]

I.

THEORETICAL PROBLEMS RELATING TO NATIONAL ART AND CULTURE

A theoretical dissertation on the meaning, nature and function of art and culture is hardly the province of a work-a-day committee set up to recommend practical measures to meet practical objectives. Nevertheless, it is hardly possible to formulate practical policies on any subject in the absence of a defined basis of approach. The observations in this section, although far from original, are intended to provide this basis.

The term 'culture' was originally used for the art of making living organisms grow and develop. When applied to human beings it is popularly defined as 'the whole way of life of a specific human group or society'. This whole way of life would obviously comprise both ideological and material components, i.e. both values and social practices. The definition postulates that:

(a) Culture, unlike the arts, is not created by a few individuals but is 'lived' and evolved by a whole community. The arts thus are abstract or symbolic manifestations of what is lived by the community.

(b) Since every culture relates to a specific human society and since every human society lives in time and space, every culture must be both historical and territorial, although its ideological components may include extra-territorial and supra-temporal elements. For instance, Muslim societies, in spite of racial, linguistic and other differences, have many cultural traits in common.

(c) Since the way of life of a community is conditioned by the social organization or system under which it lives, the culture of this community must be similarly conditioned. Any change in the cultural patterns of this community, therefore, must be accompanied by corresponding changes in its social conditions of existence. Obversely, when these social conditions change, the culture of a community must change accordingly.

(d) Since culture is a way of life and not merely a way of thought, its quality and complexion are determined more by what is actually practised and not so much by what is merely professed. It is not inconceivable that a particular society may strongly believe in one set of values and actually practise, out of material considerations, values which are totally different.

It should be obvious from the above that cultural problems do not relate to the arts alone, or to any other specific department of national life, but form an integral part of the basic structural socio-economic problems of every society.

The solutions to these problems, therefore, must also lie with the solution of these basic socio-economic problems. Thus the culture of a society fragmented into different social classes with varying levels of intellectual development, must also be fragmented into different patterns of varying quality. To evolve a common or unified culture for such a society we must presume the evolution of a unified and equitable social structure.

It should be equally obvious that in periods of social change, there is likely to be a conflict between the patterns of culture inherited from the past and new patterns demanded by environmental exigencies of the present. In such a period, it becomes incumbent on the community to re-evaluate its historical traditions and to integrate them with new elements created by new social conditions. A complete negation of the past would destroy the roots of cultural growth. A complete negation of contemporary conditions would destroy its chances of survival.

Thus even though culture cannot transcend the limitations of a given social structure, it can certainly lag behind it. In other words, while cultural activity cannot exceed the progressive potentialities of a particular society it can certainly fall short of what is both possible and desirable. The reasons for such a situation arising are many, e.g.:

1. Dominative influences of vested interests opposed to any social change.
2. The lack of adequate creative enterprise by enlightened elements within the community because of insufficient resources, patronage, or opportunity.
3. Apathetic, indifferent and fatalistic attitudes which permeate under-privileged majorities in societies characterized by marked social inequalities.

Thus while an hypothetical ideal culture must await an hypothetical ideal society, it is given to every society, in the imperfect present-day world, to accept or reject attitudes, and to adopt or ignore measures in the cultural field, which are conducive to social progress and intellectual enlightenment within its limitations.

Art thus has an important dual political role. Internally it holds up the mirror to a nation or society and helps it to discover its own image and its own personality. The consciousness of this personality helps a nation to bring about a closer and more harmonious integration among its component elements. It is thus a powerful agent for national integration.

Externally it provides the most potent means to establish the identity of a nation in the international confraternity.

Art, thus, is an important medium of national projection and interpretation of national thought.

The exchange and interflow of national modes of self-expression embodied in the arts help every society to discover underlying universalities in the best of contemporary thought and feeling. Art thus is an important promotional factor in international friendship and understanding.

This Committee is not concerned with the problems of ideal culture in an ideal society. It is only concerned with the cultural situation as it pertains in present-day Pakistan. It is again not within the province of this Committee to go into the basic socio-economic problems which govern this situation or to hypothesize their solutions. We have, therefore, mainly concerned ourselves with only those components of national culture regarding which, despite all limitations, much can be, and needs to be, practically done. These components are the body of our arts.

Role of Arts

As stated earlier the arts symbolize in a finished and stylized form a society's way of life, both material and ideological. The body of the arts is, therefore, the visible representation of a nation's identity or image, by which it is known and recognised. The level and quality of these arts is taken to be the measure of the level and quality of its civilization.

Art, unlike culture, is not the raw material or social life which exists independently of individuals, but a deliberate and superior manufacture created by a body of specialists. It predicates, on the part of the artist, an awareness of things superior to the common run and a level of sensibility higher than of those who are not similarly endowed. Art, therefore, unlike culture, is not merely a passive reflection of a way of life but an active agency which can also, to some measure, change and modify it. It can change and modify the consciousness of all those with whom it communicates. It prescribes the good and bad in taste, the 'cultured' and 'uncultured' in personality and behaviour, the beautiful and ugly in material surroundings. It thus profoundly influences both value judgements and social behaviour within the community.

Art, therefore, is an important moral (and in its perverted forms immoral) social force.

The arts provide a sublimated vehicle for the expression of urges, impulses, instincts, dreams, illusions, conflicts, happinesses and unhappinesses, fulfilments and frustrations of a human group.

These means of self-expression are as natural and as necessary to a community as laughter or tears, or cries of pain and pleasure, to an individual. The blocking or suppression of these means can have the same pernicious psychopathic repercussions for a people as the forcible suppression of natural instincts for an individual.

Artistic expression, therefore, is an important factor in peoples' mental health.

Art is an acknowledged source of human pleasure. So much so that this is sometimes mistaken as its sole end. This pleasurableness together with other moral, intellectual, and emotional components, makes good and serious art into the most instructive, beneficial, and purposeful means for the utilization of a peoples' leisure.

Art thus is an important agent of human happiness.

All this and more has been repeated more than once from more than one platform in Pakistan. Why then has so little been done? Because of misconceived, fallacious, short sighted and even perverse national attitude towards the problems of art and culture. In this report, we can only briefly outline some of them.

National Attitudes

CULTURE AND IDEOLOGY

There is a school of thinking which holds that all cultural activity in general and the performing arts in particular are immoral and anti-religious. The anti-culture, anti-art attitudes fostered by this school mainly derive from the following factors:

(i) Prolonged colonial subjection subverted the native cultural patterns of our old society and the imperialist rulers sought to replace them by their own cultural imports. Everything 'native' by way of culture and the arts was held up to contempt and ridicule and their western counterparts held out as the only models fit for imitation. The resultant disruption of national life and impoverishment of all the national arts robbed large sections of our people, particularly the influential section called 'the Civil Lines', of all love, respect and understanding of their national arts.

(ii) During the declining years of the Mughal Empire in the subcontinent, as elsewhere in similar historical conditions, the arts were reduced to become handmaids of dissolute courts and instruments of their decadent pleasures. This was particularly true of music and dancing which were encouraged to become the monopoly of a socially and morally unacceptable class. After the downfall of the Mughals, the moral indignation evoked by these decadent practices and the social prejudices attaching to the class of 'singing girls' were detached from the social conditions which gave them birth and transferred, in the popular mind, to the arts themselves.

(iii) Since Independence, these anti-art-attitudes inherited from the past have been seized upon by certain factions in the country for topical political ends. They first sought to equate all culture with music and dancing and then to equate all music and dance with the lewd vulgarizations of these arts by inept professionals. From these premises, it was easy to proceed to the conclusion, as has often been done, that all art is immoral, hence anti-religious, hence ideologically unacceptable. It takes no great religious knowledge to rebut this thesis. Hamd, Na'at Salam, Marsia, Qawwali are all forms of musical expression. Khattak, Dhali, Kathi, Bhangra, Jhoomar, are all dance forms. All decorative arts partake of elements of sculpture and painting. We doubt if many people, even among the most religious minded, would object to any of these forms of artistic expression on religious or moral grounds. Any ideological objection that can be brought against any therefore, must relate to some particular form and content of a particular art and not to the art as such. This obvious platitude is deliberately ignored because the basic motivation of this school is neither moral nor religious but socio-political. This motivation seeks to promote attitudes hostile to all agencies of sensitive feeling and enlightened thought, including scientific research and artistic creation.

(iv) Culture and the arts have also been brought into disrepute by the peculiar institution which goes by the name of 'cultural show'. Thoughtless and ill-advised official and public bodies have frequently dignified by this title, cheap and prurient programmes of music, dance and clowning by disreputable performers. This practice has fortified both the anti-culture school of opinion mentioned above as well as the existing popular prejudices against the arts.

(v) The generally negative public and official attitudes towards national art and culture have opened the gates for a resolute cultural invasion by Western commercial and political agencies. Thus in the last few years many corrupt and perverted versions of Western culture focussed on sex, violence and profligacy, have provided the staple cultural fare for the sophisticated Pakistani boy and girl and the outlet for his or her natural craving for self-expression. It is ironic that the sections who are most vociferous against this deliberate perversion of our national, cultural, ethical and ideological values, are the same as have at least partially, and perhaps unintentionally, made this subversion possible by their unqualified hostility to the promotion of our own national arts and to the evolution of serious public standards of moral and aesthetic judgement. The validity of the case made out by this anti-culture, anti-art school has been repeatedly challenged from many forums, and, of course, has never been officially accepted. Nevertheless, the issue has never been squarely faced either, and no national government has clearly defined in theory or in practice the limits of permissibility or impermissibility in the field of art and culture. As a result, it has been left to individual functionaries of the state to lay down the law for the artist and the cultural worker without any policy sanction except his own personal preferences and prejudices.

This has led, firstly, to some ludicrous contradictions in official policy. Thus music and dancing were, at one time, banned in all educational institutions in one half of the country, while in the other half they formed a regular part of the academic curriculum. Since people in halves of the country profess the same religion and the same ideology, one party or the other must have been guilty of grave deviation. Secondly, it has bred a feeling among many public officials that art and culture are rather risky things to play around with and are better left alone, unless superior authorities explicitly desire it otherwise.

This Committee is of the opinion that:

(a) Most ideological objections to the promotion of art and culture in Pakistan are based not on the fundamentals of religion or ideology but on social prejudice, political expediency, or lack of discrimination between the good and bad, the pure and putrid, the moral and immoral in art and culture.

(b) Blind hostility to all forms of artistic or cultural activities is warranted by neither history, nor tradition, nor current practice of great Muslim societies. Otherwise, there would have been no such thing as Muslim culture or Islamic civilization.

(c) To rectify fallacies and confusions in the public mind regarding the true nature of the arts and their correct role in national life, it is necessary:

   (i) to evolve a consistent and unequivocal national policy regarding the arts and to create a national agency to implement it.

   (ii) to educate public mind and to train public taste in the appreciation and enjoyment of the arts, not through precept but through examples, not through argument but through demonstration, i.e. by creating conditions favourable to the promotion of serious and wholesome forms of artistic expression.

CULTURE AND NATIONAL DEVELOPMENT

A second fairly influential point of view in the country is that culture and the arts, even though they may not be morally undesirable or ideologically reprehensible, are still something of a luxury which only the rich countries can afford. Developing countries, like Pakistan, must put first things first and devote all their resources to material development, i.e. agriculture and industry, and let 'the harp and the fiddle' wait till better days come round—just as a poor man would put his daily bread before the pleasures of art.

We are unable to agree with this point of view.

In a developing society where the paucity of funds hinders all development, education constitutes personal capital and hence counts as a basic factor in development. Similarly, culture which represents the awareness of a society of its values, aims and aspirations provides an important incentive for national development. Any development efforts which ignore the emotional and spiritual aid provided by a nation's awareness of its own goals and aspirations are bound to engender antagonistic contradictions between the people and the agencies responsible for such development. Cultural activity in a developing nation is in many ways a form of socio-political activity and it is only through this activity that a people's full participation in nation-building efforts can be ensured.

If the total expenditure on the promotion of national art and culture is compared with the money spent on the construction of golf links or ski resorts or the palatial buildings of some banks and commercial houses it will be seen that the analogy of the poor man does not really hold and that Pakistan, like every other developing country, has thought it fit to invest large sums of money in 'prestige' projects, not for the sake of material returns, but to improve its 'image' both nationally and internationally. This Committee feels that for precisely the same reasons the promotion of national art and culture should have been given a higher priority in the plans of national development because the national arts are the most obvious assets of a country's prestigious capital, and the most organic component of its 'image'.

Establishment-wise, while almost every department of national life, from the eradication of mosquitoes to the promotion of tourism, is adequately staffed at more than one level, there is, to our knowledge, not one senior officer in any establishment whose duties pertain, exclusively, to the promotion of art and culture.

The analogy of the poor man does not hold in many other ways. For instance, there is hardly a poor man who does not seek to leaven his daily bread with whatever 'cultural' entertainment is available to him by way of folk song or folk dance or film or sport. And if no such outlet is available for the utilization of the leisure hours, he turns in desperation to drugs and opiates. The same applies to a human group, society, or nation. If the State or responsible public agencies do not meet the demands of popular leisure and emotive satisfaction, these demands are bound to be supplied by other irresponsible agencies with no public or moral scruples. The goods they supply can prove even more deleterious for the mental and moral health of a nation than drugs and opiates.

Secondly, the arts are as much a factor in the material processes of production as education is. Just as an investment in national education has a direct bearing on national productivity through recreating superior skills, an investment in the arts has a direct role in improving the standards and qualities of many forms of industrial production by superior fashioning and designing.

Thirdly, in the world of today, advertising and public relationing are no longer regarded as a luxury but an important charge on industrial revenues. Nations do their advertising and public relationing through cultural exchange, i.e., exchanges of art products and performances.

This Committee is, therefore, of the opinion that the priority of the promotion of art and culture, in national plans of development, should be re-examined and more correctly assessed.

CULTURE AND NATIONAL IDENTITY

Before the inception of Pakistan, there was, understandably, no such entity as a Pakistani nation. Politically the people of present day Pakistan (leaving aside some minority groups) were part of the Indian Muslim Community. Ethnically and geographically they were called after the areas they inhabited, i.e., Bengalis, Punjabis, Sindhis, Baluchis, Pathans etc. Understandably, therefore, the culture of the now Pakistani nation when it emerged was not a finished, ready made unified-entity. The differences in social development among different regions of the country, differences of climate and geographical habitat, ethnic and historical factors and administrative divisions enforced by foreign rulers, all combined to make the culture of the people of present-day Pakistan a composite of diversified patterns. Nevertheless, these people in all parts of Pakistan shared a common historical experience as well as those common ethical and cultural mores which originated from the religion they professed. It was this common religion and the sum total of these values and their expression in social life which made the Muslims of the subcontinent emerge as a separate and distinct cultural entity over a long period of history.

There is considerable difference of opinion on how precisely this culture should be defined. There appears to be some agreement, however, that the culture of the people of Pakistan includes every thing which has been integrated into the bloodstream of the social and historical life of our people. This conglomeration is principally composed of (a) the religion of Islam which provides the ethical and ideological basis for the people's way of life, (b) the indigenous cultures of different linguistic regions inherited from their own specific cultural past, and (c) elements of Western culture absorbed since the days of British occupation. Added to the above are the distinctive cultures of minority groups who form a part of the Pakistani nation.

This proposition raises two debatable issues:

1. If Pakistan is an ideological state and its ideology is Islam, isn't Muslim culture or Islamic culture an adequate definition of Pakistani culture? Is it necessary or desirable to seek or discover a cultural identity apart or beyond this generic term? This line of reasoning ignores two obvious realities.

First, it ignores the reality of the non-ideological components of culture, e.g., language, dress, cuisine, architecture, arts and crafts, non-religious customs and social observances, etc. These are mundane products of historical origin and geographical environment and cannot be dubbed Islamic or un-Islamic. Thus Urdu, Punjabi, Sindhi, Pushto, Ajrak, Ralli, Shalwar, Kurta, Lassi, Sajji, Tikka, Kabaddi, Tent-pegging, Urs at Sehwan, and Mela Chiraghan at Lahore etc. etc. are essential Components of our particular national culture but they are hardly translatable into any ideological terms. Second: it ignores the reality of nationhood. Nationhood may be a good thing or a bad thing but it can hardly be ignored as a fact of present day political life. It provides the very basis of a State and its denial amounts to a repudiation of ones own sovereignty as a State. Thus Sudan, Nigeria, Turkey, Iran and Indonesia are all Muslim States but a Nigerian, unless he forfeits his nationality is not a Turk nor can a Sudanese claim to be an Indonesian. As they all profess Islam, what differentiates the identity of one from the other must be something other than religion. This some thing else is his nationhood and his culture which are two sides of the same phenomenon.

There is little justification, therefore, for any ambivalent or apologetic attitude either towards Pakistani nationhood or towards Pakistani culture.

2. The second issue relates to regional cultures. The basic and characteristic vocabulary of our people's culture, i.e., language, dress, customs, architecture, music, folk arts etc., has naturally been better preserved in our villages and the countryside of various regions than in big towns where dominative foreign influences have introduced a cosmopolitanism composed of many elements and characteristics which are not exclusively national. The growth of these folk cultures was arrested at various levels of development with the disintegration of feudal societies, the withdrawal of feudal patronage, and the concentration of power, wealth and educational and cultural facilities in the big towns. A reversal of this process of stagnation, therefore, and a revival of these regional cultures—the most

authentic store-house of what is distinctively Pakistani—seems obviously called for. This raises two issues: First, whether such a revival would promote centrifugal tendencies of narrow regionalism and militate against the goals of national integration. Second, whether such a revival and the development of regional cultures would yield to some sort of a synthesis on the national plane.

The consensus of the opinions we have gathered may be summarized as follows:

(a) Culture, like charity, begins at home. It appears natural, therefore, that before a citizen of Pakistan comes to love or appreciate a national culture which is still in the process of evolution and which he knows only in the abstract, he must love, respect and appreciate his own regional culture which already exists, in whatever developed or undeveloped form, and which he knows and understands. In as much as all regional cultures are an organic part of the totality of our national culture, love for the part does not preclude, and in fact predicates, love for the whole. The confusion of thought which continues to plague this subject stems from one basic fallacy which seeks to counterpoise national and regional cultures as antagonistic rivals and thus postulates that one can or would develop only at the expense of the other. This fallacy can be dispelled by a clear understanding of the obvious fact that just as the country is a geographical union of its constituent regions and the nation is a political union of the people inhabiting these regions, similarly, national culture is an aggregate of these regional cultures plus the unifying bonds of faith and history. The development of national culture therefore presumes that every citizen of Pakistan must love, respect and creatively participate in the culture of his birth and upbringing and at the same time make this activity embrace and coalesce with the collective national creative process.

(b) Genuine national integration requires not merely a sharing of common values and beliefs which might be negatived by more powerful emotional or materialistic motivations, but also a sharing of collective experience—a communion of collective thought and feeling and sensibility, lectures, discussions, seminars, exchanges of individuals etc. may have their uses but they have only a cerebral appeal to extremely limited audiences, particularly at the present stage of educational and intellectual development. They cannot serve purposes of mass understanding or mass communication. The only media which can perform this function are the arts. A flowering of regional cultures, arts, crafts, literatures etc., and a widespread and consistent exchange of artistic expression will not only not hinder but should serve as the most effective means of national integration. One further point to be kept in view is that any regional cultural or artistic manifestation which gains wide acceptability through its aesthetic or emotional appeal can easily become 'national'. We already have examples of folk songs and folk arts which have become universally popular in all parts of the country.

(c) A genuine synthesis of diverse forms of regional cultures into national patterns cannot be brought about by any forcible impositions through administrative means. It can only evolve through a gradual accumulation of affinities and a gradual assimilation of 'sympathetic elements into a new compound'. This is possible only if 'diversity' is not misinterpreted as disunity and the natural process of the growth of diverse elements is not perverted or stifled by an impatience for immediate results. In any case, if the creative potentialities of our regional arts and culture are allowed to wilt and die we shall soon find ourselves with nothing left to synthesize. The only alternative left to us will be to borrow a national culture wholesale from some alien source—a process which is already piece-meal in progress.

CULTURE AND TRADITIONS

The problem of national identity also relates to the classical tradition of the arts. And this presents a different set of problems.

(a) Since this tradition, particularly in arts like music and dancing, is much older than the Muslim era, it contains many ingredients unrelated to Muslim social traditions.

(b) Since the Indo-Muslim civilization was not confined to the areas which now form Pakistan, it contains many ingredients which transcend our boundaries and cannot be deemed exclusively Pakistani.

Should this tradition, then, be owned and accepted wholesale or should it be recast into a mould nearer to the heart of a present-day Pakistani citizen? There is considerable difference of opinion over this issue. One school holds that to establish a completely different national and ideological identity it is necessary to discard all these ingredients and if this is not possible with regard to a particular artistic tradition it were best to do away with this tradition altogether. The opposite view is that by maligning a tradition evolved by Muslim society in the days of their greatest glory, a tradition which represents their main contribution to the cultural history of this subcontinent, we really malign our own history, that we are not justified in taking exception to what our ancestors, in whom we take pride, not only took no exception to but actively sponsored and patronized.

A third point of view put to us was that a distinction must be made between the non-Islamic and the anti-Islamic in art and culture. It is only to the latter, i.e., to an element obviously repugnant to a basic Islamic tenet, that we should take exception.

As for territorial limits, it should be obvious that some of the most basic components of our cultural heritage originated and evolved in areas beyond the present geographical boundaries of Pakistan. These include the Urdu language and literature and the whole body of Arabic, Iranian, Central Asian and various other influences which have been integrated into our cultural tradition.

The most cogent argument advanced in favour of preserving the purity of classical tradition was that, apart from religion, this tradition in the arts, e.g. architecture, music and dance, represents the main connecting and common link among our regional cultures. The vocabulary of the classical arts is common to all regions of Pakistan alike. Hence it should be regarded as a factor in national integration and steps should be taken to make this vocabulary, at present familiar only to a limited few, as widely intelligible as possible.

Lastly, there is the problem of re-evaluation our cultural and artistic tradition in the light of contemporary experience, the adjustment of 'from the past' with the demands of the present.'

Western societies, after thirty-two hundred years of scientific industrial add technological advancement, mainly at the expense of the peoples they dominated, have introduced to the world techniques, methodologies, tools, materials, and modes of production unknown before. These advances, in their turn, have induced new habits of thought and cultural expression, thus modifying or eliminating various traditional elements in social or cultural life. In developing and newly liberated countries, like Pakistan, this process has just begun. And along with it have emerged the horns of a dilemma—of tradition vs. modernism.

This dilemma has generated three tendencies—one of blind imitativeness of our own past in the name of tradition, the other of blind imitativeness of everything Western in the name of modernism, the third of a tasteless hotchpotch of the two in order to have the best of both worlds.

We are of the opinion that all these attitudes are incorrect, that:

(a) The continuity of tradition does not mean its perpetuation in toto. For instance, the place of our traditional arms, the sword and the spear, is no longer in the battlefield but in the museum. Nevertheless, they should be preserved, loved and respected as a part of our heritage.

(b) The acquisition of scientific, technological industrial, and intellectual knowledge from the West does not necessitate a negation of our own historic personality.

Therefore,

(c) These elements of our traditional culture which were only relevant to another set of conditions in the past and have outlived their utility cannot and should not be artificially perpetuated merely on the grounds of sentiment. The sentiments of love and respect alone should be enough.

(d) The application of new techniques in the arts, experimentation with new forms of expression, utilization of new materials, popularization of new artistic concepts, should not be discouraged merely because they have originated in the West, provided the artist retains his identity as a member of his own community.

(e) A living and dynamic culture is one which provides conditions for maximum contribution by national talent for the aesthetic and intellectual enrichment of the community, at the highest level of contemporary attainment. Our endeavour should be to create the most favourable conditions for this maximum contribution.

SUMMARY

Culture is the whole way of life of a community. It changes when social conditions change. Cultural development is not conceivable without social development.

The arts represent the level of a society's civilization. They are not a passive reflection of reality but an active agency for social uplift or degeneration.

The arts are the visible image of a nation-hence its best media of projection.

Opposition to art and culture in Pakistan stems from social prejudice and political considerations rather than religious or moral scruples.

The arts are not a luxury. They are an important factor in a nation's mental and moral health and productive efficiency.

The national culture of Pakistan is a composite of many elements. Regional cultures and folk arts are the best preserved elements of this culture.

The national culture of Pakistan is as yet in the process of evolution. This evolution can be helped by the development of regional cultures and their creative synthesis.

Classical traditions being common to all regions of Pakistan are an important factor in national integration. These traditions must be remoulded in the light of modern knowledge and contemporary conditions.

II.

PRACTICAL PROBLEMS RELATING TO THE PROMOTION OF NATIONAL ART AND CULTURE

General

CO-ORDINATION AND DIRECTION

There is almost unanimity of opinion that although the arts in Pakistan have made some progress particularly in the last decade and although some development has been registered in some limited cultural fields, there is as yet no sense of direction in any of the arts, no clear concept of social or national goals to be aimed at and no co-ordination at any level between cultural organizations engaged in different artistic pursuits.

As a result the cultural and artistic potential of the country has been fragmented into a number of isolated pockets of activity with purely local affiliations. Because of the absence of any cohesive link between them they have failed to make any impact on the social or intellectual life of the community as a whole.

It is inconceivable that any national cultural artistic movement should develop, or any unifying tendencies in the regional and local cultural affiliations emerge, in the absence of a central national organisation or organisations which should co-ordinate, direct, plan and facilitate the development of national art and culture. It is only through such an organization that a correct and continuing evaluation of the work of the present cultural organizations can be made and the utilization of public funds at present being spent on the promotion of art and culture be properly scrutinized. The establishment of such an organization is also essential to evolve some uniform pattern of work for different cultural organizations at different levels, to prescribe the most effective organizational, and administrative arrangements for different types of cultural organizations, to plan and advise on international cultural exchange and to provide a 'brains-trust' for the formulation of national policies on art and culture. It must be clearly understood, however, that freedom of expression is of the very essence of creative process and whatever the organization and apparatus set up for the promotion of art and culture it must not be allowed to deteriorate into an instrument of thoughtless regimentation or bureaucratic control.

As of present, there appears to be very little effective liaison even among policy making organs within the Government itself. There are a number of Government agencies dealing with some aspect of art and culture, e.g., the Central Ministry of Education, the Provincial Departments of Education, the Central Ministry of Information, The Bureau of National Reconstruction, The Pakistan Council for National Integration, the Department of Tourism, and the Ministry of Foreign Affairs. Since they all function more or less independently of each other there is considerable duplication of work, wastage of labour and sometimes even contradictions in policy. To the extent that their respective fields of activity do overlap this is perhaps unavoidable. Nevertheless, some mechanics for clearer definition of functions and closer integration of policies should be easy to evolve, if some co-ordinating agency of the type advocated above can be instituted.

INFRASTRUCTURE

The second most important factor which has restricted the growth of the arts is the absence of the minimal material facilities necessary for their fruitful prosecution. There is not a single properly equipped public theatre or auditorium anywhere in the country. There is not a single properly equipped art gallery for the exhibition of the plastic arts. There are no studios available with any institution where a poor artist can ply his trade. There are no proper concert halls, no proper museums for the display of folk arts, no properly organized art emporia for the sale of an artist's work, not even adequately supplied stores to provide an artist with his work materials. It should be obvious that if our arts, in general, and the performing arts, in particular, are expected to attain the maturity desirable, at least this minimum infrastructure must be provided.

We feel that the past practice of doling out developmental funds to various organizations on the basis of some arbitrary formulae without any reference to the requirements of specific projects must be discontinued. It may be more advisable to release funds for the completion of selected developmental projects in selected centres and the requirements of other projects in other centres should be considered only after these initial projects are completed. Until the other arrangements outlined in the plans for a central body are implemented, we should suggest that development funds available with the Ministry of Education may be initially allocated only for the completion of these projects which are already well advanced and need only limited additional help for completion.

Finances

The third factor which appears to have hindered a balanced growth of the arts has been the absence of any secure and guaranteed financial resources to enable various cultural organizations to plan any long-term programmes of work. Maintenance grants both from the Central and the Provincial Governments are variable, sometimes from year to year, sometimes over longer periods, and there is no certainty regarding their date of release. Consequently, grant-receiving bodies face many difficulties in planning and budgeting. An additional complaint made by various Arts Councils is that there are inordinate delays is recovering from the Government amounts spent on cultural exchange programmes. This further hampers their own plans of activity.

This Committee is, therefore, of the view that, as in other countries, a way must be found to create self-generating sources of income for cultural organisations to relieve them of their dependence on uncertain annual grant allocations.

TRAINING AND UTILIZATION OF TALENT

In Pakistan today, the traditional modes of artistic training i.e. through 'gharanas' or families or 'Ustads' and their journeymen and apprentices are neither feasible nor desirable. They are not feasible because these institutions were integral to the feudal structure of society and could only be sustained through individual aristocratic patronage which is no longer available. They are not even desirable because 'the closed shop' methods thcy followed made the classical arts so exclusive and so 'cloistered' that, with the passage of time, their appeal and accessibility became progressively more and more restricted. If these arts are to survive their training will have to be institutionalized on modern lines.

The problem of training should be viewed in the light of the following considerations:

(a) Perpetuation of traditional skills: We still have among us today some notable exponents of traditional artistic skills in music, dance, folk arts etc. But there is widespread apprehension that these masters may be the last of their line unless they are enabled to transmit these skills to others. This can be ensured only if these artists are provided with gainful employment in their own field and with facilities to teach others. At present the only stable avenue of employment open to music and drama artists is the Radio and to a lesser extent films and television. This is far from satisfactory. In the first place, neither Radio nor TV can provide a really adequate living to an artist. (The wages of well-known staff-artists of Radio Pakistan even after 15 to 20 years service average Rs.250 to 400 a month). In the second place, these organisations are in no way concerned with the training of future talent.

Again, it is hardly practicable that each individual artist should be provided with a training institution of his or her own although some of them do maintain some struggling institutions of this kind. The only practical method of ensuring continuity of artistic skills and knowledge, therefore, seems to be the establishment of properly organised training institutions staffed by the best talent available in the country and so organised as to yield maximum results.

(b) Discovery and utilization of talent: The wealth of artistic talent in the country can never be fully known unless this talent is enabled to surface and mature. Since academic education has made some progress, it is possible to spot in primary and secondary schools a student who may be talented in any particular discipline and assist him or her to pursue higher studies through scholarships etc.

There are no such prospects open to any boy or girl who may be equally gifted in any of the arts. Discovery of this talent and its subsequent utilization demands the creation of similar channels, i.e.:

(i) by integrating the teaching of the arts with the normal educational process, and
(ii) by providing adequate facilities for higher training in the same scale and on the same basis as training in other trades and professions.

Concretely this involves:

(1) A revision of academic curricula so as to make the creation and appreciation of art and culture a worthwhile academic pursuit.
(2) The establishment of higher institutions of artistic learning in the main towns on a reasonably widespread scale which should serve the dual purpose of providing trained teachers in the arts and of helping individual talent to mature and grow.

As stated earlier one of the reasons for the social prejudice against some of the art is their professionalization in the hands of a small class which is not socially acceptable. We feel that the surest way of overcoming this prejudice is to confer on the arts the same status of respectability as the other academic disciplines enjoy. This is proved by the fact that within a space of 20 years painting and allied arts have already won for themselves a popular and respectable place in our national life. The enabling factor has been the induction of art teaching in the academic, schedule of some universities and the establishment of two Government Institutes for training in Fine Arts. Similarly, since music and dance form a part of school curricula in East Pakistan they are regarded as desirable social accomplishments in that part of the country. We have no doubt that if training in all the arts is nationally planned as an integral part of national educational policy much of the present apathy, and what is worse, distaste and hostility, towards national art and culture, can be effectively dispelled.

RESEARCH

While facilities for artistic training are woefully deficient, facilities for research in our rich cultural heritage are almost non-existent. Whatever work has been done in this field is due to the efforts of some dedicated individuals who have to hunt for data as best as they can without any institutional help. As a result, apart from a few pamphlets and brochures produced by certain Governments, there has been very little authentic exposition or documentation of our contemporary cultural and artistic assets. This is lamentable in many ways: Firstly, the absence of authentic cultural data of the classical, regional and the folk arts of Pakistan debars a citizen, particularly a young boy or girl, from knowing the best of his own country and from taking legitimate pride in his own heritage. Secondly, it hinders closer acquaintance between the people of different regions because only systematic and careful research can reveal the affinities, connecting links and common elements among different regional cultures. Lastly, the absence of this data hampers the projection of Pakistan's cultural image abroad. The lack of any organized institutions or mechanism for research also placed at a disadvantage with international organizations like the UNESCO. We are thus deprived of many services and facilities which such organizations are able to offer in the field of research. Scientific research and documentation projects in the sphere of the arts should, therefore, be speedily formulated and implemented.

CULTURAL EXCHANGE

In the recent past, the Government of Pakistan has finalized a large number of bilateral pacts with a large number of European, Asian and African countries, thus relieving in some measure the anonymity and isolation which handicapped our external publicity in the past. We have, however, organized no agency capable of handling the many delicate and complex tasks that an effective implementation of these cultural pacts involves. The Ministry of Education has no machinery of its own to deal with the subject and the responsibility for handling individual items of cultural exchange programmes has generally been left to one Arts Council or another, generally at short notice and without adequate preparation. As a result, these organisations, ill-equipped as they are, have to resort to haphazard improvisations to throw together an exhibition, to assemble an troupe of performing artists, to select managerial staff, etc. They have acquitted themselves of these responsibilities as best and as bravely as they could but the arrangement can hardly be called satisfactory. There have been complaints that many of the programme items exported abroad were not truly representative of the best in the country, that paintings have been lost or damaged for lack of care, that there is lack of cohesion and understanding among artists sent out and that the leadership of delegations is not always carefully chosen. It was alleged, for instance, that one cultural delegation sent abroad was led by an office accountant.

Obviously the situation calls for some remedial action. The organization of an effective machinery and programme for foreign cultural exchange is particularly important for Pakistan because our identity has yet to be securely established on the cultural map of the world, many parts of which still regard Pakistan as a cultural appendage of its bigger and better known neighbour.

We feel, therefore, that a separate and high-powered national organization should be created and entrusted with the task of co-ordinating and supervising all cultural exchange programmes and Pakistan's cultural projection abroad.

CULTURAL TROUPES

At present, the PIA is the only organization which maintains a regular professional cultural troupe on a wholetime basis. As a result, the PIA Arts Academy now enjoys a virtual monopoly as the purveyor of our national culture abroad. The enterprise shown by PIA is an excellent pioneering effort but it is doubtful whether a single small group can sustain its position as the sole exponent of Pakistan's performing arts for very long. Firstly, the repertoire of such a group is bound to be limited and will not bear much repetition before the same audiences. Secondly, only a limited number of artists can be employed in such a professional ensemble and it cannot possibly accommodate the entire talent of the country. Moreover, such an organization is compelled to demand very high performance charges in view of heavy maintenance expenditure. This limits accessibility to bigger towns and richer audiences. It was, therefore, suggested that:

(a) Other organizations who have adequate resources at their disposal, for instance, the three armed services, major banks etc., may be encouraged to organise similar ensembles specializing in some particular field, e.g., choral and martial music, acrobatics, dramatics, etc.

(b) It may be suggested to PWR and EPR to attach special recreational carriages to passenger trains and teams of folk performing artists, e.g., jugglers, acrobats, musicians, storytellers etc. may be organised to give way-side performances in the moffussil and outlying areas.

(c) Regional cultural organisations may be advised to organise regional cultural troupes from among the best available regional talent. These artists may be assembled periodically and rehearsed for, let us say, 2 to 3 weeks for which remuneration should be paid. This should mitigate the necessity of maintaining these troupes on an expensive wholetime basis. Such diversification would make for better representation of national talent and greater freedom of choice in their selection for cultural exchange both inside and outside the country.

Administration

In many countries of the world today, both developing and developed there are full-fledged Ministries of Culture. In others, there is at least a separate Department, or Division, devoted exclusively to cultural affairs under the Ministry of Education or some other parent Ministry. We doubt if there is any country of the size of Pakistan today where national culture is as starved of administrative care as ours. Financial stringency can hardly be the reason for crowding Culture and Sports on to the desk of a single, meagrely-manned section in the Ministry of Education when some other Ministries have far larger, establishments for much more limited items of activity. We suggest that until other larger projects are taken in hand, as a minimal measure, a separate division, section or cell should be created in the Ministry of Education to deal exclusively with the problems of art and culture.

Personnel

Like everything else in the present-day world the planning and organization of cultural activities has also become a specialization and it is presumed that the personnel in charge of such activities have some acquaintance with modern techniques and methodology of organisation, programming and production. UNESCO and perhaps some other international organisations offer regular courses of training in this field. Similarly, individual projects and programmes, e.g., art exhibitions, design and display centres, national stalls in international fairs and festivals, decorations of public buildings, etc., all require professional training and skill. For various reasons the matter has received little attention so far and in the absence of any plans or facilities for personnel training in this field responsibilities in both the administrative and production spheres have been largely handled by amateurs and dilettanti, sometimes even by busy public officials or their wives. These voluntary efforts probably deserve some appreciation rather than criticism but if it is desired to put the organisation of cultural affairs on a scientific and modern footing, the problem of creating a cadre of trained personnel must be given some priority. UNESCO fellowships and the aid of advanced and friendly countries should be available to enable senior cultural workers to study and train in the modern methodology of planning, organization, programming and production. In any case the execution of those cultural programmes and projects for which trained professional artists are available in the country, must not be entrusted to influential amateurs whose technical knowledge may not match their enthusiasm.

Problems Relating to the Specific Arts

Architecture

Architecture is an important component of people's everyday life and therefore as important component of a people's culture. One of the principal functions of this art is to provide the common man with the infrastructure of comfortable living within his given means. Architecture in any given society, therefore, has to harmonise with the people's way of life at a given period and this implies a satisfaction of both the needs of physical comfort as well as the fulfilment of emotional and social values. This requires a careful balancing of basic factors like climate, material costs, town planning and the social mores of the community. Such knowledge only qualified and scientifically trained artists are in a position to provide.

Architecture in Pakistan has not made satisfactory progress because:

(a) Most architectural construction in the country, both public and private, is entrusted not to qualified architects but to unqualified amateurs or draftsmen who have no concept of either functional or aesthetic requirements of the community.

(b) New constructions, private and public or Government, imitate either the past feudal Mughal patterns, which do not harmonise with modern construction methods and materials and with modern living conditions, or equally blindly imitate modern western architecture which has no relevance to climatic conditions in various regions of the country or to the normal living habits of our people.

(c) A qualified architect is regarded as a luxury which only the rich can afford, He is not normally associated with the planning of community housing schemes at the village or the low income group level. Obviously individuals with low incomes cannot afford an architect on an individual level. An architect's services can only be utilized on a communal basis by the Government or by public bodies to plan and build not individual houses but communal housing projects.

(d) Foreign architects brought into the country are not sufficiently conversant with the climatic and social conditions nor are their professional credentials scrutinized closely enough. As a result, the structures put up by them do not help in the evolution of a national style of architecture nor are they entirely functional. Many of these architects borrow indiscriminately from the old Mughal architecture and transplant these features to modern western models thus creating a hotchpotch of architectural style.

(e) There are not enough training facilities in the country to meet the ever-increasing demand for qualified architects in view of the accelerated pace of developmental construction. Facilities for advanced training, which are absolutely essential to equip our architects with more advanced techniques and theoretical training, are so severely restricted that they may be regarded as almost non-existent.

(f) There are no facilities for research in the regional styles of architecture or in climatic, material or costing factors.

It was suggested to us that:

(i) The Institute of Architecture should be given more resources to set up facilities for research. The Institute should be more representatively organised and the services available with them should be better publicized among the public and should be more fully utilized by Government and public bodies.

(ii) It should be made a statutory obligation that the designing of all Government and public buildings be entrusted to qualified architects and the use of draftsmen, overseers and unqualified amateurs in public bodies like the P.W.D. should be discontinued.

(iii) The employment of foreign architects should not be left to the whim of officials in different departments who are not qualified to check their credentials. The choice of all foreign architects must be processed through the Institute.

(iv) Above all, the National Institute of Architects, after any constitutional modifications which may be necessary, must be elevated to a regular statutory body, on the lines of the British Institute of Architects, and empowered by charter to award memberships and fellowships. It should function as a permanent advisory body to the Government in all matters pertaining to theoretical, academic, and practical aspects of architecture.

(v) An Institute of Architectural Research—in all its aspects— should be established either as a part of the Institute of Architects or as an autonomous organization under the supervision of the Institute.

(vi) Trained manpower needs at various levels, in the field of architecture, must be assessed over a long-term period and training facilities adjusted and expanded accordingly.

(vii) The priority of advanced architectural training in the provision of scholarships and other facilities overseas should be re-examined and more correctly assessed.

PAINTING AND ALLIED ARTS

It was pointed out that above all the other arts painting and sculpture are subject to a process of constant development because of the discovery of new techniques, new forms and new materials. These forms and techniques were international and a modern artist had every right to utilize them but his themes, his way of viewing and expressing reality, should reflect his own national identity and social environment. This is not always obvious in the work of many modern Pakistani painters who have isolated themselves from the life of the community and paint either in a social vacuum or as a form of personal protest against a society which has failed to find use for their talent.

One reason for the isolation of the artist from the community is that since the disintegration of the feudal system he has not been assigned any social role or social function. Before the industrial era, the artist at the city level, and the craftsman at the village level, were an integral part of the social system. The artist was permanently employed to build, to decorate and to furnish churches, mosques and the houses of the rich. The craftsman provided the rural population with all goods of daily use which had both aesthetic and decorative as well as functional utility. In the West with the rise of industrialism the artist became a purveyor of the aesthetic needs of the new rich class as well as a mass producer of cultural goods for commercial purposes. In industrialised societies culture became a commodity which like all other commodities was subject to the laws of supply and demand and as a result gave rise to a new class of cultural entrepreneurs. In developing countries like Pakistan no such class has arisen and the artist therefore has to struggle on his own as an individual. The craftsman is being forced out of existence through neglect or competition with the machine. As a result the artist is no longer in harmony with any section of the community and his isolation has driven him into subjective, non-communicative, abstract, and negative forms of expression. This is the main reason why in Pakistan today a good deal of contemporary art does not reflect the life or the hopes or the aspirations or the identity of the people of Pakistan.

It is, therefore, desirable that:

(a) The work of artists should be brought into harmony with the new social system of the community, progressing from a feudal land economy to an industrial urban community. This can be encouraged by the utilisation of artists' services in all Government and public projects from the district level upwards by regular purchase of paintings for public buildings, commissioning artists for murals, interior decoration, etc. It was suggested that, as in some other countries, 40% of the budget for every public construction should be set aside for artistic decoration. It was also suggested that apart from main construction, the decorative elements in public building, e.g., friezes, murals etc. should, in no case, be left to contractors and illiterate craftsmen as their atrocious creations brought disrepute to national taste and talent.

(b) Most of our practising artists are self-made and self-taught who have discovered their talent through instinct. There are no facilities in the country for artistic talent to mature and develop through external training. It was deplored that in a country with a population of over 10 crores there are only two full-fledged art institutes in Dacca and Lahore and even these are not fully equipped by way of libraries, research facilities or facilities for specialization in a specific branch of art.

(c) Art training in schools and educational institutions is hopelessly out of date. Art teachers as a rule are totally unqualified to develop or train creative talent. At the university level there is either no department of Fine Arts at all or it is not properly staffed and equipped.

(d) Very little effort has so far been made to promote the work of national artists, by organizing special exhibitions of their work abroad, placing their work in reputed galleries, or publicising them in the international or world market through art magazines, books, etc.

(e) Very little effort has been made inside the country to acquaint the audiences of different regions with contemporary national art through exchange and display of work of artists of different parts of the country. A national exhibition of paintings and sculptures which was instituted some years ago has been discontinued, The Arts Councils find it difficult to invite the work of artists from considerable distance owing to heavy transport expenses. The artists themselves are reluctant to send their work to distant centres because according to some of them much of it is lost or damaged in transit due to indifferent handling.

(f) There is no plan or project to discover artistic talent in the moffussil and outlying areas, nor do the people in these areas get much opportunity to view the work of prominent national artists. The creation and enjoyment of art therefore has become the monopoly of a limited section in big towns.

(g) For some years now, the artist in Pakistan is gradually being deprived of the basic tools of his trade, namely, art materials, paints, canvas, drawing paper, etc. owing to prohibitive prices. As a result, unless an artist has considerable resources of his own, he is no longer able to paint.

It was therefore suggested that:

(i) Art education and art training throughout the country from the primary school upwards must be revised and brought up-to-date.

(ii) The utilization of artistic talent in Government and public projects, industrial projects, etc., should be put on some systematic basis.

(iii) Exchange of artistic products on an inter-wing and inter-regional level should be put on a systematic basis.

(iv) More art institutes with proper facilities should be established.

(v) Systematic promotional efforts should be made to publicise and to sell the work of national artists both at home and abroad.

(vi) Research facilities through academies and institutes should be provided for the study, preservation and utilization of folk arts and handicrafts.

(vii) Regular exchange allocations should be made to Art Institutes.

Art Departments of Universities, and other suitable bodies, should be given requisite bonuses for the import of art materials and some system should be evolved for their sales to practising artists at reasonable prices.

Arts Councils and other cultural bodies should be reorganised with a view to:

(a) organising artists in different areas into guilds and art societies who should be made responsible for running their own affairs as a separate entity for which the cultural organizations should provide adequate facilities;

(b) setting up separate agencies to organize art exhibitions and to promote the sale of art works on commission basis—the commission being payable not to the parent organization but to the promoters and salesmen themselves;

(c) setting up art stores for the sale of art materials at marginal profit;

Performing Arts

DRAMA AND THEATRE

It was widely suggested that theatrical production is perhaps the only art from whose appeal is not limited to any particular class or section of the community nor conditioned by the level of social or intellectual sophistication. It is of particular importance in a country with a low rate of literacy like ours, and perhaps the most important medium of mass communication after the film. In an economically backward country, its accessibility is much wider than that of Radio or Television whose services are available only to a limited section. This is why, in spite of the total absence of state patronage or private investment, the theatre has managed to survive through the efforts of devoted amateurs long after the death of the professional theatre. Thus in Karachi alone nearly 150 plays have been staged during the last 10 years and there are 12 drama groups actively engaged in theatrical production. None of them receives any aid from any source and their income is mainly derived from publicity brochures and gate money. Apart from Lahore Arts Council's own theatre group which enjoys some facilities, the situation is more or less the same in Lahore.

The lack of Government and commercial patronage is one handicap. Prejudices associated with the old professional theatre is another. This prejudice naturally inhibits young educated people from adopting it as a whole time occupation.

Above all the basic facilities for stage and dramatic activity, i.e. properly equipped theatres, whole-time workers, a sufficient repertoire of plays etc. are non-existent. Consequently, there is no such thing as a stage career.

The cost of individual productions is now prohibitive, i.e. rent of premises, lights, sound equipment, stage properties and payments to the cast now average from Rs.10,000 to 17,000 per production. Amateur groups working on a non-commercial basis, therefore, are finding it extremely difficult to continue their activities.

Drama and theatre are still regarded as a means of entertainment and recreation rather than instruments of social education and intellectual uplift. As a result a correct concept of the theatre has yet to be evolved. We still have in some moffussil areas remnants of the old theatrical tradition or remains of old theatrical premises and properties which could be revitalized and brought back into use. For instance, in Multan, in West Pakistan, there are still groups and individuals actively engaged in dramatics in the old style and in East Pakistan there are a number of old theatres at Bogra, Kishoreganj etc. with manually operated revolving stages. These buildings are now lying derelict but can still be rescued. Even in big cities i.e. Lahore, Rawalpindi, Hyderabad, there are modern open-air theatres which are rarely used because they happen to be in the care of disinterested official departments rather than active cultural bodies. A national theatre movement and properly organised local cultural organizations could salvage all these assets.

In most higher educational institutions dramatics now form a regular part of extra-curricular activities but no attempt has yet been made to provide adequate technical and professional knowledge to raise the standard of these productions. It was, therefore, suggested that:

(1) There is an urgent national need for training institutes in this art, a need which also stems from the requirements of new communication media like television. A State-subsidised professional theatre could combine both training and production, provided it were run not on bureaucratic but on purely professional lines.

(2) There is also a need to coordinate local and sporadic activities in the field of the theatre into a broad based national theatre movement. This obviously needs a central organising agency.

(3) It is desirable that theatre groups should have separate organizations of their own instead of being dependent on the Arts Councils as at present. These organizations should be directly subsidized.

(4) Conditions should be created to promote original dramatic writing on serious and educative themes. Dramatic literature at present is limited to the adaptations of foreign plays written in completely different social context or old feudal, romantic and legendary themes inherited from the professional theatre with no relevance to contemporary social problems.

(5) Dramatic literature in both the national and the regional languages should be encouraged and the needs of audiences in big towns as well as the mofussil areas should be kept in view. These dramatic groups should be frequently exchanged to learn from each other.

(6) Exemption from entertainment tax for Arts Councils' productions alone is not adequate and should be generalised to cover all bonafide amateur theatrical productions.

(7) There is a need to study and promote folk dramatic forms at the village or district level and to discover and utilize dramatic talent in these areas through observation, study and research.

MUSIC AND DANCE

In Pakistan today music and dance are perhaps the most maligned and at the same time the most popular of the arts. Some of the factors making for this contradiction have been explained earlier. On the one hand these arts are the most ancient, the most deeply embedded and almost instinctive forms of human self-expression. On the other, they are easily susceptible to abuse and debasement and because of their visible impact on social attitude and behaviour such falling from grace arouses righteous, and some times not so righteous, indignation. Contemporary opinion regarding these arts, therefore, is a baffling medley of attitudes. This confusion continues to inhibit the development of these arts on refined, wholesome and socially acceptable lines and at the same time abets the deterioration in their formal and thematic standards which everyone deplores. Apart from the school which seeks to outlaw these arts altogether some of the popular controversies centre round the following:

(1) Amateurism vs. Professionalism

In East Pakistan almost every child with a musical talent receives same training in folk and classical music and Tagore and/or Nazrul songs as a part of his school education. Girls coming from even the most conservative families learn some dancing in their childhood. At least in music both men and women, if they have the talent, are encouraged to continue this pursuit for higher attainment and no social stigma attaches to a public display of their talents-but only as amateurs. Professionalism is very seriously frowned upon and music even for the most eminent artist is a pastime rather than a career. Amateurism and respectability are almost inseparable. In West Pakistan, on the other hand, the practice of these arts is largely in the hands of professionals of two categories. In the first category are eminent masters and earnest students of these arts with family traditions of long standing. In the second category are professional entertainers who use these arts as a vicarious supplement to other pleasures. It is because of these latter that professionalism has come into such disrepute and even eminent artists because of being professional are denied the respect and recognition they deserve.

The first practical problem, therefore, is, and it can only be solved over a long period, to create conditions which make a professional career in music or dancing as respectable as any other trade or profession.

(2) Folk vs. Classical

There are four lines of approach:

(a) Folk music and dance are too crude and too unsophisticated to deserve serious consideration as art forms.

(b) Classical music and dance are too complex and too erudite to appeal to any sizeable section of the people.

(c) Folk music and dance are typical of various regions of Pakistan and therefore deserve encouragement but their classical form can hardly be called exclusively Pakistani and therefore should be discouraged or discarded.

(d) Classical music and dance in their present form are an integral part of Muslim cultural heritage of the subcontinent; some of the greatest contemporary exponents of these arts are Muslims and it is both unwise and undesirable to forego this valuable part of our own heritage.

The consensus of knowledgeable opinion we have been able to gather holds that:

(a) A correct approach to the subject should be eclectic, broadminded and forward looking rather than sectarian or narrow-minded.

(b) Folk and classical forms of expression are complementary and inter-related rather than antagonistic and mutually exclusive. All classical music and dance derive from the elaborate on folk dances and melodies and in their turn are re-absorbed to enrich and diversify folk forms of expression.

(c) Classical music and dance inherited by us are merely a 'methodology', or grammar, of voice and movement expression, which has been changed and modified over the centuries, both in form and content, by various creative influences in our history of which the Central Asian Muslim influence has been the most dominant. Until we evolve a completely new system of basic 'grammar' or 'methodology' for these arts, therefore, we have no option but to train in the discipline of our present classical modes.

(d) Music and dancing, like all other arts, must adjust themselves to the demands of progressive evolution. Hence while traditional, folk and classical skills must be preserved and new creative processes must also be engendered to absorb and new advances in experience, techniques, modes and instruments of expression.

(e) Above all it is necessary to dispel the appalling ignorance that prevails in present day society regarding the elements of the language of music and dance, folk or classical, eastern or western. An elementary knowledge of these arts presumes the capacity to recognize a note and its purity, a movement and its grace, a composition and its mood and intent. The absence of this knowledge deprives our people of the joy of appreciation of these arts and deprives the artist of the happiness of creation which demands the participation of an appreciative audience.

It was, therefore, suggested that training in these arts must be institutionalised on modern lines by incorporating both folk and classical music and dance, and new creative combinations of both, into the educational system, to enable the younger generation to appreciate, enjoy, and participate in their own national forms of self-expression.

(ii) More institutes and academies for higher training in these arts should be established which should prescribe standards of attainment and institute degrees and diplomas as professional qualifications. Until academically qualified personnel become available, honorary degrees may be awarded to eminent musicians, as has been done in some other countries, to qualify them for academic posts.

(iii) Western technical advances in harmony, orchestration, notation, choral and operatic singing, etc. should be incorporated in our schemes of musical studies.

(iv) Facilities should be provided for exchange of technical knowledge and experience by sending our own musicians and musicologists abroad and inviting foreign artists, particularly from Asian countries who are in the same stream of tradition, to train our artists in modern techniques of production and expression.

For the preservation and development of classical music and dance it was desirable to:

(i) provide eminent national exponents of these arts with adequate means of living and gainful employment in institutes and academies;

(ii) record and document on a comprehensive basis a repertoire of compositions popular with all the existing masters and schools of music;

(iii) popularise a system of notation to facilitate teaching, standardization and preservation of these skills;

For the preservation and development of folk music and dance, it was desirable to:

(i) explore and discover local talent by some regular system of surveys and talent scouting;

(ii) record and document folk melodies of all regions.

(iii) organize regional performing troupes under the aegis of regional cultural bodies.

(iv) arrange for exchange of folk artists and cultural troupes within the country and the projection of their best talent abroad.

(v) institute more national fairs with competitions, honours and awards for folk artists. As a beginning at least two national festivals, one in East and one in West Pakistan, let us say on Pakistan Day and Independence Day, may be instituted. This should prove a good tourist attraction besides stimulating folk talent.

FOLK ARTS

Apart from the conventional arts the country also has a wealth of talent, which is constantly diminishing, in other folk arts e.g. puppeteering, acrobatics, jugglery and various types of indigenous sports, which also deserve to be preserved and encouraged. The regional cultural organizations could profitably engage in the discovery and promotion of such talent. Folk arts and handicrafts, ceramics, calligraphy, costumes, jewellery, textiles, woodwork, metal work, leather work etc. offer a vast field for indexing, collection, research and documentation, provided this work is entrusted to expert and trained specialists and is not allowed to be corrupted by commercial entrepreneurs or by well meaning but aesthetically ignorant official agencies. Academies of plastic and performing arts suggested in this report should incorporate this task in their work-schemes in collaboration with regional cultural organizations.

NOTES

1. In May 1968, Mr Q.U. Shahab, the then Secretary of Education. Government of Pakistan, convened a meeting of representatives of various grant-aided cultural organizations and some prominent cultural workers to review the activities of various Arts Councils and other Cultural Organizations to survey the organizational, constitutional and financial aspects of their functioning and to recommend ways and means for their improvement.

At the conclusion of the meeting, it was unanimously decided that a committee designated as the Standing Committee on Art and Culture should be set up with the following members:

1. Mr Faiz Ahmad Faiz, (Chairman), Principal, Haji Abdullah Haroon College, Karachi.
2. Mr Jamiluddin Aali, (Member), Pakistan Writers Guild, Karachi.
3. Professor Munir Chaudhury, (Member), Department of Bengali, Dacca University, Dacca.
4. Mr Salahuddin Mohammad, (Member), Chairman, Pakistan Features Syndicate, Dacca.
5. Mrs Rukiya Kabir, Eden Girls College, Dacca.
   Later replaced by
   Mr Qamrul Hasan, Chief Designer, East Pakistan Small Industries Corporation.
6. Mrs Bano Qudsia, (Member), Writer.

   The Committee remained in session for nearly six months. The Committee visited practically all important cultural centres from Peshawar to Chittagong and interviewed over 300 artists, writers, scholars and cultural organizers. I submitted its report to the then Ministry of Education towards the end of 1968. Before this document could be taken up for official consideration, however, the country was overtaken by serious political upheavals. As a result, it never saw the light of day, nor was it officially accepted or rejected. The report was compiled in a different political climate and obviously, the drastic political developments that have taken place since could not then be foreseen. Nevertheless it is felt that some of the basic conclusions arrived at by this Committee might still be relevant to the situation prevailing in present-day Pakistan. Some extracts from this report, therefore, are being reproduced for discussion and further consideration by those interested.

Faiz Ahmed Faiz
14 April 1975

9

WHAT WOULD YOU HAVE?

Let us think of a few names at random, Harun al Rashid, Shah Jahan, Ishaq Mosuli, Amir Khusrau, Tansen, Behzad, Mansur, Mutanabbi, Hafiz, Ghalib—all artists or patrons of art. Were they also plagued in their time by cavillers, or denounced as purveyors of sin, perverters of faith, corrupters of public morality? Perhaps, but their detractors, if any, are now dead as dust, nameless as ghosts. Now suppose for a moment that the kings and nobles and peoples of old had paid ear to these nameless ghosts rather than to their great music-makers, their painters and poets and dreamers of dreams. In event of such a calamity what is it that you could hold up today as our cultural heritage? There may be a small minority among us who are as vengeful towards the dead as they are towards the living, who would be as glad of a past without Mansur, and Shah Jahan and Tansen as they would be of a present without, let us say, Chughtai and Roshan Ara Begum and Ghulam Ali Khan, Their number must be small and they do not greatly matter. There are others, however, who do matter. These would not deny the past its Haruns and Mamuns and Shah Jahans, its music and painting and poetry and other splendours. They only insist on denying these splendours to our own present. Music may have been good food for the Abbasids but for the Pakistani of today it is deadly poison. Painting may have done no harm to the Mughals and the Iranians but its votaries today are dreadful delinquents. Culture is an adornment, a thing of pride, so long as it is confined to the page of history; in the living present it is a thing of shame, a cloak to hide the dagger of nefarious designs.

Perhaps somewhere at the bottom of this perversity there may be an unconscious modicum of sense. There is no doubt that in the confusion of values that prevails among us today a great deal of trash is allowed to masquerade as art or culture. There is much grotesque caricature of the fabulous Mughal Court, much debasement of beautiful folk legends, much flippant, perversion of national history, much bad music, bad cinema, bad painting, and bad literature. All this should be condemned. It corrupts public taste and therefore also corrupts public morals. It perverts values and debases the intellect and is, therefore, truly subversive. In the incoherent outpourings of the anti-culture partisans, however, this modicum of sense rarely comes to the surface. For them there is little to choose between a reverential melody sung by Roshan Ara Begum and a demonstration of lascivious hip swinging, between a Chughtai and Zainul Abedin and a poster of *Yakke Wali*, between a serious cultural organization and a coterie of charlatans.

This is precisely what makes the blind, indiscriminate hate-campaigns against all cultural activity and all art so harmful. In the commercial world of today bad art needs no patronage. Only good art does. An unscrupulous charlatan knows how to pick his way about in the social maze of self-interest and greed. A genuine artist is not even interested in doing so. Anti-art and anti-culture campaigns, therefore, do not inhibit bad art or debased cultural pursuits; they only promote them at the expense of the good.

This is one consideration. The other consideration is that our today will sometime be our posterity's yesterday. The main pride of all our yesterdays is what the great builders and musicians and painters and poets of old bequeathed to us, thanks to the patrons who looked after them. Today you and I are the only patrons the artist has left and the artist is a part of you and me. What is it that we propose to leave behind in our turn, apart from *Kabaddi* and *gulli-danda* which we did not invent any way. The choice lies between the love and ecstasy, the passion and the pain of the genuine artist and the hate, ignorance, and callousness of his many adversaries. What would you have?

10

SHACKLES OF COLONIALISM

The idea of national identity is of fundamental importance to a developing nation. Without a clear identity of nation, no national directions can be determined, no conscious efforts can be made to maintain, to retain or reject, tradition, and thus no meaningful development can be made.

National identity, in brief, can be the soul (psyche) of a nation, and unless it is clearly defined and comprehended by all concerned, all kinds of confounding variables may affect a nation's thinking, consequently affecting and impending its development and growth.

This is true of all aspects of a nation's 'existence' including comprehension and practice of (national) ideology, religion, morality and ethics, culture, the arts etc.

The formation and development of national identity is similar to the formation and development of the identity of a person. This process of formation and development can also be described as the process of identification with an external object, person or group.

The factors which influence, determine and facilitate the process of identification are the externally imposed rewards and punishments attached to each pattern of behaviour and thought in the process of identification.

Those patterns of behaviour and thought processes which facilitate the process of identification are highly and positively reinforced or rewarded. And those behaviour and thoughts which impede and hamper the process of identification are highly and negatively reinforced or punished.

Thus a nation's identity is a continuing process of identification with a given system of behaviour and thought and this system of thought and action is imposed by the forces which control the contingencies of rewards and punishments. These forces may be the governments of the countries, the pressure groups, or the colonisers, or all of them together under any given name.

In colonised countries, the process of identification with the coloniser is most pronounced and clear. In reference to Pakistan, the coloniser had attached very high rewards to the patterns of behaviour and thought, on the part of the locals, which served, facilitated and advanced the cause of the coloniser.

The coloniser had attached very high punishments to those patterns of thoughts and behaviour, on the part of the locals, which did not serve his (coloniser's) interests.

The locals therefore, like the white rats of the psychologists, were made to learn to identify themselves with the coloniser in order to survive and advance socially, mentally and materially. This process went on for a number of centuries in the area now called Pakistan.

The major part of national identity of Pakistan can then be described as consisting of nothing more or less than the interjected value systems of thought and behaviour of the coloniser, the English.

Once the process of identification takes a coherent form in a person, then it becomes a self sustaining system, i.e. it may not need external rewards and punishment to sustain itself. The same is the case with a nation; once the identification with the coloniser took its roots in the psyche of the nation called Pakistanis, it became a self-sustaining system.

There were (are) attempts to be more and more like the English, even when being and becoming English did not (does not) carry any externally imposed rewards (by the coloniser). This is, perhaps, true of all colonised countries, may they be Asian, African or Latin American.

Tradition, national goals and the process of national development is influenced and determined by thoughts and acts of the people of a nation. When the main motivation behind the thoughts and acts of a nation is an attempt to identify itself with the coloniser, then tradition and development would also be affected by this motivation.

All those traditions and national goals of development which serve the purpose of satisfying the motive of identification with the coloniser, are maintained, sustained and overplayed. Conversely, all those traditions and national goals of development which do not serve the purpose of facilitating the process of identification or satisfying the acquired need for identification, are discarded and underplayed. Maintenance, or otherwise of a tradition, and national development, therefore cannot be isolated from national identity, which in a newly decolonised country, is the interjected need for identification with the coloniser.

The only way in which this process of identification with the coloniser can be broken, is the same in which this process started: i.e. to reverse the contingencies of rewards and punishments.

Those thoughts and acts which are attempts at identification with the coloniser must be negatively reinforced or punished, and those acts and thoughts that tend to break a person/group away from identification with the coloniser, must be positively reinforced or rewarded.

Once this has been achieved externally, by governments and pressure groups, only then the true elements of identity of a nation may begin to emerge.

Section III
ART

11

THE CONCEPT OF BEAUTY[1]

'What is life', wrote the poet Ghalib, 'but the manifestation of harmony (orderliness) among the elements.' The same may be said of beauty as its prime attribute—a harmony, a symmetry, an equilibrium or whatever the name one may give it, in its formal composition.

This phenomenal beauty may be God-given as in a human face or form, in a naturally sculptured landscape, or a star-studded night. But, by and large, it is the product of human endeavour. The music-maker, the artist, sculptor or architect, the poet, the weaver of cloth, the moulder of metal or the jeweller of gold are all manufacturers of beauty—all minor god-heads seeking to recreate a medley of sounds, colours, stones, words, fibres or metals, sensory phenomena of what Byron calls 'Beauty truly blent'—as harmonious in the miniature as the music of heavenly spheres.

Nothing Negative

And yet this beauty is not merely the negation of ugliness. The mere absence of a discordant note in music, a garish colour, or a disproportion in a material structure, or a physical deformity does not answer to 'the joy forever'. The mere perfection of form as in a Taj Mahal, a 'ghazal' by Dagh, a painting by Mondrian, or a finely sculptured face certainly brings us pleasure but not necessarily excitement. The perceptual experience is static and not effervescent. It holds no surprises, it creates no tension, it brings no turbulence. As Bacon has acutely observed, 'There is no excellent beauty that hath not some strangeness in the proportion.' This 'strangeness in the proportion' obeys no laws, is subject to no discipline and can be neither described nor codified. It is the magic casement opening on the foam of imagination's perilous seas forlorn. And this magic lies in ambush not in corporeal things alone. It can be just a movement ('She walks in beauty'), a state of feeling, a line of thought or even a scientific formula. This is why 'How beautiful!' is always an exclamation and never a mere statement of fact.

The beauty of human face and form is something else again. Here face and figure are but outer accoutrements expressing or disguising another reality within; the human personality. You may admire this visual or purely sensory element as you may admire a Taj Mahal but you cannot really 'experience' it without penetrating into the reality within—the human person. And sometimes appearance and reality maybe completely at variance. Thus when you say 'What a beautiful person!' the face or figure of the person concerned may be the last thing you are thinking of.

Not So Mad

Even the madness called 'love at first sight' is perhaps not so mad after all and includes some cognitive element besides visual dazzlement. And add to all this one more element—the supplemental dimension of memory which makes the saddest thoughts sweet. Sensitive memory is selective like a sensitive artist. It suffuses the remembrance of things past with the same haunting quality as an artistic masterpiece.

What then is Beauty? It is both the tranquillity of harmony and the turbulence of 'some other proportion', it is as tangible as reality, and as elusive as ghost, it is ecstasy, torment, experience and memory all rolled into an 'infinite variety', it acquires an emotional and perceptual permanence which age does not wither, nor custom stale.

NOTE

1. *Viewpoint*, Lahore, 23 November 1980.

12

THE UNICORN AND THE DANCING GIRL[1]

In Pakistan as elsewhere in Asia
and Africa, time past is time present
And in the past—the past
which neither man nor history remembers—
there was no time.
Only timelessness!
The timelessness of the city of the dead
And of the graves of nameless saints
with their tattered flags
which never rallied anyone to any cause
And their earthen lamps which shed no
light on the mysteries of human darkness.
The timelessness of the unicorn
Presiding over the pots and pans
over weapons and vanities
of the city of the dead
who is not even a unicorn
is not even a legend
For even a legend is a memory
And the memory is in time
But the past is timeless
like the eternal snows of
Timeless mountains
The eternal sands
of timeless deserts
And the waters

of the timeless sea
And written within this eternity of silence
The music of time began.
in the leap of a lonely spring
out of the encrusted womb of a wilderness of rocks
The joyous limbs of the dancing girl
defying the motionless unicorn
And dancing waters on their festival
march to the sea.
Thus time was born
And cities arose on the plains
Attracting an unending caravan
of human feet marching in and
out of the timeless mountains
Parthians, Bactrians, Huns, and Scythians,
Arabs, Tartars, Turks, and White Men.
But as Time unwound its first thread
The unicorn which is the past
grabbed it in its blind hoofs
And spun it round and imprisoned it within itself.
And time became
The endless drone of the waterwheel
The creaking of the wooden cart
The hum of the spinning wheel
The closed spectrum of light and shadow
The heat and cold of the seasons
Although men matched their strength
against the wheel
to fight and to create
much that was good and beautiful
Buildings
Gardens
Paintings
Carpets
Ornaments
Music
But everything moved within

its own remorseless orbit
Even the dance of the dancing girl
imprisoned within the circular whirl
of her own limbs
and the gaze of eager eyes in a close-set circle.
For the wheel was fate
and custom
And the will of the unknown powers
which predestined all beauty
To death and decay after its span
And mighty cities to dust.
And small men gave up the fight
And accepted the yoke
to circumambulate their
allotted round of days
like blindfold oxen.
And the wheel was fate
And the yoke was 'karma'
And fear and want and pain
And the withering of age
And death with its mercy
And the tyrant with no mercy in his heart.
Until the present
And then the stirring and the strain
The sorrows and dreams and passions and yearnings
of numberless beings
over untold centuries
snapped the yoke
and broke the wheel
to unleash an orgy of frenzied movement
The wheel clanking away on steel tracks
speeding on metalled roads
whirling on airfields
in giant factories
Explosives ripping up the timeless
mountains to release power
Earthmovers ploughing through timeless sands

to admit the festival march of life-giving water,
men and women
boys and girls
unyoked from fate and 'karma', and
Custom and the dream of an unknown will,
The joyousness of the dancing girl
rippling in abandon through the young flesh
of countless limbs
And the unicorn reduced
at last to a mere design on a fabric
A mere decoration on the wall.
And yet
Time present is still time past
in faces
in places
in custom and ritual and the grave of the nameless saint
In hunger and want and pain and the withering of age
The birth of time out of timelessness
is beset like all births
with travail, and hope, and joy and apprehension.
And its birth in Pakistan as elsewhere in
the newly liberated countries of Asia
and Africa
is as yet only a small flag of freedom
raised against
The bannered and embattled host of
Fear and want and hunger and
Pain
And the death of human hearts.

NOTE

1. *Civil and Military Gazette*, Lahore, 3 March 1961.

13

THE WORLD OF SADEQUAIN[1]

In spite of his considerable preoccupation with the solution of technical formal problems, Sadequain has never been a purely formal painter. Recordist, abstractionist, social critic, emotional visionary, within a few short years, Sadequain has sped from one role or compulsion to another with equal impetuosity. Although the still centre round which his creative vocabulary will eventually stabilise is, perhaps, as yet difficult to foresee, some aspects of his work both formal and thematic, appear long past the interim phase. The articulate line, calligraphed, woven, chase or tapestried, the muted colour stemming from darkness rather than light, the thirst to drain the cup of every new-found image to the last, the suffering without the pity and the agony without the ecstasy appear too enduring to depart.

Retrospectively he began quietly enough painting living things as appearances, but even then in selection and treatment, he was more of a commentator than a mere naturalist. From things phenomenal, he chose only those which were alive and trying to 'kick' however, ineffectually. And in his social community the only living ones are those who suffer. For they are the only ones who toil—the camel, the ox, the hewer of wood, the drawer of water, the famished cactus, the root under the stone. And to paint the figure together with its suffering obviously dictated a distortion of visual appearance, a juxtaposition of the conceptual and the material. Naturally enough in Sadequain's work of this period, the composition is not entirely unself-conscious and the colour treatment is at times somewhat conventional but evidence of formal control and intellectual commitment is already unmistakable.

Then with the commencement of his phantasmagoric exploration of form and substance, there emerges a series of abstract visual statements, strong and subtle, stripping, anatomising and recreating the skeletal forms beneath the visual flesh—Skeletons of streets and cities, weeds and plants, men and women. In the process, he also evolved a new social and emotional credo of the essential unity of material things, all caught in the agonising toils of an evolutionary process of struggle goading them upwards. And now, since his return from Paris, Sadequain has once more reverted to direct social comment to depict a loveless and macabre world—a world of the scare-crow acting as the Lord of blood-thirsty crows, of the harridan decked out as a beauty queen, a world of trapped tongues and cobwebbed hearts, of debased flesh and servile manners. Flittering across this world, we see a Christ-like figure, perhaps meant to be autobiographical, his body one with thorns, his head encircled by the crown of atrophied oblivion. This bitter vision of reality may not be the whole truth but it is certainly a part of it and if some of those immediately confronted with the hypocrisy and the heartlessness of a particular environment fail to own the hope beyond the despair, the failure is not entirely theirs. That Sadequain is not unaware of the hope is borne by his huge canvas, rather stylised and deliberately contrived though it is, depicting the conflict of peaceful forces and their antagonists.

The most obvious feature of the work displayed in this exhibition, however, is Sadequain's virtuosity in whatever medium he operates and his varied and electric idiom based on a wealth of sources, from medieval calligraphy to modern posters, from classical sculpture to modern expressionism.

NOTE

1. This article was written specially for an exhibition of Sadequain's paintings organised by the State Bank of Pakistan in May 1968.

Section IV
LITERATURE

14

THE LITERARY HERITAGE OF PAKISTAN

Present day Pakistan has a population of nearly 70 million souls. The people are predominantly Muslims but there are also a number of minority groups: Christians, Parsees, Hindus, Buddhists and Sikhs. While the cultural heritage of Pakistan in its manifestations other than literature can be traced back to the great Indus civilization of the fifth millennium BC, its literary heritage may be more appropriately equated with the Muslim period commencing with the advent of the Arabs in this region early in the eighth century AD. The Arabs ruled over the Sindh region and a part of lower Punjab with two separate seats of government: one in Mansura in Sindh and the other in Multan in the Punjab. During this period, Arabic was the official, academic and cultural language of the areas under Arab dominance. The spoken language of the indigenous population was Sindhi in the Sindh region and various dialects of the Punjabi language in the lower Punjab. During the early decades of the eleventh century, Northern Punjab and some adjoining areas were overrun by the Turko-Afghan armies of Sultan Mahmud of Ghazna and thus a new Muslim kingdom was established with its capital at Lahore. Sultan Mahmud had gathered in his court some of the greatest Persian poets of his age and in his wake, Persian language first came to be introduced to this land and later held sway over a major part of the subcontinent for a number of centuries. The admixture of Persian and local dialects of the northern areas of the subcontinent gave birth to the national language of Pakistan, namely, Urdu. The literary heritage of Pakistan, therefore, has been trebly enriched by three classical languages: Arabic, Persian and Urdu. Parallel with these three literatures there is the wealth of folk classics in various regional languages, Sindhi, Punjabi, Pushto, Baluchi and some smaller and more localised Brohi in Baluchistan, Kashmiri in Kashmir, Shina in the northern areas of Gilgit and Chitral.

Arab Period (710–1020)

The educational system during the Arab period and later almost down to the British days centred primarily round religious studies called *Manqulat*, although some secular subjects were also added to the curriculum during the reign of the Delhi Sultan Sikander Lodhi (1489-1516) and the Mughal Emperor Akbar (1556–1605). Even to this day in all the religious seminaries in Pakistan, Arabic writings of earlier epochs are still being studied and, therefore, continue to be a part of a live tradition. Understandably the bulk of this literature in Arabic is mainly religious and theological, i.e. commentaries, expositions and exegesis of sacred texts or jurisprudence, dialectics and discursive exhortative pamphlets based on religious themes. Nevertheless, a number of important works were also produced on historical, biographical, geographical, philosophical or sociological subjects. Mention might be made for instance of Najih-bin-Abdur Rehman al-Sindhi (d. 787) whose *Kitab al-Maghazi* was used as a source book by the well known Arab historians Waqidi and Ibn Saad, or the great Abu Rehan Alberuni (d. 1048), historian, mathematician, and jurist. His *Kitab al-Hind* is still regarded as the most authentic source book on the history, religion, philosophy, geography, social life and anthropology of medieval India. Then there were lexicographers like Sanaani (d. 1252) and jurists like Badr bin Taj of Lahore who are also internationally known in the scholarly Muslim world. In religious literature the work of exegesis by scholars like Ali bin Ahmad Mahaini (d. 1341), particularly his *Tayassar al-Mannan fi Tafsir al Quran*, writings on the life and sayings of the Prophet of Islam by Sheikh Abdul Haq Muhaddis of Delhi like his *Madaraj-al-Nabuvvat* or historical treatise like, *Tarikh-i-Haqqi*, were also compulsory reading in Muslim religious schools for centuries. Shah Waliullah of Delhi (d. 1762) is perhaps the greatest name in this line. As a political thinker, social reformer and religious ideologue, his writings particularly his definitive work, *Hujjatullah Al-Balighah* influenced both popular and scholarly thinking in many Muslim lands. His eldest son Shah Abdul Aziz was an equally gifted scholar and his expositions of the traditions of the Prophet of Islam and his compendium of Muslim case law are also internationally known. This tradition of religious scholarship has continued unbroken to the present day and among contemporary writers mention might be made of Maulvi Abdul Haye of Lucknow (d. 1923) whose monumental work *Nuzhat ul Khawatir* is a many-volume biography of famous Arabic scholars and Muslim Divines of the subcontinent. Later scholars, and there are many distinguished names among them, wrote mostly in Persian or Urdu and their names appear elsewhere.

The Legacy of Persian

Unlike Arabic literature of various periods which is mainly religious or theological. The literary legacy in the Persian language is far more varied and richer by far. It encompasses, with the exception of drama of which there was no tradition in Arabic or Persian literatures, practically all forms of literary and scholastic expression, poetry, history, biography and autobiography, epistles, fiction, reminiscences, dictionaries, commentaries on juristic and religious classics, and *belles lettres*. The pride of place in this vast storehouse, however, belongs to poetry which has been the daily food of innumerable generations over the centuries. All through the Muslim period of Indo-Pakistan history, after the consolidation of the Delhi Sultanate in the thirteenth century, this literature was being constantly enriched, apart from the contribution of the many gifted writers indigenously born and bred, by a stream of talent from Iran and other Persian speaking lands. This resulted in the evolution of a new and distinctive school of Persian poetry, which the Persians called *Sabke Hindi* (the Indian School) because it was very differently flavoured from the products of classical Persian. It introduced to Persian poetry new nuances of feeling and expression, deeper and more delicate explorations of subjective experience and subtler modes of social and political comment.

The main forms of poetic expression in Persian are *Qasaid* (panegyrics with a semi-philosophical exordium or historical narrative) *Mathnavies* (narrative poems on erotic, historical, mystic, philosophical or metaphysical themes) *Rubaiyat* (epigrammatic quatrains) and *Ghazal*, (short lyrical poems of a limited number of couplets each more or less self-sufficient in meaning). It is this last highly symbolical form which was later adapted and perfected by Urdu poets and attained the greatest popularity.

The earliest poets in Persian, i.e. Abul Faraj Rumi (d. 1114) and Masud Saad Salman of Lahore (d. 1121) may not be much read today but the *ghazals* of their illustrious successor, Abul Hassan Amir Khusrau (d. 1325) historian, thinker, musicologist, linguist, and political theoretician, are still current coin and are permanently included in the musical repertoire of *qawwali* singers (chorus singers of mystical or devotional songs).

Among other great names, mention may be made of Urfi (d. 1591), Faizi (d. 1595), Naziri (d. 1614), Ghani Kashmiri (d. 1668), Abdul Qadir Bedil (d. 1720), Asadullah Khan Ghalib (d. 1869), and the renowned poet Mohammad Iqbal (d. 1938) of contemporary times. Of these Urfi with his poignant lyrics and almost modernistic diction Faizi with his versatile mastery of narrative and descriptive verse, Naziri's delicate handling of social and philosophical problems and Bedil's deeply intellectual approach to metaphysical themes, have all left their stamp on the great tradition bequeathed by them to their successors.

Towards the middle of the eighteenth century, the rise of Urdu and its growing popularity displaced Persian as the favourite of princely courts and their retinue of talented poets. Although Persian retained its place as the official language and the language of scholarly discourse or correspondence, its poetic tradition was partly eclipsed by a succession of Urdu classics. Its glory was revived once again, however, by two great masters Asadullah Khan Ghalib (d. 1869) and Mohammad (Dr Sir Shaikh) Iqbal (d. 1938) who wrote with equal facility in both Urdu and Persian. Ghalib articulated with great insight and passion the intellectual ferment, soul-searching and heart-break of the generations which witnessed the final decline and fall of the Mughal empire and the vanishing of their beloved of life and Iqbal did the same for the bewildered Muslim intelligentsia which grew up during the turbulent three or four decades of the present century. Their fame has travelled far beyond the borders of the subcontinent and their Persian verse is widely known and widely read in many West Asian lands where Persian is spoken or understood.

In Persian prose, generally cadenced and highly ornate as a rule, there is voluminous literature as already stated, particularly in historiography and related fields. Almost every ruling dynasty or important monarch commanded some gifted chronicler and their works are a valuable record of contemporary life and times in various eras. *Tarikhe Firoze Shahi* and *Fatawa-e-Jahandari* of Zia-ud-Din Barni (d. 1357), *Akbar Namah* and *Ain-e-Akbari* of Abul Fazal (d. 1602), *Muntakhebut-Tawarikh* of Mulla Abdul Qadir Badayuni (d. 1615), *Gulshan-e-Ibrahimi* or *Tarikh-e-Farishta* of Mohammad Qasim Farishta (d. 1623), *Badshah Namah* of Abdul Hameed Lahori (d. 1647), *Maasr-e-Alamgiri* of Nemat Khan Aali (d. 1710) and, *Siyar-al-Mutakhirin* of Ghulam Hassan Tabatabai (d. 1781) are some of the most noteworthy accomplishments in this field with their first-hand account of historical events, doings at court, racial and cultural affairs and some times perceptive analysis of state-craft and court policies.

In the field of biography and autobiography perhaps the most interesting documents are the writings of kings and princes themselves, for instance, *Babar Namah*, autobiography of the founder of the Mughal Empire, Zaheer-ud-Din Babar, *Humayun Namah*, an account of the second Emperor's life by his sister the Princess Gulbadan Begum, and *Tuzk-e-Jahangiri*—an autobiography of the third Mughal Emperor, Jahangir. There is also a whole body of literature on the lives of saints, scholars, poets and notables.

In the field of religious studies, there are a number of important works on mysticism, and related subjects which have influenced not only religions, but also social and political thought of many generations. Included among these are *Kashf-al-Mahjub*, of Syed Ali Hajveri, known as Data Ganj Bakhsh of Lahore (d. 1072/88), perhaps the first extant work on Sufi doctrines, discipline and practice in the Persian language, the *Fawaidul Fawaid*—a collection of the teachings of Nizamuddin Aulia of Delhi compiled by his poet-disciple Hassan Sijzi, and *Maktubat-e-Mujjadid Alf Thani*—the credo of the militant religious divine and reformer Shaikh Ahmad of Sirhind (d. 1625). All these books are still popular reading both in the original Persian and in Urdu translations by religious scholars and disciples of these holy men.

The Evolution of Urdu

The origins of Urdu language can be traced back to the eleventh and twelfth century when the first Muslim kingdom was established in Lahore and the Persian speaking settlers learnt to communicate in the local language which they named Hindvi. Masud Saad Salman (d. 1121) one of the Ghaznavid court poets composed a *divan* (collection of poems) in this language which is no longer extant. However, the songs, riddles, doggerels and musical compositions of the great thirteenth century poet Amir Khusrau which first brought respectability and general acceptability to the Hindvi and Punjabi languages are popular to the present day. Strangely enough, it was not in the north of the subcontinent, where it was born, but in the south that the new language, which later came to be known as *Rekhta* or *Urdu*, matured and developed. This is because towards the middle of the fourteenth century the principalities of upper Deccan broke away not only from the Imperial court in Delhi but also from its court language, Persian. The rulers of these small kingdoms of Golkunda (1518) and Bijapur (1489) in their efforts to identify themselves more closely with the native population actively patronized literary endeavours in the spoken language and poets and writers of great eminence rose in the Deccan or Urdu language—an admixture of Persian, Turkish, Deccan, Hindvi and Punjabi dialects (a large number of Punjabi soldiers had settled in Deccan as contingents of imperial garrisons).

The first long narrative poem in Deccani-Urdu, *Saiful Muluk-wa-Badi-ul-Jamal*, was composed by Gavasi (1618) and the first major book of prose *Sab Ras* by Mulla Vajhi (1637).

It was, however, towards the middle of the eighteenth century when both the Mughal court and the court language Persian were already on the decline, that Urdu came into its own in its own homeland—the northern areas of the subcontinent.

In the early years of the eighteenth century, a gifted poet from upper Deccan, Wali Deccani, migrated to Delhi and his Urdu *ghazal* and lyrical poems found immediate and widespread response in the literary circles of Delhi. He may, therefore, be truly regarded as the Chaucer of Urdu poetry. He was followed almost immediately by a whole line of distinguished poets, Mir Taqi Mir, (d. 1810), Mohammad Rafi Sauda (d. 1782), Mir Dard (d. 1784), Mir Hassan (d. 1874). Mir Taqi Mir is known for his tender and nostalgic lyrics in the *ghazal* form which continue to sung and recited in literary and music gatherings up to the present day. Sauda introduced Urdu poetry to incisive social and political satire; Mir Dard is about the only mystic poet of the classical period while Mir Hassan composed the most celebrated romantic fairy tales in the form of *Mathanvi* (rhymed couplets). Nazir Akbarabadi stands in a class by himself because he sang not for court circles but for the common man, not in the classical idiom but in the language of the market place. And he wrote not on romantic themes but on every day experiences of the common man. Mir Anis popularised a completely new school of poetry, the school of the *Marsya* (elegy) writers. The *Marsyas* are a cycle of poems devoted to the martyrdom of Hussain, the grandson of the Prophet of Islam, at Karbala in Iraq and the various episodes connected with this tragedy. Mir Anis's elegies are part descriptive, part narrative, part dramatic and part declamatory. They are recited all over the subcontinent when the anniversary of the tragedy of Karbala is observed by Muslims of the Shia sect.

The most eminent name in this hierarchy of poets, however, belongs to Asadullah Khan Ghalib whose name has already been mentioned in the context of Persian poetry. His slender volumes of Urdu *ghazals* has had a profound and many sided influence on practically the entire stream of Urdu poetry since his days. He liberated Urdu poetry from various types of clichés that had become current in the form of conventional imagery, diction and symbolism. He instilled in his work firstly the entire tragic experience of his age for he saw the final extinction of the old feudal order and the complete political suzerainty over his land by a foreign power, secondly, the philosophical and metaphysical questionings that this experience gave rise to in sensitive minds of his times and thirdly the new rational and enlightened forms of thought and expression introduced by Western rulers.

The end of the nineteenth century saw the birth of what may be called the modern movement in Urdu poetry actively directed and sponsored by the British elite. It was based on the critical dicta of Mathew Arnold and other Victorians and modelled after William Wordsworth, Alfred Tennyson, Robert Southey and H.W. Longfellow etc. The two main exponents of this school were Mohammad Hussain Azad and Altaf Hussain Hali whose contributions to Urdu prose in the form of literary criticism, history and biography are of equal importance. With the passage of time and the closer acquaintance of Urdu Writers with modern literature of the West, this movement has proliferated into a number of different schools. The towering figure among the moderns, however, was the great Mohammad Iqbal who is the subject of a separate study.

Before 1790, whatever prose there was in the Urdu language generally followed the ornate and florid type of Persian writings but about that time two gifted religious scholars Shah Rafiuddin, Shah Abdul Qadir (sons of Shah Waliullah) brought out their translations of the Quran in simple Urdu, in a style very near to the spoken idiom.

In the beginning of the nineteenth century with the consolidation of British power in the subcontinent, some British scholars gathered round themselves talented Urdu writers of the time to translate some well-known Arab and Persian classics into Urdu as well as to produce educational instructive or scientific literature on Western lines. The first centre of learning with these objectives was set up by Dr John Gilchrist in Fort William College, Calcutta to be followed later by similar centres in Delhi and Lahore. The pioneers of the Calcutta School gave to Urdu a simple direct and un-encumbered prose style which served as a model for the more gifted writers of Delhi and Lahore. Of these Sher Ali Afsos and his translation of *Gulistan-e-Saadi* called *Bagh-e-Urdu*, Hafiz-ud-Din Ahmad and his excellent rendering of Abul Fazal's *Bahar Danish* named *Khirad Afroz*, Mazhar Ali Khan Vila and his translations of *Baital Pachisi* from Sanskrit deserves special mention. In the evolution of this new prose style, a special place belongs to the collection of letters of the poet Ghalib, intimate and colloquial in tone, sparkling and witty in content.

During the 1870s of this century, the school of Sir Syed Ahmad Khan, scholar, educationist, historian and social reformer brought into being a flood of high class literature on social, political, scientific and educational themes. A parallel school of religious learning was led by another great scholar Maulana Shibli Nomani. His monumental work on the life of the Prophet of Islam—*Sirat-un-Nabi* and his scholarly history of Persian literature *Sher-ul-Ajam* are both regarded as authentic works of reference up to this day. In fiction, a *Dastan* (a fanciful long tale of incredible adventures and extravagant love) was penned by the Emperor Shah Alam under the name of *Ajaib-ul-Qasis*. This tale served as a forerunner of a string of other tales in similar vein produced by the Gilchrist School of Fort William College. Most famous of these is the *Dastan of Amir Hamza* adapted from the Persian by Khalil Ali Ashk of Fort William College. This work was later revamped and blown up with additions and interpolations into a many-volume literature of fantastic extravaganza. This rambling and rather formless escape literature later gave place to the Urdu novel proper. The first of these is a gigantic picaresque romance written by Rattan Nath Sarshar entitled *Fasana-e-Azad*. The idea of this book was probably suggested by Don Quixote which Sarshar translated into Urdu. The thread was picked up by two other distinguished writers, Abdul Halim Sharar and Moulvi Nazir Ahmad. Sharar produced, on the one hand, a number of historical romances concerning Muslim heroes of old in a style vaguely reminiscent of Sir Walter Scott, and on the other, realistic novels of purely contemporary social content. Moulvi Nazir Ahmad wrote a number of novels in the form of, perhaps, what comes nearest in Urdu to 'the novel of manners,'—domestic tales of every day life with every day characters picked up from the lower middle class and with a strong moral and reformist message. Both are current household reading.

In the present century when a number of literary magazines came into vogue, the popularity of the novel was eclipsed by the short story under the influence of great storytellers of the West: Guy de Maupassant, O. Henry (pen name for William Sydney Porter), W. Somerset Maugham, Anton Chekhov, Maxim Gorky, and others. For a short period in the early decades of our times a number of stage plays were also written, for the short-lived professional theatre, by a team of professional playwrights led by Agha Hashr Kashmiri, some times called the Indian Shakespeare, because of his eloquent adaptations of the great master.

Regional Languages

Punjabi, which for this account, will include Seraiki/Multani, the speech of Southern Punjab and Hindko-Pothowari, dialects of north-west Punjab, is the most widely spoken and one of the most ancient of the indigenous languages, while the doggerels, quips and riddles of Amir Khusrau can be claimed by both Punjab and Urdu, the *dohas* or epigrammatic verses of his contemporary Baba Farid Shakar Ganj (d. 1265) can certainly be identified as the earliest compositions in Punjabi verse. These are still in print and sung in devotional gatherings both in Pakistan and in Indian Punjab. By the sixteenth century, the language had developed sufficiently to produce the first notable classics by poets like Peeloo, author of the ringing metrical romance *Mirza Sahiban*, Damodar, the first major poet to versify the celebrated tragic story of *Heer Ranjha* and Lal Hussain, the first major mystic poet. These themes were perfected and elaborated by later writers into a vast body of metrical romance and legend which, apart from love or romantic interest, gave a vivid depiction of customs, beliefs, superstitions, and the sacred and profane practices of the Punjabi in various periods. The five or six best known among these are: *Heer Ranjha* by Waris Shah, Maqbil,

Ahmad Yar and about forty other. Major and minor poets, *Mirza Sahiban* by Peeloo and Hafiz Barkhurdar, *Saif-ul-Muluk* by Mohammad Bakhsh, *Yusuf Zulaikha* by Ghulam Rasul, *Sohni Mahinwal* by Fazal Shah and Shah Hashim, *Sassi Punnu* by Shah Hashim Qadir Yar and Moulvi Ghulam Rasul, *Puran Bhagat* by Qadir Yar and Kalidas. Strongly enough while classical Urdu produced only one mystic poet of any worth, in Punjab, there are at least four great names, Lal Hussain of the times of the third Mughal Emperor Akbar, Sultan Bahu (d. 1691) Bulleh Shah (d. 1764) and Khwaja Ghulam Farid (d. 1901). There is besides an enormous store of anonymous, folk songs, ballads, and legends which continue to be improvised to this day.

In Sindhi, oral tradition tells of popular romances in verse going back to the Arab times of the eighth century, the earliest written records belong to the fourteenth century. As in many other languages, these early poems are of a religious, mystical or didactic nature, called *Gunyay*—in Sindhi. In this genre, verses of some divines, and Peer Nur-ud-Din, Peer Shams-ud-Din and Peer Sadar-ud-Din of Uch (circa 1358) are extant. The earliest political poetry was composed by Sh. Hamad Jamali (d. 1438) when Jam Tamachi, the then Governor of Sindh, was deposed and arrested for anti-state activities. The real wealth of Sindhi literature, however, lies in mystical and devotional poetry. The name of Shah Abdul Latif Bhitai (d. 1752) is a household word, even in those areas of Pakistan where Sindhi is not spoken or understood. On the occasion of his anniversary celebrations, thousands of pilgrims flock to his mausoleum to listen to the rapture and the music of his ecstatic verse. Sachal Sarmast (d. 1826) and Rahol Faqir (d. 1797) are two other mystic poets of eminence while Shah Inayat Rizvi (d. 1621) is famous for his metrical romances, *Momil Rano, Leela Chanesar, Jam Tamachi and Noori*. These poems, like their counterparts in Punjabi, also reflect social patterns, economic conditions and value areas of contemporary society.

Pashto, another ancient language, has been most fortunate in one respect. The earliest extant poem is believed to have been written by Amir Karore (d. 756) although he was not a native of the subcontinent. The first prose work is *Tazkiratul-Aulia*, by Sulaiman

Maka (d. 1215) and the first historical narrative is *Tarikh-e-Suri* by Mohammad Ali Abasti (circa 1349). The first love poem in the *masnavi* form was authored by Akbar Zamindari (d. 1369). Later epochs saw the emergence of great mystic poets, Mirza Ansari (d. 1630) and Rahman Baba (d. 1706), heroic and romantic poets, the greatest of them being Khushal Khan Khattak (d. 1689), warrior and lover, preacher and patriot, His family produced five major poets, his sons Abdul Qadir, Sadar Khan and Sikander Khan, grandson Kamgar Khan and daughter Bibi Halima. The Afghan king Ahmad Shah Abdali who ruled over this area for a time was also no mean poet.

In recent years these has been a considerable revival of interest in these languages and a number of talented writers and scholars have addressed themselves to the task of bringing these languages into line with the more developed classical and modern languages by creative writing, critical studies and historical research.

15

THE LEGACY OF LITERATURE[1]

Literature was born when the first ray of consciousness enlightened the mind of the primeval man and craved for expression. His wordless cries of pain and pleasure, anger and endearment thus got defined in sounds specific to each experience and the word unit was born. At the same time, the loneliness of the primitive hunter was replaced by close grouping in families which demand community of response and action. Thus, the word took on an additional function besides expression, namely, communication. And then these communities discovered that the word was not merely a vehicle for expression or communication but could be bent to perform many other functions as well. It provided a productive factor in communal labour by facilitating rhythmic movement. It was an instrument for increased knowledge through an exchange of observation of the material world. It served as an invocation to the mysterious and unknown forces of fire and light and rain and thunder which governed human plenty or want. It was also a repository of events and experiences of men and women memorable in the history of each community. Thus, the combination of words called literature combined judgement, magic, memory and inspiration all at the same time.

And thus it has remained.

Exploitative Factor

With the passage of time families and groups coalesced into powerful tribes and tribes united into nations. The increasing mastery of man over material resources produced a surplus of wealth and wealth meant power. A new factor then entered into human social existence, the dominative and exploitative factor. The wealthy and the powerful within the tribe came to dominate over the rest of their compeers and the more numerous and powerful tribes subjugated others less fortunately placed. Kings and empires and classes arose and with them arose the division between the privileged and the leisured, on the one hand, and the toiling and the deprived, on the other. With this division, literature also began to speak in two different languages: the language of kings and captains and their dependents, on the one hand, and the language of the hewers of wood and drawers of water, on the other.

These two parallel traditions, the classical tradition of the courts and folk tradition of the masses is the past of all our literature in Afro-Asian countries. In some cases, the division into these two languages was not merely metaphorical but even literal as in the case of Sanskrit and the Prakrit literatures in our subcontinent, of Latin and the local national languages in Europe or of Persian or Arabic and the various native dialects of the Middle East and Central Asia.

Classical literatures of old flourished or decayed according to the fortunes of the dominative feudalism and their representatives, but the folk tradition suffered much less from such fluctuations and enjoyed a greater measure of continuity. This literature of the past, lyrical, devotional, heroic or epigrammatic has, thus, produced two parallel series of classics: orthodox classic of the courts by authors whose names are well preserved and folk classics by bards and sages who with few exceptions have remained largely anonymous.

This entire body of literature, both folk and classical, forms one part of the literary heritage of the present and the coming generations. As stated above, it embodies the wisdom, the experience, beliefs, the history and the collective dreams and aspirations of their forefathers. It, thus, provides both a testament of their national identity as well as sustenance for their continuity of collective experience.

Resistance

After the seventeenth century, with the rise, first of powerful mercantile and later of capitalist classes, in the Western world, together with the revolutions wrought by them in the modes and relationships of production, the era of imperialist, colonialist expansion began. One by one, the countries of Asia and Africa fell before this onslaught and the long night of imperialist, colonialist slavery descended on the two continents. The new masters were not content with economic exploitation and political enslavement of their subjects alone, because they realised that this process could never be wholly fulfilled without destroying the national cultures of subject people, in other words, the effacement of their individual personalities as cultural entities. This necessitated an onslaught on whatever constituted this personality, literature, beliefs, values, modes of thought and feeling, language and habits of social existence. It was a planned and determined effort to alienate them from their own past and to reduce them to faceless, heartless and spiritless dummies fashioned after the image of their masters. But the best and the bravest among the peoples of Asia and Africa never accepted defeat and waged an unremitting struggle both against political enslavement and cultural depredation. In this struggle, the writers participated fully with their pen and sometimes with their blood. Thus, a new body of literature was born—the literature of resistance. Its main components were first a re-discovery and re-evaluation by the writers of their own literary heritage of the past. Second, a moving and realistic portrayal of the sufferings and deprivations of their people; third, a fierce protest against this slavery and oppression; and fourth, dying hope and a burning faith in their liberated future. Over laid on all this was an impassioned love for what makes life good and beautiful—peace, freedom and social justice. This literature forms the second half of the literary legacy of the present and the coming generations. It is both a record of what the Afro-Asian people have gone through during the period of foreign domination as well as an inspiration for the struggle yet to be won.

October Revolution

Half a century ago, after the success of the Great October Socialist Revolution, the long march towards freedom and liberation gradually terminated at one victorious post after another. This march became a rally after the defeat of the Fascist hordes at the end of the Second World War and today with the exception of a few pockets, practically all Asia and Africa is free. This led to another development. The peoples of Asia and Africa long isolated from each other by the barriers put up by the imperialist Powers were not able to communicate and come together to join hands not only in thought but also in practice for the pursuit of their common ideals. Thus, the Afro-Asian movement was born. Among the writers of these two continents it took shape in the form of an Afro-Asian Writers' Organization, which was born in Tashkent in 1958. Thus, Afro-Asian writers were able, firstly, to discover and to learn from the creative efforts of their contemporaries in other lands. Secondly, they were able to pool their strength in support of their less fortunate brethren still locked in bloody battles in different parts of the world, in Korea, in Indo-China, in Algeria, in the Portuguese colonies, in Rhodesia, South Africa, Palestine and the Arab occupied lands. Some of these battles have since been won; some are yet to be won. The literature produced in this period, thus, provided a powerful addition to the weaponry of the freedom fighters in all these battles of the past and continues to do so in the battles still being fought.

This is, in brief, what literature has bequeathed to the present and the coming generations. It has furnished them with a mirror of their own identity, a code of rational belief in humanism, peace, freedom and justice, a climate of feeling and sensitivity towards human suffering and human pain, an articulate battle-cry against cruelty and oppression, a repertoire of tender songs of love and compassion, of beauty and of truth.

NOTE

1. *Viewpoint*, Lahore, 15 July 1977.

16

KHUSRAU: CATALYST FOR SOCIAL CHANGE[1]

Of the many great names that adorn the pages of Muslim history in South-Asia, the name of Hazrat Amir Khusrau ranks among the greatest. Scholar and statesman, soldier and savant, courtier and mystic, writer and musicologist, philosopher and wit, he combined in his person, the best of all the accomplishments that contemporary society offered. He lived, besides, in one of the most formative periods in the social and cultural evolution of Muslim society as a separate and distinctive entity on the subcontinent—the period of the Sultanate of Delhi. It was during this period that the process of ethnic and cultural assimilation of Muslim West-Asian and indigenous South-Asian and indigenous South-Asian peoples matured—the process which reached its culmination during the days of the great Mughal Empire.

Muslim immigrants from across its borders gradually came to accept their new habitation as a land of their own: the barriers of racial exclusiveness and social elitism which divided the Turkish aristocracy and the native masses were effectively pierced and out of the fusion of their two cultures a new civilization was born. This cultural synthesis found expression at different levels in language and religious practices, and in the idiom of every-day living.

Humanist

Amir Khusrau was one of the main catalytic agents in this ferment and strode like a colossus over this vast panorama of social, political and cultural changes. He was a humanist in the truest sense of the word, equally opposed to the aristocratic ideals of nobility of birth and purity of blood and the heartless fanaticism of bigoted priestocracy. He was equally at home in the company of the highest in the land, kings and emperors, and the most lowly born, weavers and washermen, peasants and working women. And he wrote and sang for them all. He wrote ornate eulogies of kings and captains, profound historical and philosophical dissertations for the learned, tender and moving lyrics both devout and profane, alongside with riddles and jingles for children, word games for housewives and homely songs for lovesick maidens and tired old men. And he taught the music makers of his times to sing these compositions in a mode that touched every heart. Thus, apart from his very significant contribution to contemporary history, it is by this ineffable body of music and verse that he is best remembered by posterity.

Amir Khusrau was born in the year Hijra, i.e. 1152–53 AD at Patiali a village near the present-day town of Badaun (according to some authorities, in Delhi). His father Amir Saifuddin Mahmood, a chieftain of the Lachin Turkish Tribe, was forced to flee his territory in the face of the Mughal onslaughts and took service with Sultan Shamsuddin Iltutmish at Delhi. He married an Indian lady Daulat Khatoon, daughter of Imadul Mulk, one of the most powerful nobles at the imperial court. Khusrau, one of three brothers, Izzuddin Ali Shah, Abul Hasan Khusrau, and Husaluddin Qutlugh, lost his father when he was only seven years old and was brought up by his maternal grandfather who was equally distinguished as a scholar and statesman.

It was under his care that the child Khusrau was introduced to all the branches of contemporary learning. It was also in the same household that he sat at the feet of his spiritual mentor and beloved master, 'The King of Saints', Hazrat Nizamuddin Aulia of Delhi, who stayed with Imadul Mulk for two years after obtaining his Khilafat from Hazrat Fariduddin Ganj-e-Shakar.

Khusrau was a precocious child and fame as a poet came to him early, but it was at the age of 20 that his political and literary career really began. During the same year, he published his first *Divan* and at the same time took service with Malik Chajju, a nephew of the emperor Balban and a generous and powerful prince.

From 1273 to 1290, Amir Khusrau served in the courts of various nobles and princes, travelled with them and fought their battles all over the subcontinent from Bengal to the Punjab and from Sindh to Telangana, with a long sojourn at Multan. This was the formative period of his long life during which he mastered, apart from the classics of Arabic, Persian, and Turkish, the various dialects of the country, (he mentions twelve), and acquired a detailed and intimate knowledge of the peoples and places of various regions.

He wrote tirelessly all this while but it was after 1290 AD, when he finally returned home to Delhi from his wanderings and spent the next thirty-five years at the Imperial Court that his genius truly flowered and the voluminous body of his historical, lyrical and descriptive verse was composed. He wrote with equal facility in Persian, Arabic and his native Hindi or Hindvi, although much of what he wrote in the indigenous dialects appears to have been lost.

In the year 725–1325, the voice of this great 'Songster of Sugared Tongue' was stilled and he was rejoined, as he ardently wished, with his beloved master, 'the King of the Saints', who had died six months earlier.

NOTE

1. *Viewpoint*, Lahore, 3 October 1975.

17

MIRZA ASADULLAH KHAN GHALIB (1797–1869)

Consumed by the agony of remembrance
The remembrance of nights' festive company
The one remaining candle flickers and dies.

So wrote Ghalib, the last and the greatest of classical poets of the Urdu language. The image is characteristic. The flickering candle battling to the last breath, hopelessly and alone, against an inexorable end may well be the poet himself. He is the last articulate spectator of the glory that has departed—the colour and the gaiety, the warmth and good cheer, the '*Saqi* of incandescent beauty,' the 'singer of the ravishing voice'—and all else that peopled the emptiness of now deserted pleasure halls. Thus, in two symbolical lines the poet envisions the passing away of an age, a civilization and a way of life, his own nostalgia for happier times gone by, and an experience timeless and universal, in the life of all human individuals and human groups—the experience of the evanescence of time.

The great empire of the Mughals was an unconscionable time a-dying. The disintegration of the Empire, and together with it the disintegration of feudal society and the way of life organic to this system, began towards the beginning of the eighteenth century after the death of the Emperor Aurangzeb and culminated with the formal British annexation of the whole subcontinent after the abortive national uprising of 1857. Of the many turbulent epochs in the history of the subcontinent, these years were perhaps the most troubled. Following on the sack of Delhi by the Persian adventurer Nadir Shah (1739 AD) wave after wave of murderous strife and disorder ravaged the Empire and hordes of marauders scoured the land at will, leaving behind them a disastrous trail of toppled kingdoms, ruined cities and a populace sick with loss and despair. And into this confusion, the foreign invader insinuated himself, first as a trader, then as an ally of one warring faction against another, biding his time until all of them were equally prostrate. After one final convulsion in 1857, the subcontinent resigned itself to the domination of an alien people, to their strange ways, their incomprehensible language and novel values. The long and festive party of the feudal order was over; gone were the *Saqi* with the wine cup and the lights snuffed out in gracious pleasure halls.

And yet this worst of times was also, in some ways, the best of times. During this very period, particularly towards its close, Urdu poetry flowered and attained maturity; there was a significant revival of Muslim learning, and eminent religious reformers sought to rejuvenate the faith by reasserting its moral and social content. Contact with western civilization and western thought, an introduction to scientific and empirical modes of reasoning, engendered new curiosities and new bewilderments. The rapid erosion of a social edifice, long regarded as fixed and unalterable, demanded new social, cultural and intellectual adjustments. And beyond the ruins of their shattered world, the poet, the scholar, the mystic and the reformer saw the vague glimmer of a world as yet unborn. It was an age of intense preoccupation with the fundamental problems of life and reality, of heated literary, theological and philosophical controversies, of doubts and questionings, hopes and fears, sensual abandon and intellectual diligence, of the catharsis of physical suffering through emotional and spiritual expression.

And of the many notable poets of this period, Muhammad Taqi Mir (1723–1810), Muhammad Rafi Sauda (1713–1780), Vali Muhammad Nazir (1735–1830), Momin Khan Momin (1799–1851), it was Ghalib, above all, who captured in its entirety this 'moment of humanity', the collective emotional, intellectual and spiritual experience of over a century, and made it timeless. He distilled into his Urdu and Persian verse the pain, the nostalgia and the despair of successive generations who watched in bewildered helplessness their great society drift to its destined doom. At the same time, he sought to discover for them through subjective, meditative efforts the why and wherefore, not only of this particular predicament but of the human situation *per se* and to fortify them with his faith in the eternity of life's renewal and human regeneration.

Ghalib wrote both in Urdu and in Persian, both prose and verse, although he is best remembered for the briefest of these writings— his thin volume of Urdu poetry in the traditional 'ghazal' form—a rather severely restricted composition of a number of two epigrammatic lines in a uniform metre and rhyme. Even the themes and diction of this form were largely conditioned by popular usage and as the poet had to 'prove' himself not in print but in oral recitation before the audiences of 'Mushairas' or poetic assemblies, he generally suited his tune to the demands of popular or courtly taste. Ghalib for the first time liberated the Ghazal from the tyranny of custom and usage, cut away ornamented frills and conventional trivialities, and in a diction all his own, with a montage of telescoped images and multi-associational meanings, made it into an all-purpose instrument of expression for both personal experience and abstract thought. The bewilderment this aroused at first, he treated with contempt, 'For mead nor praise I care; if my verse is incomprehensible, so let it be'.

The bewilderment soon gave place to comprehension and acceptance and his experiments gave to Urdu poetry completely new dimensions in expression—earnestly thoughtful, deeply truthful, wonderfully plastic and evocative, in diction, methodology of expression, and analytical perception of experience, Ghalib was the first of the moderns in Urdu poetry. For his models Ghalib turned to the great treasure house of Persian poetry, particularly to the poets of our own subcontinent, Bedil, Urfi, Naziri, thus restoring to Urdu poetry its broken links with this great heritage. He carried this process a step further by making the Persian language his vehicle for the expression of more expansive themes, descriptive, philosophical, discursive or narrative, an example, so eminently followed, later, by Allama Iqbal.

Ghalib's contribution to Urdu prose, although perhaps not so deliberate was equally significant. In his letters with their wealth of anecdotes, critical observations, pen-portraits, he departed once again from the highly ornate and laboured style of prose-writing common at the time and introduced the language to the rhythm of colloquial speech, the beauty of the simple word, and a type of sophisticated wit which came spontaneously to his pen.

> A talisman for the Treasury of Thought
> Is the word which finds its way to my verse

So Ghalib claimed. And the claim is true of both his prose and verse.

Ghalib began his poetic career at the age of about ten and by his middle teens had already become known as something of a literary figure. At the age of 24 he compiled his first *Diwan* or collection of Urdu poetry. A good deal of juvenile verse included in this edition he later omitted from the revised versions brought out during his maturer years but his title to fame was already secure.

During the next five or six years in the company of the most discriminating scholars and critics of the day gathered in Delhi, he chiselled and perfected his characteristic style and then ventured forth on a new exercise in poetic expression. For nearly twenty years after 1847, in some ways the richest and most arduous years of his life, he wrote mainly in Persian. In 1842–43, he published the first revised version of his Urdu verse and a little later his first collection of Persian poetry. When Ghalib joined the Royal Court in 1850, his indefatigable Muse turned to Urdu once again and simultaneously he began pioneering in a completely different field—Urdu prose. It was during this period that he began to correspond with his friends and pupils in Urdu and these inimitable letters were later collected and published in two separate volumes named *Ood-i-Hindi* (1868) and *Urdu-i-Mualla* (1869), towards the end of his life. His collection of Persian prose entitled *Panj Ahang* and a portion of his history of Mughal kings, a commissioned work, called *Mihri Neemroze* also came out during the same time, i.e. 1850–57.

The period of violent disorder during and after the uprising of 1857 Ghalib spent mostly confined to his house and utilized this enforced leisure to write a diary of his experiences in a Persian pamphlet called *Dastambo*, a picturesque and moving account of those calamitous days. In 1862 he published a polemical pamphlet entitled *Qaata-i-Burhan* seeking to correct what he considered to be inaccuracies in a Persian Dictionary called *Burhan-i-Qatae* very popular with Persian scholars of the day, thus reopening old wounds of his literary skirmishes in Calcutta and in the ensuing uproar, he was called upon to return repeatedly to the fray to answer his many critics.

During the closing years of his life he saw the publication of his collected works both in Urdu and Persian, never received a penny in royalty, and had to beg and borrow from his friends to buy his own books for distribution to the persons he valued.

Mirza Asadullah Beg Khan as he was named at birth, was born at Akbarabad (Agra) on 27 December 1797. The non-de-plume which made him famous, he assumed in his twenties when he first turned his pen to Persian verse. In his early Urdu writings the pen-name he used was Asad. Ghalib was descended from a family of Aibak Turks of present day Uzbekistan. His grandfather Mirza Fauqan Beg Khan left his native Samarkand in search of adventure somewhere early in the eighteenth century and found service with the Mughal Governor of Lahore. Ghalib's father Mirza Abdullah Beg Khan married into a family of rich noblemen of Agra but this appears to have been the only stroke of good luck he ever had. He was killed in battle in the service of the Prince of Alwar, when Ghalib was only five years old. The orphaned child was given into the care of his uncle Mirza Nasrullah Beg Khan—a man better favoured by fortune. Nasrullah Beg was appointed to the governorship of Agra by the Marathas and after the city fell to the British he was enlisted in the Imperial forces in a fairly senior rank. He too died in service four years later. As Nasrullah Beg had no children of his own, the considerable annuity and properties the British had bestowed on him devolved to his collateral heirs, of which Ghalib and his brother Yusuf Beg Khan were the nearest. For Ghalib this proved both a blessing and a bane. While his share of this endowment did ensure for him a subsistence, he was not given what was rightfully his due and until the end of his days he fought an interminable and heart-breaking battle to obtain redress. This hopeless battle with its unending series of defeats, reverses and humiliations, petitions, appeals, an arduous and fruitless journey from Delhi to Calcutta, and knocking at the doors of various British bureaucrats, big and small, is perhaps, the longest shadow which overcast Ghalib's life, a life beset by many other cares and other sorrows.

But to return to his childhood. After the death of his uncle, Ghalib spent the rest of his early years with his mother's affluent family at Agra and from all accounts, these were the happiest and most carefree years of his life. He never completed his formal education, a lack he often regretted, but he did receive instruction in the then popular branches of learning, theology, astronomy, logic, jurisprudence, literature and medicine from a noted local scholar Khalifa Mohammad Muazzam. According to Ghalib's own avowal, however, his real mentor was a wandering Persian scholar, who spent two whole years with him during his early teens, a Zoroastrian, Hormuzd, by name, who later took on the name of Abdus Samad after his conversion to Islam. No other evidence regarding the existence of this person is available but Ghalib claims that he was incomparable in his knowledge of Persian language and literature and generous with imparting this learning to his gifted pupil.

At the age of 13, Ghalib was married to Umrao Begum, daughter of Nawab Ilahi Baksh Maruf of Delhi. Nawab Ilahi Baksh was brother to Nawab Ahmed Buksh Khan of Loharu, one of the most influential noblemen of Delhi and a brother in law of Ghalib's uncle Nasrullah Beg. Two or three years after his marriage Ghalib set up house in Delhi although until he was nineteen or twenty he still spent a good deal of his time in Agra. He was a gay youth and probably the old haunts of his childhood held a greater store of forbidden pleasures than the staid metropolis.

Ghalib's fame as a poet had preceded him before he settled down in Delhi. He was related by marriage to one of the foremost families of the capital and had a claim to rank among the nobility. In spite of his haphazard schooling, he could hold his own in learned discourse. What he lacked in material means, he made up by liberally borrowing from local moneylenders on the strength of the family fortune he someday hoped to reclaim. He was, therefore, soon accepted as a member of the metropolitan elite, the elite of poets, scholars, and accomplished nobleman, and for the first few years, his life followed the happy and leisurely pattern of the privileged aristocracy. Reading, writing, entertaining friends, poetic assemblies, learned discussions, formal calls.

But the holiday was short-lived. By 1824–25 debts and other financial difficulties he had so blithely ignored began to press heavily upon him and for the next twenty years he was deeply involved in the struggle already referred to, the struggle to retrieve his family pension and other assets. In 1827, he set out for Calcutta to present his case personally to the Governor-General, stopping at Lucknow and Benares on the way. Nothing came of the representation but the journey enriched the poet in many ways. The stay at Benares produced a beautiful long poem in Persian, and the sojourn in Calcutta gave him his first intimate glimpse of European society and the new cultural mores they had brought with them. Experience gave him a new awareness of the progressive march of human social history, confirming his faith in the future of new human societies and in his own zest for the joys of living. On the negative side were the heavy and unrecompensed expenses of the journey and of the two years' stay in Calcutta and what was worse, a bitter, acrimonious literary controversy he landed himself into, by denigrating the accepted master of local Persian poets and scholars, a Punjabi poet and philologist by the name of 'Qateel'. 'I do not accept any son of a Khatri as an authority on Persian', said Ghalib, and exposed himself to a stream of vituperation and abuse which he fought back as doggedly as he fought for his pension.

In 1817, at the age of 50, he was visited by what he considered to be an even greater misfortune than the loss of his pension. He was arrested on the charge of running a gambling den and sentenced to six months in prison. This wrote finis to his dreams of regaining his rank and status and three years later, he accepted a lowly job at the court of the last Mughal king Bahadur Shah. Technically its incumbent enjoyed the distinction of being the king's people tutor'; in actual fact he ranked only as a scribe and hanger-on.

In 1857 came the fearful holocaust after the failure of the nationalist uprising. The victorious British subjected the Muslim populace of Delhi to unspeakable atrocities. Many of Ghalib's dearest friends were hanged, banished or rendered destitute. His only brother, mentally deranged for some years, died. Ghalib's meagre pension was discontinued. The fair city he loved was reduced to a wasteland.

Ghalib survived the calamity for eleven years. To add to all this Ghalib had his share of personal bereavements. His seven children all died in their infancy. Then he adopted a nephew of his wife whom he dearly loved, Zainul Abedin Arif, and he too died in the prime of youth. There was probably also an affair of the heart, mourned in a very moving poem, of which little is known.

Such then was the life of this poet. Of his personality and temperament, his friends, pupils and above all his own letters have left us a wealth of material. He was a man of great warmth of heart, a devoted friend, a gracious teacher, as punctilious in his formal duties towards his friends and relatives as he was neglectful of his own interests, as proud of his genius and his station before the world as he was humble towards men be loved and respected. He suffered no fools and was fiercely intolerant of pompous obscurantists and pseudo-scholars. And yet in his personal dealings he was gentle to a fault, even gullible to a degree; a man of great application and industry in his art and yet so lazy in physical habits that he would let a house collapse over his ears rather than shift to a more comfortable residence in some other area. But perhaps the dominant and most endearing quality about him was his wit and unfailing good humour, his cheerfulness which kept breaking in on the gloomiest of situations, and a stout resoluteness to see every problem and every situation through.

This cheerfulness abided by him all through his long and painful sickness until on 15 February 1869.

his flawed heart ...
burst smilingly

'What a free, untrammelled man he was, May God rest his soul', as he wrote of himself.

18

MOHAMMAD IQBAL

'No man was ever yet a great poet,' wrote that very discerning critic, Samuel T. Coleridge, 'without being at the same time a great philosopher.' This formulation may or may not be entirely acceptable in the West, but in the East, particularly among the Muslim peoples, a succession of great names bears it testimony: Jalaluddin Rumi (1207–1273), Moslehuddin Saadi (d. 1313), Shamsuddin Hafiz (d. 1389), Khusrau (1253–1325), and Asadullah Khan Ghalib (1797–1869). It is to the same distinguished line that the poet, Iqbal or 'Allama' Iqbal (1877–1938), as he is reverentially called, unquestionably belongs, with this difference that, unlike some of his medieval predecessors, he was not only equipped with intensive education in various philosophical schools both ancient and contemporary, but also commanded sufficient prose in more than one language to articulate his own answers to the problems of reality with logic and precision.

Like all great 'poets of affirmation,' Dante Alighieri, John Milton, Johann Wolfgang Goethe,[1] Iqbal was no abstract thinker. Like them he was closely involved with the affairs of the social world around him, and for many successive generations of Muslims in the Indo-Pakistan subcontinent he was not the un-acknowledged but the acknowledged law-giver for the norms of their social religious, and political thinking.

For the Muslin community of undivided India, the closing decades of the nineteenth century and the early decades of the twentieth century, were a period of acute mental confusion and emotional distress. The downfall of the Muslim Mughal empire, the bloody reprisals that followed the uprisings against British authority in 1857, the extinction of the privileges, values, and usages of the old feudal order, the ascendancy of their non-Muslim compatriots to most available positions of power and wealth, sorely lacerated the collective mind. Adversity had also made them kin to other Muslim peoples beyond their borders who were similarly afflicted: the Ottoman Turks, Arabs of the Middle East, Libyans, Moroccans, and Tunisians of North Africa. They awaited a consoling and uplifting voice to lead them out of their wilderness of despond. Leading voices of an earlier era, the timid voice of liberal reformists urging them to come to terms with the alien ways of their British rulers and the strident voice of religious divines exerting them to reject the blandishments of the infidel and return to the fold of ancestral tradition, no longer appealed to the new intelligentsia. Iqbal, the poet, was far better attuned to the sources of their discontent, and Iqbal, the thinker, far better aware of the nature of their intellectual and spiritual malaise—of the giants of modernism and tradition pulling at their wrists. He loved them both wisely and too well. Over the years he chiselled out his answers to contemporary problems of Indian Muslims, the Muslim people in general, and of the abstract trinity of God, Man, and Nature.

While Iqbal sympathised with and assimilated many elements from Western philosophic and scientific thought, e.g., Hegel's concept of man and history being 'man's own work', Kant's critique of pure reason, Marx's denunciation of capitalism and class exploitation, Nietzsche's rejection of liberal bourgeois morality and his glorification of the will to power, Bergson's defence of the validity of intuitive knowledge, Einstein's four-dimensional time-space continuum, etc., he considered that both idealist and materialist philosophies of the West were largely irrelevant to the social and ideological predicaments of his own people. He devoutly believed that it was only the authority of their own religion, Islam, and the sanction of their own sanctified tradition, the life and sayings of the Prophet of Islam, that could truly validate the message he carried.

And on these he focused the searchlight of his vision. Concurrently, the Muslim mind had to be liberated from the sterility of nearly five hundred years of social and intellectual torpor and

the tyranny of backward-looking, anti-intellectual orthodoxy. As a
first step, therefore, like the prophets of old, he sought to cleanse
the House of God of all false idols, of scribes and Pharisees, the
obscurantist Mullah, the withdrawn mystic, the charlatan and the
demagogue.

> Why these curtains draped between the Creator and his creatures.
> Drive out of my Church these elders of the Church!
> I am weary and displeased with these slabs of precious marble.
> Build me another sanctuary of humble clay.[2]

Only thus could this House be made deserving of the 'vice-regent
of God' on earth, Man.

Iqbal is a humanist not only in the formal but in the literal sense
of the word: for him 'no form of reality is so powerful, so inspiring
and so beautiful as the spirit of man.' The fall of Adam was not a
falling from grace but the opposite: his elevation to the position of
a 'Co-worker with God' in the process of creation; a process which
is still continuing. For 'our universe is not a complete factor. It is
still in the course of formation and man has to take his share in it
inasmuch as he helps to bring order into a portion of this chaos.'[3]
The terrestrial world is as much man-made and God-made with the
difference that while the creation of God, Nature or Matter is
relatively static and immobile, the creative energies of man are
geared to the dynamics of an evolutionary process which is both
timeless and measureless.

> There are other worlds beyond the stars,
> Other testing grounds for the passion of love.
> Don't stay enmeshed in your (earthly) nights and days,
> There are other measures of time for you in other spaces.
> (Yonder)

> You created the night, and I the lamp.
> You created mud, I made it into a wine-cup.
> You created deserts, mountains, wastelands,
> I made them into orchards, gardens, flower-beds.[4]

As a corollary to this, Iqbal applied the Muslim concept of 'Tauheed'; the unity or Oneness of God, to the unity of the terrestrial and the celestial worlds, thus replacing the concept of transcendence of God by His Immanence[5] and obliterating the duality of sacred and secular, spiritual, and material. 'The spirit finds its opportunities in the natural, the material, the secular. All that is secular, therefore, is sacred in the roots of its being.'

Further, since the process of human evolution through a progressive mastery over material forces is continuous and unending, it follows that the only abiding element in the cosmic scheme is transition and change.

In this world, only change has permanence.[6]

And this applied as much to subjective and ideological as to social and material factors; even the edicts of religion. 'Eternal principles when they are understood to exclude all possibilities of change, which according to the Quran is one of the greatest signs of God, tend to immobilize what is essentially mobile in its nature'.[7] Having already parted company with the traditional mystic who dismisses the physical world as an illusion and physical endeavour as mere vanity, Iqbal discards equally emphatically the dogmatic theologian and his static orthodoxy.

Finally, the principal agent in this creative process is the human Ego, or Personality or Self—*Khudi*, as Iqbal calls it. To meet the challenge of creation, the human self has to be fortified both by perceptual knowledge of the physical world and intuitive passion (or love, 'Ishq' in Iqbal's terminology) for the realization of higher values and ideals. It logically follows that 'the idea of personality gives us a standard of value—that which fortifies personality is good; that which weakens it is bad. Art, religion, and ethics must be judged from the standpoint of personality.[8] But this personality or self cannot develop or fortify itself in isolation. It can do so only in the context of the totality of social relationships. And here Iqbal's Perfect Man (*Mard-e-Kamil*) disengages himself from Nietzsche's superman, for Iqbal's categorical imperatives rule out all forms of nationalist chauvinism, imperialist domination, racial discrimination, social exploitation, and personal aggrandisement, since all of them make for the debasement and perversion of human personality.

Understandably, the bulk of critical literature on Iqbal is devoted to the study and analysis of his message and thought content rather than to an appreciation and evaluation of his poetry. And yet it is his vibrant and impassioned verse and the persuasive appeal it carried which accounts for much of his influence. In his poetic works, form and content, theme and style move along well defined lines and their evolution over a long span of continuous creation makes an interesting study. In the first phase, lasting up to 1905, most of the poems relate to the wonder and questionings inspired by isolated phenomena of nature; mornings and sunsets, mountains and rivers, the moon, the start, and the causeless nostalgia of youth. This lyrical period of short pieces is followed by a series of long poems, passionate and rhetorical, mostly devoted to political themes—nationalist or Pan-Islamic. All this work is in Urdu. In 1915, Iqbal brought out his first long philosophical poem in Persian, *Asrare-Khudi* (Secrets of the Self), which initiated the next phase of philosophic speculations mostly in Persian. And lastly, the early thirties saw the final perfection of his teachings and poetic art in the form of three volumes in Urdu, *Bal-e-Jibreel* (The Wing of Gabriel), *Zarb-e-Kaleem* (The Rod of Moses) and the posthumous *Armaghan-e-Hijaz* (The Gift of Hijaz). By this time his restless quest had travelled from bits and pieces of subjective experience; the wonders of nature, the travail of Indian Muslims and the Muslim world, to a calm contemplation of the ultimates of reality—God, Nature, and Man.

With this progressive expansion in the field of his poetic vision there is a corresponding reduction in his poetic themes, from profusion to orderliness, from dispersal to integration, terminating in the monolithic thought of his last years. There is a similar transformation in style from prolixity to precision, from ornate and involved phraseology to lucid direct statement, from flamboyant rhetoric to unadorned poetry. The long poem, philosophical or political in the *Mathnavi* (rhymed couplets) or *Musaddas* (six line stanza) form gives way to epigrammatic verse in the form of *Ghazal*,

Qita or *Rubai*. The emotional climate also undergoes a change from sentiment (*Mohabbat*) to passion (*Ishq*) or love. In this mature body of verse, Iqbal, after discarding the normal conventional embellishments of oriental poetry, employed a number of devices of his own to relieve the austerity of his verse and to maintain its heightened tenor. The first among these is the musicality of sound patterns and a number of prosodic innovations which are utterly lost in translation. Second, the introduction of highly evocative proper names, hardly known to Urdu poetry before him—the sands around Kazima, the snows of Mount Damavand, the deserts of Iraq and Hijaz, the blood of Hussain, the Majesty of Rome, the beauty of Cordova, the glories of Isfahan and Samarkand. Third, he gave currency to unfamiliar words which are antique without being archaic, unused without being obscure. And he counter-matched them with rhymes and meters which had rarely been used in Urdu poetry.

At this stage, after much piecemeal thinking and intense subjective exploration, he at last arrived at a theme big enough to fill the whole of his vision, the twin theme of Man's grandeur and his loneliness. The theme of human loneliness, around the immensity of the odds arrayed against man; oppression, exploitation, and various meannesses within and a hostile heartless nature without. The grandeur of man—the tragic hero—lies in his acceptance of this challenge; his destiny of unending struggle, of perpetual frustration and fulfilment to attain to the wholeness of God. He sang of this glory and this pain, the hopes and anxieties, the fulfilments and frustration of the world of man with great tenderness and compassion, at times with great wrath and indignation. And he did so with a conviction and a sincerity, with a sweep and amplitude of expression unequalled in his age.

NOTES

1. V.G. Kiernan, Introduction to *Poems from Iqbal*, John Murray.
2. God addressing the angels, *Bal-e-Jibreel* [The Wing of Gabriel].
3. M. Iqbal, *Reconstruction of Religious Thought in Islam*, Lahore, Ashraf.
4. Dialogue between 'Man and God', *Pyame Mashriq* [Message of the East].

5. W.C. Smith, *Modern Islam in India and Pakistan*, Lahore, Ashraf.
6. *Bang-e-Dara* [Call of the Caravan Bell].
7. M. Iqbal, *Reconstruction of Religious Thought in Islam*, Lahore, Ashraf.
8. Iqbal in his Introduction to Professor Nicholson's translation of *Secrets of the Self*, Lahore, Ashraf.

19

IQBAL—THE POET[1]

I wish to talk to you this morning on a rather neglected aspect of Iqbal's work, namely, the artistic aspect or what you might call the purely poetic aspect. As you are no doubt aware there are any number of studies on the thought, philosophy, message and various other aspects of Iqbal's works; but so far as I am aware very little analysis has been done of his poetic technique or the secret of his poetic magic. For this the poet himself is partly responsible because, as you are aware, there are a number of injunctions in Iqbal's works imploring his readers to ignore his poetry and to concentrate on his message. It is also due, I suppose, partly to the very low social evaluation that we put on the poet or the artist in our country. The serious people among us consider a poet to be a rather disreputable character who is not to be taken very seriously. If they wish to elevate his worth then they must classify him among thinkers, or philosophers or preachers or even politicians—a poet as such is not worth much bothering about. I suppose Iqbal was aware of this prejudice and did not want to get mixed up with the decadent songsters with which our community abounds. Anyway, I am not going to quarrel with this approach today. I merely wanted to say that whatever the rights or the wrongs of this approach there is no doubt that a poet of Iqbal's calibre would be great by whatever name you call him. The one thing which I don't think will be seriously contested is that even though Iqbal was a philosopher, a thinker, an evangelist and even a preacher, what gave real force and persuasiveness to his message was his poetry. This is borne out by the fact that his prose lectures, excellent as they are, have hardly a fraction of the readers that his poetry has, and hardly command a fraction of the influence that his poetry has wielded on more than one generation in more than one country. This by itself should be a sufficient proof that in addition to his thought the supplemental excellence of his poetry is not only important but it is all-important. Therefore, I think it is worthwhile to pay some attention to the purely poetic side of his work.

In the very brief time that is available to me, I can only indicate a few focal points from which this study might be made. I have no time either to elaborate or to illustrate these points but I think most of them are so well known that my elaboration would hardly be necessary. First of all I might clarify that Iqbal himself was deadly opposed to art for art's sake and, therefore, we cannot study his art or his style or his technique or his other poetic qualities in isolation from his theme because even though there is steady progression in his style, even though he wrote in different styles, yet all these styles were fashioned according to the themes which he was trying to put across. Therefore, the evolution of his style is parallel to the evolution of his thought and it would be superficial and misleading to study one in isolation from the other. Keeping that in mind, if you look at Iqbal's work, the first thing that strikes you is a very strong contrast between the style and the expression of his earlier works and the style and expression of his mature and later works. The second thing that strikes you is that in spite of these differences, there is a continuity in all his work. I think this is due to two reasons. Apart from his juvenile and very early works, even the things that he wrote about in his youth are imbued with a sense of solemnity and earnestness which persist throughout his works. The second aspect of this continuity is the element of quest and inquiry—a persistent desire to know and to explore the secrets of reality, the secrets of existence. Now these two subjective elements provide the continuity to his works while the stylistic element provides the element of evolution. How does this evolution take place? What are the elements in this evolution? I would say there are four elements, each determined by the progression in his thought. Firstly, the style of his earlier works, as you know, is ornate, florid, Persianised, obviously under the influence of Bedil, Naziri and Ghalib and the school of Indo-Persian poets which was popular with our intelligentsia in the nineteenth century and the beginning of the twentieth. As examples of his earlier work, you have the following type of verses.

Kis qadar lazzat kishod uqda-e-mushkil main hai
Lutf sad hasil hamari saee bay hasil main hai

or

Gaysoay Urdu abhi minnat pazir-e-shana hai
shamma yeh saudai dil sozi-e-parwana hai[2]

This is generally the style which is, as you can see, a bit florid, a bit diffused, a bit undefined. So you find that so far as the pure style is concerned the progression in his work is from ornateness and ornamentation to austerity, from diffuseness to precision, from rhetoric to epigram. It does not require any great elaboration because it so obviously strikes one. In his later works, all the ornamentation has been cut out. There is no imagery or hardly any imagery. There is hardly any element of the sensory or the perceptive, the approach is purely cognitive and intellectual, austere and precise. This is a process of reduction, or what I might call contraction. The other is the process of expansion. This process is in the thought, in the theme; because Iqbal begins with himself in his very early works,—in the work that he wrote in his youth. He talks about himself, about his love, about his grief, about his loneliness, about his disappointments. Then from himself, he progresses to the Muslim community, to the Muslim world, in the later half of *Bang-e-Dara*. From the Muslim world, he goes further to mankind and from mankind to the universe. So beginning with himself his thought progresses to the cosmos and his thought determines the style, and the expression which he uses. In his earlier works, when he is talking about disjointed things, about sensation, about perception, about experiences, about objective bits and pieces, the style is also disjointed, it is varied, sometimes simple sometimes ornate. Later on when his own whole thought is welded into one monolithic entity his style also becomes monolithic. It becomes almost uniform, having no ups and downs, practically keeping the same pace and the same level. That is the second progression. The third progression is a process of what you might call integration. In his earlier works, for instance, there are a number of poems on the sun, the moon, the clouds, the mountains, the rivers, cities, but there is no connection between them. Later on when he developed his thought, then everything, the whole universe, is really welded together by the single concept that Iqbal has evolved with regard to the role of man in the universe and his destiny. When he has determined this role then everything falls into its place. In his later work if you find poems about natural phenomena and external objects, like his *Kirmak-i-Shab Taab*, *Shaheen*, the moon, and the sun, then they are no longer external phenomena: they are purely symbols, symbols to illustrate some inner subjective theme which Iqbal wants to illustrate through these symbols. They are no longer things in themselves. He is not interested in the Eagle or *Shaheen* as such, I don't think he has ever described what the Eagle looks like. He is not interested in the firefly as such; nor in the eagle or the moon or the sun, they are no longer for him external objects but merely symbols to illustrate certain themes. This is the third progression in his work and style; the progression which integrates disjointed phenomena disjointed experiences into a single whole through a process which is both intellectual and emotional. And fourthly there is a transition in emotional climate. In his earlier works you will see that the word he in fond of is *Mohabbat* whereas in his later works, as you are all aware, the main burden of his song is *Ishq*. For instance, in his earlier work you will probably remember some of these lines:

Mohabbat he say pai hai shifa bimaar qaumon nay
Sharab-e-rooh parwar hai mohabbat nau-e-insan ki

But you hardly find this word *Mohabbat* later on in his mature works where the word used is always *Ishq*. So this is the progression from sentiment to passion. A progression from a purely external attachment to something which comes from within, a something which is the essence of your being, something which is not an acquired trait that merely makes you love certain things or hate certain things, about which is an innate fire, which is all-consuming.

I want to emphasize another point. When Iqbal attained to his matured style, a style which is unadorned, austere, and unornamented, then how does he heighten his statement? How does he compensate for the absence of the other ornaments that poets generally use, the frills with which the poets generally attract attention? This, I think, is a very fascinating subject and very little study has been done on it. Three or four things are very obvious which no one has attempted in Urdu poetry before. For instance, something which is completely Iqbal's addition to the poetic style in Urdu is the use of proper names. Apart from one or two names which have been traditionally used, like Majnoon, Farhad, Laila and Shirin proper names are not a part of our poetic vocabulary. It was Iqbal, I think, who for the first time popularised the use of the proper names:

Ghar mera na Dilli na Safahan na Samarqand
Misr-o-Hejaz say guzar, Paras-o-Sham say guzar[3]

You will see a profusion of such names as Koofa, Hejaz, Iraq, Furat, Isfahan, Samarkand, Koh-i-Adam, Nawah-i-Kazima, Qurtaba, etc. Knowing the poetic implication of these, when you come across a proper name like this, you do not need any simile or any metaphor. This word by itself evokes a sense of distance, a sense of time, a sense of remoteness and what you might call a sense of the romantic because romance after all is a sense of distance, of distance either in space or in time. So this use of the proper name is something which compensates for the absence of other ornamentation in Iqbal. The second thing which he does, which again is rather new, is the use of words which are simple but unfamiliar, words which are neither difficult nor obscure, words which are crystal clear and yet were never used before—words like *Nakheel, Tailson* and *Parnian.* Similarly, you will find a number of such words which Iqbal has deliberately introduced. Take, for instance, the famous line which I consider to be a masterpiece:

Khatoot-i-Khamdar ki numaish

Mariz kaj-e-dar ke numaish[4]

Everybody knows what *Khatoot-i-Khamdar* is; *Mariz* is rather an unfamiliar word, but even as such as intelligible. This is his second, what you might call, trick but I would rather call it his second weapon to relieve the austerity of his statement and to heighten the emotive atmosphere of his verse. The third element which he employs, is to use the unfamiliar metres, for instance the metre of *Masjid-i-Qurtaba*. He has used at least half a dozen metres which were not used in Urdu poetry before and which he introduced for the first time.

Thus, he creates a sense of unfamiliarity by unfamiliar metres, by unfamiliar words, by the use of proper names and, above all, by a very contrived pattern of sounds. I do not think any poet in Urdu has used the patterns of consonantal and vowel sounds deliberately as Iqbal has done. He does not go after the obvious tricks like onomatopoeia and assonance. You will find that his phonetic arrangement of consonants and of vowels is very deliberate. The only other poet who does it in that way is, as far as I know, Hafiz. But in Urdu no such thing was known before Iqbal. Nobody has used a whole line or passage as a deliberate sound spectrum.

These, I think, are some of the stylistic elements which are very characteristic of Iqbal. If you study Iqbal, you find that this was the only style which could fit the ultimate theme which he evolved during the course of his poetic career. This ultimate theme, as far as I know, has many aspects, and one can choose any aspect that he likes. But I think the final theme that Iqbal arrived at was the world of man-man and his universe, man against the universe, man in the universe or man in relation to the universe—I would call the world of man. I might point out that in spite of Iqbal's deep devotion to religion he never mentions the other world or hardly ever mentions the other world except symbolically. There is very little talk of the hereafter in his poetry. There is no mention of any rewards or any punishments in the other world, for the very simple reason that since he is the poet of struggle, of evolution, of man's fight against the hostile forces of nature, the forces hostile to the spirit of man, the hereafter in which there is no action, in which there is no struggle, is entirely irrelevant to his thought. Anyway, the ultimate thing is this theme, the theme of man and the universe of man, of man's loneliness and of man's grandeur. He speaks of Man's loneliness because man is pitted against so many enemies. First against the forces within him, like the forces of greed, cowardliness, of selfishness, exploitation and, secondly, the forces outside him like the forces of inanimate hostile nature. So he speaks of man as a small atom of passion set against the entire universe. He speaks of man's greatness, in that man is the only creature to accept the challenge of creation, man the microcosm of pain accepts the challenge of the stars and the moon and the sun and the universe. It is this great theme which elevates the verse of Iqbal, towards the end of his days, from the beautiful to the sublime.

NOTES

1. Transcription of recorded speech.
2. *Bang-e-Dara*.
3. *Bal-e-Jibreel*.
4. *Zarb-e-Kaleem*.

20

IQBAL

Iqbal (Dr Sheikh Mohammad Iqbal, reverentially known as Allama, or the Sage) is unquestionably the most important writer of Pakistan in modern times. We call him a writer of Pakistan only retrospectively because he died nearly ten years before the establishment of Pakistan and his influence was therefore or is by no means confined to the geographical boundaries of present day Pakistan. Nor is it confined to literature alone. In fact his poetry coloured the social and philosophical thought of many generations of all Muslims of the Indo-Pakistan subcontinent and this influence is still operating. He is perhaps the most written about contemporary writer in any language and the body of literature about his life and work is already voluminous. Unfortunately, however most of these commentaries and evaluations of his work are far from satisfactory, because most of them have been written in order to uphold some particular point of view, mostly some narrow reactionary point of view. These critics, therefore, either isolated some element of Iqbal's thought and elaborated on it in purely abstract terms to the exclusion of other conflicting aspects of his writings, or they overemphasized some particular work of a particular period throwing the rest of his work out of perspective. For instance, most of these writers have put a great deal of stress on the religious element in Iqbal's work without clarifying that Iqbal's concept of religion was in many ways totally opposed to the concept of the orthodox Muslim theologian. In fact the Mullah or the orthodox religious preacher is the subject of some of the bitterest satirical verse written by Iqbal. On the other hand, progressive critics have made much of his admiration for Marx and Lenin in some of his poems and his genuine appreciation of the egalitarian character of socialist society. But again these critics ignore that Iqbal's approach to social and economic problems was idealistic and abstract and the scientific basis of Marxist materialism did not enter into his concept of socialism. Actually he frequently confused the materialist and the capitalist points of view and according to his way of thought a materialistic approach to reality without some idealistic or spiritual belief inevitably lead to exploitation and self-aggrandisement.

To understand Iqbal correctly, therefore, it is necessary to keep in mind that his work reflected all the inner intellectual contradictions, all the conflicting impulses, all the confused dreams and aspirations of the middle strata of Indo-Pakistan Muslims during the first three of four decades of this century and it is precisely because of this that his work is popular among progressive and reactionaries alike and makes for his title as the national poet of Pakistan.

What then is the substance of his thought, how did it evolve and how was it related to the social reality of the poet's times.

In the first phase of Iqbal's poetry belonging to his young days his themes are either descriptive and colourful delineations of natural phenomena, the sun, the moon, clouds, mountains, flowers, etc. or subjective experiences typical of adolescent years, experiences of nostalgia and romantic melancholy. His style at the time is rather flamboyant, ornate and highly Persianized, nevertheless there are some beautiful lyrics belonging to this period like *The Evening on the River Nekkar, Loneliness*, etc. To the same period belong some excellent poems written for children, which still continue to the popular. In early years of the twentieth century the first wave of nationalist anti-imperialist sentiment, after the great uprising of 1857, arose in undivided India and saw the birth of various political organisations like the Indian National Congress, the All-Indian Muslim League, and of political movements like the great movement against the partition of Bengal. This period saw the second phase of Iqbal's verse when he transferred his attention from personal subjective observations and experiences to the collective sentiments and experiences of his country—his nationalist, patriotic phase. It was during this period that he wrote in simple unaffected but very effective words, quite unlike his previous style, some of his immortal patriotic poems like *The New Temple* and *Our India*, preaching national unity and expressing pride and love for the country, which were for many years afterwards hummed, chanted and sung by practically the whole of the literate population of North India, from school-children to venerable patriarchs.

In the years of the great nationalist anti-imperialist movement after the First World War these poems were generally sung as a prelude in every political meeting before the speeches began.

Shortly before the First World War, during the war years and in the decade after the end of the war the subcontinent was convulsed by a series of widespread anti-imperialist movements. Indian Muslims, while fully participating in these movements shoulder to shoulder with the non-Muslims, had some additional emotional and political motivations which were distinctly their own, and which found expression in what came to be known as the Khilafat Movement. During and before the war the Ottoman Empire was being steadily dismembered by the western imperialist powers; mainland Turkey itself was threatened by British and Greek armies and the Sultan of Turkey. The national religious head, or 'Khalifa', of all the Muslims, together with the institution of the Caliphate or Khilafat was in imminent danger. Previous to and concurrently with this development there were bitter struggles between the Muslim peoples of the Mughrib, or North Africa, and Italian, French and Spanish colonialists. The anti-imperialist movement of the Indian Muslims, therefore, took on a Pan-Islamic character and sought to identify itself with the anti-imperialist struggles of other Muslim peoples in other Asian and African lands. The main leadership of this movement was also in the hands of anti-imperialist religious divines like Mahmud-ul-Hasan, Obaidullah Sindhi and Abul Kalam Azad. Iqbal's poetry correctly reflecting the emotional and political impulses of his people also turned from Indian patriotic to Pan-Islamic anti-imperialist themes, which is the third important phase of his poetic evolution. This was one of the most fruitful periods of his writing when he composed a series of long, almost epic, poems concerning the sufferings and travail of Muslim peoples, the glories of their past and their hopes for the future. The appearance of each poem, which he recited himself annually to a tremendous gathering in Lahore was an event eagerly looked forward to throughout the year and each poem was published as a separate booklet and sold out immediately.

For these poems *The Poet and the Lamp*, *The Divine Guide*, *The Plaint to God* and *God answers the Plaint*, etc. he found a yet different style again, rhetorical, passionate and extremely eloquent.

The period immediately succeeding the war saw the abolition of the Caliphate by the young Turks, thus depriving the Pan-Islamic movement of one of its main pillars. The blood bath in Europe revealed the deadly contradictions of the capitalist system, it exposed the pious hypocritical pretensions of the imperialist powers and the dangerous fallacies in bourgeois nationalist thinking.

The same period also saw the birth of the first socialist state in the Soviet Union and the challenge of a new social and ethical system to the established capitalist-imperialist order. For Iqbal these were the years of deep study and meditation resulting in the fourth and last phase of his work, the most mature and the most valuable, the phase of his philosophical humanism. In these years, he evolved and perfected his own personal poetic creed and integrated worldview and finally a theme grand enough to suit the magnitude of his poetic genius. After travelling from his subjective self to his people and from his people to the comity of Muslim peoples, he finally took the whole of mankind as his subject, and took up as his final theme, Man and his Universe.

What is the essence of this theme? First, that human life is a continual process of evolution and that the evolutionary potentialities of the human species are unlimited. The domain of man is not confined to this earth it extends to other unexplored worlds in the universe. There is no final goal which can bring him complete fulfilment, each higher stage of evolution is merely a step to the next stage and thus each human success is always a partial failure and each fulfilment a partial prostration. The dynamics of this evolutionary struggle are provided firstly by what Iqbal calls 'Ishq' or passion in the sense of dedication to a humanist ideal, and secondly by what he calls 'Amal' or action as opposed to more passive contemplation or meditation, advocated by the mystics and idealist philosophers. The goal of the struggle was the realisation of fulfilment of what he called 'Khudi' or the Self, but the individual self could attain to its full potentialities only in the ideal collective social order, an unattainable goal, because no social order could remain ideal if it failed to move forward, and became immobile.

This struggle, therefore, was a dialectical process in which the positive element of human greediness came into conflict with variety of negative elements, first within human society, in the form of exploitation, greed, oppression, and fear, and secondly outside human society in the form of the great challenge posed by the physical universe and the material forces fighting against human subjugation. Therefore, Man was both a heroic and a tragic figure challenged from all sides by forces bigger than himself but accepting this challenge with undaunted courage in the passionate belief of his eternal and instantly triumphal march.

The style which Iqbal finally evolved to express these themes contrasts strongly with what he had practised before, it is austere, precise, unadorned, almost without imagery and without the general poetic frills, almost epigrammatic with the lucidity and expressiveness of the great classics. To relieve the severity of style he introduced some completely new poetic devices unknown to Urdu poetry before, first a very conscious use of subtle sound patterns based on the Persian classics, second the use of proper places and personal names with symbolical overtones, names like Samarkand, Isfahan, Cordova, Damavand, thirdly by the use of unfamiliar metres, and fourthly by the usage of ancient classical words and expressions, unfamiliar without being ambiguous or obscure.

As stated earlier, Iqbal's approach and exposition of these themes was abstract and philosophical which frequently gave use to contradictory expositions by his followers and admirers. But there is no denying the fact that his poetry contributed a great deal to the rise of the progressive movement in the Urdu language, firstly because its high and purposeful seriousness demolished many decadent notions regarding the function of poetry as trivial, entertainment like the notion of art for art's sake, and secondly, because the core of his humanist thought held up for admiration

the great human ideals of freedom, justice, progress and social
equality.

21

PAKISTAN MODERN URDU SHORT STORIES[1]

In early Urdu literature, story-writing, or more correctly story-telling, was largely modelled after the age-old *dastan*—a cycle of picaresque romances, an admixture of fact and fable, social observation and supernatural fantasies, human characters and creatures conjured up from imaginary worlds. The archetypal classic, *The Thousand and One Nights*, provided one of the main sources of inspiration. Popular legends relating to the lives and loves of princes and warriors of native origin were another store-house to draw upon, as were the moral and didactic tales of the Persian classics like the *Gulistan of Saadi*.

Fiction in the modern sense first became known towards the end of the nineteenth century when some gifted writers took to the novel under the influence of their British mentors of the Victorian period. The short story, as we know it today, was a later arrival because, as elsewhere, it had to wait for the advent of another communicative medium, the literary journal or magazine. Although literary monthlies in Urdu came on the scene in the early years of the present century and contributed a great deal to the development of modern Urdu poetry and critical or descriptive prose, their contribution to the art of the short story right up to the mid-twenties was almost negligible. This is because, apart from translations or adaptations from western languages, the short stories of this period were still wrapped in the traditional aura of romantic unreality, even though the locale had shifted from mythical lands to the native soil and the characters had come down to earth. This was engineered by various escapist devices: characters were chosen from socially remote, rich and emancipated classes and action was located in equally remote aristocratic quarters of metropolitan towns or cloistered hill resorts.

Short story writing in Urdu, as in some other languages in the subcontinent, really came into its own with the rise of what is known as the Progressive Movement in Urdu literature, during the thirties. In this period political and economic pressures as well as closer acquaintance with the work of western writers, induced the new generation to come to grips with the basic technical and thematic problems of this particular genre. A sizeable and wide-ranging literature of the short story was thus born within a few years—impassioned stories of social protest, explorations of subjective experience, the complexities of human relationship and joys and sufferings of the common man. A new school of realistic writing arose which brought its readers into intimate contact with the mundane environment and everyday life around him in the by-lanes of the city or the mud-huts of the village. And this tradition originally popularized by a handful of gifted writers has proliferated into a vast and various schools after Independence.

The stories included in this compilation are but a few specimens of what writers, old and new, have contributed to the art of short story writing in Pakistan but they are representative enough to provide a good introduction to this emporium. It is hoped that these stories will be of interest to readers abroad, particularly in the friendly RCD countries, and the reading will provide some enrichment to their under standing of our country and our people.

NOTE

1. Foreword for *Pakistan Modern Urdu Short Stories*, compiled by S. Viqar Azim, RCD Cultural Institute, Islamabad.

22

MUSIC RESEARCH CELL[1]

In June 1974, a small Cell for research in classical music of Pakistan was established under the auspices of the Office of Consultant for Cultural affairs, Ministry of Education, Government of Pakistan. The Cell was intended to conduct and to sponsor research in all branches of classical music and to arrange for publication of research material, to re-appraise, by research and investigation, the contribution made by Muslim musicians, both by individuals as well as by schools or *gharanas*, to the development of classical music, vocal and instrumental, to collect all types of printed material on music, i.e. books, manuscripts, articles, magazines etc. with a view to set up a reference library, to obtain photographs of portraits of eminent musicians together with their biographical data, to establish a sound library of magnetic tapes, cassettes, gramophone discs etc. of famous Muslim musicians. The other objectives visualized for the Cell included a collection of musical instruments of Muslim origin from foreign Muslim countries; to prepare gramophone discs, tapes and cassettes for the popularization of classical music and to educate public taste in its appreciation. (Under this scheme a set of 20 LP records of seven famous Muslim *gharanas*, viz. Agra, Delhi, Gwalior, Kirana Patiala, Sham Choorasi, and Talwandi sung by their renowned representatives in their own characteristic style has already been prepared and will be available for sale soon).

The Cell began to operate with these very large objectives but with practically no funds and with a one man staff. The same situation continued for nearly two years when a small grant was made available for the cell by the Federal Ministry of Education. Nevertheless, as the pages of this progress report will show, it has succeeded in amassing a fair body of research material of considerable value despite these seminally prohibitive handicaps. This was made possible through the generosity of a large number of private donors whose names appear in the report, a small grant from the Ford Foundation, and above all the resourcefulness and dedicated efforts of its one man establishment namely Mr M.A. Sheikh who was assisted in his difficult task by various institutions e.g. Pakistan National Council of the Arts, EMI (Pakistan), Pakistan Television Corporation, United States Information Service, Lahore, Goethe-Institute (Pak-German Cultural Centre) Lahore, Iran Cultural Centre, Lahore, and a large number of eminent musicians and music lovers.

This report bears ample testimony to the fruits of these labours. The Cell can already boast of a reference library of over 400 rare books, manuscripts, microfilms, and a large collection of journals, magazines and learned articles which are available for all students of music. It has also managed to collect well over a hundred photographs and portraits of eminent musicians, past and present, together with their detailed biographical data categorized according to various schools and various periods of musical tradition. Copies of these photographs are made available to interested parties. It has also set up a free service in a small recording studio for recordings of this large library of music records, tapes and cassettes including music from forty-eight foreign countries that all music lovers can avail of.

The work done so far represents only the beginnings of a stupendous task, namely comprehensive archives, the compilation of the vast body of our classical music. It is hoped, however, that with more generous assistance and suitable encouragement being provided, the Cell will be able to meet its responsibilities as successfully in the future as it has done in the past.

NOTE

1. Preface to the report on the music research cell, 1 July 1977.

23

MAJOR LITERARY QUESTIONS

Q. How do you view the present literary situation?

A. The literary situation, today, like the present human social situation is in some ways very similar to the situation in the thirties. As you will recall the euphoria brought about in the twenties by the end of the First World War (the War to end all wars), the breakdown of Victorian moral and social constraints, the hopes aroused among all oppressed peoples like us by the October Socialist Revolution, and the rise of nationalist movements, the brief prosperity enjoyed by the mercantile citizen through war profits and the rural masses by rising prices of their produce all combined to produce a general air of emotional abandonment, intellectual freedom and creative gaiety. By and large this was the era of romantic lyricism and art for art's sake. This era was soon overtaken however by a double crisis in the thirties. The world economic depression hit the underprivileged classes in east and west alike giving rise to a sharpened sense of class consciousness and an intensification of class struggles in both eastern and western societies supplemented by the ideological basis provided by socialist philosophies. The rise of Nazi Fascism in the West and Japanese militarism in the East gave rise to sharpened antagonism among the Western Powers to complicate the existing confrontation between the socialist and capitalist systems on the one hand and the democratic and the authoritarian value systems on the other. As in all periods of social and political crises, this phenomenon was reflected in the world of literature by a great divide between the two major schools of literary thought and expression both creative and critical, of 'progressive realism' on the one hand and 'subjective escapism' cloaked as aesthetics formalism on the other. Thus the great debate began, on the role, function and evaluation of literature, between 'functionalists' on the one hand, who believed that the writer as an exponent and interpreter of social realities was an engineer of human souls, and the aesthete on the other, who held that literature was no more than an artistic compendium of linguistic devices and the writer was no more than an engineer of words. On the theoretic plane, this Cold War has been revived in contemporary literature once again by theories of structuralism, formalism, expressionism etc. and by the incursion of linguistics, what VS Pritchett (1900-1997) calls the 'iron mongery of words'. As an anti-thesis the post war years have produced a new concept of the literature of commitment and a more analytical approach to the theories of social and critical realism to relate the non-literary, ethical and social content extrinsic, exponents of literature with its 'intrinsic' aesthetic standards.

Q. What about the anti-form movement?

A. The anti-form movement so called like some other forms of 'pop' art has two sides. On the one hand it was or is a kind of protest against the norms and conventions of what 'angry young men' considered to be a decadent and played out literary and social establishment and on the other, an attempt like all anarchistic activity to set individual self fulfilment by adjuring all social responsibility to your audience. However to continue with the literary situation. The crises of the thirties that I mentioned earlier had both global and local dimensions. On the global level, the world economic depression the great body of the literature of 'social commart' in the west and the second most significant literary movement after the nineteenth century in our literatures, the Progressive Writers Movement. The menace of Fascism united the conscientious and politically conscious writers of East and West into a great sweep of antifascist sentiment, particularly after this menace was made more manifest by the Spanish Civil War and the Japanese invasion of China. It also sent the timid of heart and the myopic of vision, scurrying into the recesses of their own subconscious, the dream world of myth or legend or the play ground of linguistic and stylistic devices.

As I said we are faced with a similar world situation today. On the global plane the escalation of the arms race, particularly the ever ascending spiral of thermo-nuclear weapons manufacture initiated and led by USA coupled with the brinkmanship of the new US establishment has brought to the whole of mankind a wholly and qualitatively new menace of total annihilation. This is accompanied by all pervasive efforts of the newly risen Mafia of international monopolies to maintain their stranglehold on the resources of the Third World and to reverse the process of history, by perpetuating or bolstering up the backward social and political structures in these countries more amenable to such exploitation. On the national plane, the erstwhile euphoria of newly won freedom has evaporated in many Asian and African countries by the replacement of foreign domination by domestic tyrannies and by the emergence of new class structures as or more exploitative than the one they displaced. The post-liberation literature in these countries again reflects conflicting mores of confronting realty or evading it, of protests and hope or disillusionment and despair.

Q. What about the Afro-Asian Writers movement?

A. The disintegrating of some western imperialist empires in Asia and Africa after the Second World War and the liberation of many Asian and African countries, lifted after many centuries the barriers of communication interposed between them by the imperialist powers. Tentative groupings then began to go in search of each other again and to restore some of their ancient cultural links severed by foreign domination. At the initiative of some Indian writers a conference of Asian writers of various schools of opinion was convened at Delhi in 1956 which decided to enlarge the circle of their confraternity by including their conferrers from Africa and thus at the invitation of Soviet writers, the foundations of the Afro-Asian Writers Association were laid in Tashkent in 1958. Its secretariat was first established in Colombo in 1959 and later shifted in Cairo in 1963. Subsequently the Association enabled to congregate after every four or five years in a general conference in Cairo, Delhi, Beirut, Alma Ata and more recently in Luanda in Angola. Thus eminent writers from both these countries some of who were only distantly acquainted with one another through meagre translations by Western publishers got together for the first time to exchange views and pool their experience in detailed discussion on the basic technical and ideological problems faced by the present day writer in their respective countries. In 1968, the Association produced its quarterly journal, *Lotus*, in English, French and Arabic which is now in my charge.

Q. Could you enumerate some of these basic problems?

A. With few exceptions, the basic cultural problems in Asian and Africa stem from one primary source, the era of colonial domination and demand one basic solution, the decolonization of their cultures including literature. Apart from this common feature, however, there is little uniformity of pattern as the advent of imperialist colonialist domination hit different levels of development. Among them were advanced feudal societies like ours with developed languages and literatures of their own. There were, on the other hand, also pre-feudal, tribal or even pre-tribal societies, as in parts of Africa whose ancient traditional cultures had already disintegrated through other historical factors and whose languages, and literatures, therefore, had not progressed beyond folklore and oral discourse. In the former case the successors of the old feudal class, the new middle class eagerly largely accepted western norms and conventions of both literary creation and evaluation to veneer their urban classical heritage on the one hand and to alienate them from their folk tradition on the other. In many African countries, however, their native languages were swamped altogether by the invading English, French, Spanish or Portuguese and gave to each country instead, a by hybrid patois of its own. When these countries were liberated, therefore, and they were the last to be liberated, the writer's reaction to this colonialist depredation was more fierce and his quest for his own native cultural and literary roots in his folk heritage was more impassioned than in ours. Even while writing in their acquired foster language, they tried to rediscover the tilt, the idiom, and the nuances of perception and expression native to their folk traditions. To some extent this process is also under way in our past of the world where the literary elite are trying to bridge their class and cultural alienation from their own masses by re-learning the idiom of folk literatures like Punjabi. In addition to this problem of re-discovering national cultural and literary identity and relieving it from the debris of spurious overlays of colonialism, the modern writer is also faced with the task of adjusting their continuities of the past with the demands both of present day experience and social realities as well as of the new advances in the techniques and stylistics of expression. In multi-lingual and poly-cultural societies like ours, there is the additional problem of finding a productive and acceptable relationship between the official or national linguistic medium such as Urdu with the regional languages which ensures progressive development of both. Then there is the almost universal problem of raising the level of comprehension and appreciation of the culturally underprivileged masses without sabotaging basic aesthetic values of literature. In short, a writer's work like a woman's is never done.

Q. Any suggestions for widening the dissemination of Afro-Asian literatures?

A. This is firstly the problem of translations which is at present the monopoly of certain Western publishing houses. It is time that this monopoly should be broken and taken over by private or State, perhaps the idea of an Afro-Asian Literary Corporation or Consortium may be worth exploring. Secondly it is time that our academic institutions concerned with literature should break themselves free from the apron strings of western literatures and introduce into their syllabi, the story of African and Asian literatures instead. Thirdly, more extensive facilities should be provided for cultural exchanges among writers of the two continents, in addition to the platform provided by the Afro-Asian Writers Association.

Q. Literature and propaganda?

A. In a sense all literature is propaganda unless it totally fails to communicate when it is no literature at all. Even nonsensical literature propagates nonsense. Literature fails to be literature and becomes journalism or pure propaganda only when it lacks the additional aesthetic dimension required of all literature.

Q. Finally, what value do you believe to be basic to all good literature?

A. Basically there is only one value-humanism. All other values, love of peace, freedom, social justice, compassion, alleviation of human suffering, self realization, adoration for goodness and hearty flow from it.

24

MOSCOW FILM FESTIVAL

Mr Farid Ahmad joined me in Moscow on 9 July and Mr Jamil Dehlvi, on 15 July to participate in the Moscow International Film Festival. Two other delegates who were expected and whose names had been communicated to the festival authorities failed to arrive.

We had entered three films for the competition. Two of them never arrived. Even the third, Jamil Dehlvi's *Towers of Silence*, was received long after the festival deadline and if the festival authorities had not been so accommodating and our Embassy not so persistent, this too may not have been accepted. The other non-competitive film for commercial showing, *Aas*, was also received long after the deadline given for the exhibition of such films and regrettably without any publicity or display material. Film stars draw the most crowds and receive the most publicity in such festivals but no film artist was included in our delegation.

I was given to understand before I left for Moscow at the end of last month, that funds for entertainment and other incidental expenses normally involved in a delegation's activities on such occasions would be forwarded later. No money was however, received, not even for my personal expenses, nor any instructions sent to the Embassy in this regard.

In short, we joined the Festival without a film, without any publicity material, without any stars and with no money. We were supposed to discuss the project of a co-production, with the Soviet Film Authority but the script for the proposed film was also not received. Under the circumstances, the scope for the projection of Pakistani cinema to Soviet authorities or audience or to producers and distributors from other countries gathered here was severely limited.

Nevertheless, the film *Aas* received for commercial showing was exhibited in an excellent and very spacious cinema on 17 July, and all the three shows during the day were packed to capacity. The audience response was very favourable. *Towers of Silence* was shown in the festival hall reserved for short films where admission is restricted to participants of the Festival. In view of its technical and artistic merits and the painstaking work of its director, we were rather optimistic that it would win some recognition from the jury. Some members of the viewers we talked to, agreed with us. The hope was not fulfilled but I still feel that it should do well in some other festival elsewhere. In this Festival, most of the prizes went to films with a straightforward story content and with social or political comment, obvious to the average viewer.

The Ambassador Mr Sajjad Haider was good enough to attend both our film shows with his family, and the gesture was obviously appreciated by the festival authorities. The Minister Mr Humayun Khan, kindly hosted a reception at his residence which was largely attended by some prominent delegates to the festival from friendly countries, some local journalists, officials of Soviet Film Export organization and of the Soviet Pakistan Friendship Society. This was about the only organized PR effort we were able to make and I think, successfully so. In other ways too, members of our Embassy, the Ambassador, the minister, and the third secretary Mr Mohammed Khan, who had to do most of the running about, were extremely helpful and cooperative and but for their efforts, we might have drawn a complete blank in the Festival.

I had a long talk with Mr Frolov, who is in charge of the Pakistan-India section on the Soviet Film Export organization, regarding their purchase of the two films sent to the Festival. He promised to help, but opined that, during the last financial year, Soviet Union had paid Rs. 5 lakh for three Pakistani films. Pakistan had purchased five Soviet films for only Rs. 1 lakh. The Soviets were prepared to buy more Pakistani films, he said, but something should be done to modify this large disparity in the balance of payments, obviously by our buying more Soviet films. Mr Farid Ahmad also had some discussions with other distributors from other countries which he will doubtless mention in his own report.

In conclusion, despite the handicaps mentioned above participation in the festival was useful in many ways. Many new contacts were made with filmmakers and producers from many countries, particularly, the Afro-Asian countries and I think we did manage to get some of them interested in films from Pakistan. The two films we exhibited, certainly attracted notice and should prove a good introduction of our film production to international audiences.

It must be stressed, however that international film festivals should be taken a little more seriously, i.e.

i) no under production film should ever be entered in an international festival as it can never be ensured before hand that the film will be finished in time or that the finished product will come up to the required standard.

ii) Preparations for a festival should be taken in hand well in advance to ensure that publicity literature, display material, etc. is made available to the festival authorities in time, that the entire are nominated well in advance, and arrangements for some advance publicity made.

iii) The cooperation of the national film industry and the participation of some film artists must be ensured.

iv) Some effort should be made to ascertain in advance, the orientation of the festival jury and to enter films likely to prove most acceptable.

v) In a film festival apart from formal entertainment, funds are always needed even for day-to-day small get-togethers and adequate provision for such expenditure should be made. And if this is too much to ask, it is best to stay at home.

25

VISIT TO THE SOVIET UNION[1]

I arrived in Moscow late in the evening on 13 May (the flight was delayed by 24 hours) and arrived in Riga the next morning, a day after the literary symposium had commenced.

This was not a formal conference but some thing in the nature of a social get-together for informal discussions. The topics for discussion were: first 'the importance of classical legacy in the formation of the modern writer' and second 'peace and cooperation as a precondition for cultural development in Asian countries'. The proceedings, in the main were confined to vague generalities and nothing of much consequence transpired. On the second topic, I observed that while peace, security and cooperation were obvious pre-requisites for the development of all social and cultural life there were also certain preconditions for the establishment of lasting peace. These included inter alia respect for the sovereignty of all nations big or small, non-interference in one another's internal affairs and foregoing the use of force of the threat of force in the settlement of international disputes.

No resolutions were presented or passed except a general press statement that the discussions had been useful and might be held again at some unspecified date and time in the future. Both India and Bangladesh offered to play host to the next gathering if and when it was held but the question was left open.

On my return to Moscow on 19 May, I visited our Embassy and learnt of the Indian nuclear explosion. There were no public functions held after that day but in meetings and conversations with intellectuals and writers whom I know the reaction to this development was uniformly unfavourable. Even Indian and Bangladeshi writers appeared to be unhappy and the consensus of opinion was that Mrs Indira Gandhi had agreed to this measure to placate the increasingly hostile domestic opinion.

The next day Mr Mazhar Ali Khan arrived in Moscow and we had informal discussions regarding his forthcoming visit to Paris for a meeting of the World Peace Council. Mr Mazhar Ali Khan also met the Indian Minister of Education Dr Noorul Hassan and both of us were invited to the house of the Bangladesh Ambassador Mr Shamsur Rehman, an old acquaintance. Apart from social pleasantries to which the conversation was generally confined, Mr Shamsur Rehman opined that the Bangladesh Prime Minister and Foreign Minister were rather upset over the message of the Pakistan Government advising him not to press for the admission of Bangladesh into UN at this stage. He said that they felt resentful over this type of 'older-brotherliness'. Besides that, the same attitudes were developing in Bangladesh towards India as they previously harboured towards Pakistan and the communal situation was also worrying the Bangladesh Government apart from their other pressing problems.

I was invited by the Progressive Publishing House in Moscow for a discussion on further exchange of publications between Soviet Union and Pakistan. They were anxious to obtain up-to-date information on the latest publications in Pakistan as well as some indication of what we considered suitable for translation into the Russian language. I believe the National Book Centre in Karachi publish a periodical directory of Pakistani publications. It might be helpful if this Publishing House is put on their mailing list. During my previous conversation with this organization I had pressed them to obtain the services of some Pakistani translators for their Urdu publications as the translations done by their Indian translators were far from satisfactory. My previous notes on the subject refer. I was informed that subsequently at their request, the Ministry of Information had nominated a translator for them but the specimen of work submitted by him was found to be very unsatisfactory. It seems to me that this is a matter for the Ministry of Education to decide and I can recommend the names of suitable persons if desired.

I was also invited by Academician Dr Gufuror, Head of the Institute of Oriental Studies for a talk in his office regarding his impending visit to Pakistan and other matters of common interest. He emphasized once again his desire for the participation of Pakistan in the coming Amir Khusrau Celebrations as well as in a conference on Persian Literature proposed to be held in Iran next year. He was not certain of the exact date of his visit to Pakistan but he told me that he was mainly interested in visiting cultural and learned institutions in Lahore as well as in meeting representatives of the Ismaili community which is his special study. In this connection, apart from Karachi, a visit to the Northern Areas may be desirable.

I was later invited to join fifteen other international delegations for a visit to Leningrad in connection with the anniversary celebrations of the poet Pushkin commencing on 26 May. While in Leningrad I visited the famous Leningrad Oriental Institute with its priceless collection of Oriental books and manuscripts. The head of the section dealing with the subcontinent informed me with considerable embarrassment that his section continued to be known as the Indian section as no approach had been made by any party so far to get the nomenclature changed. He also informed me that he had repeatedly addressed some of our learned bodies for some material from Pakistan but had received no response. As this institution is one of the most prestigious treasure houses of oriental learning, which includes much of our own cultural heritage, I suggest that some action may be initiated through appropriate channels to put Pakistan on its map.

NOTE

1. Report on the visit to the Soviet Union, 14–30 May 1974. 4 June 1974, to Dr Mohammad Ajmal, Secretary, Ministry of Education, Government of Pakistan, Islamabad. Copy to the Ministry of Foreign Affairs (Dr Maqbul A. Bhatti).

26

HOMAGE TO TOLSTOY[1]

It was in the later twenties and early thirties that Russian classics became popular with students of literature in India and Pakistan, the major reason for this was the intense interest aroused in the popular mind by the Great October Revolution and the general desire to have a closer look at the land and the people that had given birth to it.

The was the period when our subcontinent, like most other Eastern lands, was convulsed with nationalist, anti-imperialist movements of great power and intensity, and the October Revolution naturally added to these movements a new revolutionary content. This was accompanied by a movement among the intelligentsia to look beyond the store of Western, particularly English, literature, on which all previous generations had been spoon-fed ever since the days of British occupation. So we eagerly absorbed whatever Russian writings we could lay our hands on, from Pushkin and Gogol to Gorky and Mayakovsky.

Variety of Types

But it was Tolstoy above all who brought home to us 'the awful majesty' of the land of all the Russias, its snows and forests, steppes and taigas, the steaming samovars and the tinkle of troika bells, the glittering drawing rooms of the aristocracy and the hovels of their serfs, and introduce us to the variety of its social types: the spendthrift lords and ladies, the toilworn muzhiks, the lovelorn maidens and their dashing lovers. Within a few years, his books were read, translated, discussed, talked over, imbibed and accepted as the bible of the new school of realistic writing which arose during the thirties and later became crystallized as the great Indian Progressive Writers Movement.

This year, on the occasion of the 150th anniversary of Tolstoy's birth, we join his countless readers all over the globe to pay him homage.

The statue of Leo Tolstoy in the compound of the Soviet Writers Union, clad in snow, drenched in rain, or dyed in sunlight, brings to mind the image of some ancient god eternally brooding over the doings and misdoings of the human brings populating the earth beneath his feet. He is not the wrathful lord of ancient testaments sitting in judgement over his disobedient subjects, seeking to repay their iniquities with fire, flood and pestilence. He is, on the contrary, a fatherly figure watching, with tenderness and compassion, the giant arms of impersonal social forces pulling at the wrists of the helpless human individual born in a social structure foredoomed to destruction.

Whole Collectivity

Human characters merely individualize some facet of the social dynamics operating at a particular moment in history. Thus, young Prince Bolkonsky, immobilized in front of the shell that is going to blow him to bits, or Anna Karenina, setting herself alight on the pyre of her own passion like the Hindu widow of ancient India, all typify the suicidal canker of decay implanted by social and material forces inside the feudal order of their days. And wars are but an accentuation and collectivization of the same social process operating concomitantly in peace it is merely a larger exercise in mass futility and collective self-destruction. Thus, Tolstoy imparted a completely new dimension to classical tragedy. Instead of the tragic flaw in his own character, hero being pursued by his fate or the Furies, fighting against more powerful gods, handicapped by a tragic trait it is, for Tolstoy, not an individual but a whole collectivity, not a person but a social structure, that undergoes a similar dispensation, not through the intervention of a supernatural agency but through conditions of their own making.

A New Dimension

And he added a new dimension to orthodox realism by visualizing, almost on a cosmic scale, the totality of a social and historical process, not through didactic or discursive comment, but through the personalization of class forces and the dramatization of their interacting relationships. By divesting war of its aura of myth and legend, by debunking the glorification of its half-crazed heroes and elevating the real protagonist in all social or national conflicts, the common man and the common soldier, he gave to subsequent generations of writers a new methodology of historical evaluation. To write about beauty because there is beauty, and ugliness because there is ugliness, and about good because there is good and evil because there is evil of hope because there is hope and despair, because there is despair, of love because there is love and hate because there is hate, and to distil from a correct alignment of these contradictions faith and fervour for a better, world and a happier humanity, a world free from wars and a humanity free from chains-that is perhaps, the essence of what Tolstoy taught the writers to be come. And that is, perhaps, what most of us have learnt from him-of course, each according to his ability.

NOTE

1. *Viewpoint*, Lahore, 10 September 1978.

27

WRITERS, WHERE DO YOU STAND?

A few years ago when I was working in Karachi, I persuaded some writers to address to their fellow-writers the following message drafted by me. Nothing much came of it then, but perhaps it will bear repetition in the hope that some of them might be induced to take it up again.

As fellow-readers and fellow writers we ask you:

Are you content with the present climate of creative writing in Pakistan? Do you feel that the present-day writer brings to you the same agony and ecstasy as his predecessor of the Pre-Independence days (who might be yourself), the same clarity of word and vision, the same integrity of personality and experience, the same courage, the same truthfulness, the same love and compassion, the same artistry, the same confident hope in a brighter tomorrow?

Or, do you feel that much of what is being written today is socially purposeless, intellectually superficial, ideologically confused, emotionally insincere, inhibited by fear and corrupted by greed; that the body of our literature is gradually sickening from a lack of faith and integrity and an excess of hypocrisy and cynicism?

Time to Act

If the answer to the first question is even a partial 'no', and the answer to the second even a partial 'yes', is it not time to put our heads together and try to do something about it?

What then should be done?

We consider that:

(a) It is necessary to redefine for the writer, in the broadest terms, the basic tenets of his creed as a writer to enable him to rediscover his individual collective responsibilities.

(b) To re-establish for vital links of comradeship, communication with those who share his briefs and, thus, to liberate him from the burden of loneliness and alienation.

Regarding (a), we believe that:

It is a precondition of all serious and significant writing that a writer should be committed.

He is committed to himself and his art. He must not, out of fear or opportunism, forswear his convictions, falsify his experience or prostitute his art for expediencies not his own, or external dictates not freely acceptable to him.

Nation and Humanity

He is committed to his country and his people. As a guide, philosopher and friend, he must lead them out of the darkness of ignorance, superstition and unreasoned prejudices, into the light of knowledge and reason, out of the labyrinths of tyranny into the ways of freedom, out of the realm of personal despair into the kingdoms of collective hope.

He is committed to the entire human community living in his time. He must learn, and help his readers, to identify its friends and its enemies in the contemporary world, those who seek to liberate, ennoble, enlighten and enrich the lives of their fellow beings through the agency of a just social order, and those who seek to enslave, exploit, corrupt and debase the weaker and the less fortunately placed to perpetuate their privilege of power.

Concretely, this means that in Pakistan today a serious writer must openly and fearlessly not only advocate but practise his basic right of freedom of expression, to denounce all old wrongs as well as all new injustices, all irrationalities, all cant and all dishonesties, social political intellectual.

Concretely, this means that in the world of today a serious writer must denounce all imperialist, racialist and colonialist agencies and to support, admire and love all peoples in the East and the West struggling for freedom and basic national and human rights. He must make his pen a barricade against the threatened march of imperialist forces towards human destruction and a banner for the forces seeking to lead mankind towards universal freedom and universal peace.

While we believe that every writer should find his own road to salvation and it would be wrong to restrict his pen to any narrow and fixed confines of a particular political programme, we also believe that the acceptance of the broad objectives outlined above is the minimal concom, that of all conscious and serious writing.

Regarding (b), we consider:

That an effort should be made to bring together all those writers in Pakistan who agree with what goes above to discuss and spell out a new testament of their creative creed which should help to guide their own thinking and writing and, what is even more important, the new generations who will replace them.

28

POETRY AND SENSE

Must poetry make sense? But first of all what is sense? It is, of course, most easily defined as what 'I think'—for we all labour under the common fusion of being very sensible fellows, unlike most of our friends and neighbours. When we all agree our sensibleness becomes undeniable. Common sense, sheer Common sense!' governments exclaim, as they lead their countries from slumps to wars and from wars to slumps. A few years ago, many tribes in Uganda thought it equally sensible to plan their campaigns in the light of omens obtained by boiling a young child alive. Conservatives in Uganda would have pooh-poohed the notion of running a war on any other lines. The test of theory, however, is practice, and when the machine-gun made its benevolent appearance in Africa, their boiled children failed to protect the local conservatives against it.

Now, the causes of wars, repressions, shortages, etc.—well, they are so obvious that I need not specify them. Will modern poetry be 'making sense' if it fails to recognise them? I think it will not, in any real sense, though grammatically speaking it may be as sensible as a writ of habeas corpus. Dr Johnson composed the well-known parody: 'I put my hat upon my head, and walked into the Strand, and there I met another man, whose hat was in his hand.' This is extremely sensible; it comes straight to the point—only the point is not worth coming to. In grammar and logic, it is perfect, and unassailable. But suppose we change Johnson's parody a little and turn it into this:

I put my flowers upon her head;
And led her to the sand;
And she sorrowfully said;
My lover, take my hand.

Pretty Stuff

The average reader of English would undoubtedly take this for part of a good poem, while it is, of course, nothing of the sort; we have done nothing except put in the sort of words that usually occur in poetry, and therefore make the casual reader feel poetical, just as a flag makes him feel patriotic. In fact, we could define conventional poetry, the sort that is imparted to school-children or printed in popular magazines, as stuff that looks pretty and makes sense on the surface, but not underneath. People would scarcely trouble to read it if they knew how easily they could write it themselves. Press through your memory and pick out a number of words such as 'love', 'moon', 'flower', 'star', 'death', etcetera, and string them together with the aid of a rhyming dictionary, and the thing is done. It was again Dr Johnson who said of some similar production: 'A man might write such stuff for ever, if he would but abandon his mind to it.' A good many people do abandon their minds to it. To take an instance, the word 'death', brought in at suitable intervals, is an extremely useful one. It impresses the reader by itself. The writer's business, however, is to use it in a fresh and arresting way, as in the famous lines of Webster's strategy, when the dying Duke cries:

On pain of death, let no man name death to me;
It is a word indefinitely terrible.

An inferior writer, and a careless reader, would be satisfied with the same obvious idea in equally obvious terms—like this, perhaps:

Death is a horribly unpleasant word;
I will kill the first man who makes use of it.

The first is inspired by the most intense feeling, the second, by none—the difference in value between the two is enormous. But let us take Tennyson's *Lady of Shalott* as a familiar specimen of poetry constructed by piling up 'poetical' words without any organic connection:

There she weaves by night and day
A magic web with colors gay.
She has heard a whisper say,
A curse is on her if she stay
        To look down to Camelot.
She knows not what the curse may be,
And so she weaveth steadily,
And little other care hath she,
        The Lady of Shalott.

This is not precisely 'nonsense', or at least not quite the kind of nonsense for which a certificate of lunacy could be awarded. Technically speaking it is clever, as Tennyson always is, still, the plain man, when not hypnotized by the memory of being taught this poem at school, may well ask, 'What is the sense of it? What on earth do I care about an early mediaeval legend of a young lady who was afraid to look out of the window? Bring me a bottle of coke instead!'.

And surely the plain man is right. He must be hard up for entertainment if he can find nothing better to do than read *The Lady of Shalott*. Tennyson, the highly respectable Poet Laureate, understood to be on good terms with Queen Victoria did a great deal to fix in the public mind a conception of poetry as a conventional rigmarole to be recited by little girls at Christmas parties, such poetry has no vital feeling and poetry without feeling is nonsense.

Reaction

A reaction against this academic tradition was sure to come. Now, the easiest way of curing a man's headache is to cut his head off, and the easiest way of preventing the meaning of a poem from being trivial and silly is to give it no meaning at all. Hence, there has been a great deal of experimentation the general aim of which is to communicate feelings directly from the writer's mind to readers, without translating them into ideas. Ideas, it is true are merely crystallisations of feeling. Or perhaps we should have a better metaphor if we said that the conscious mind is a beach washed by a deep sea of feeling, and that ideas are the occasional flotsam and jetsam left on it by the tides. The function of the critical intellect is to combine these bits of wreckage, to build them up, as it were, into a house. You can invite your friends into your house, but hardly into a heap of wreckage, though the material may be the same. The experiments of the surrealists, of automatic writing, and so on, banish the critical intellect, and retain nothing but pure personal feeling. The plain man is left even more baffled than before.

We can detect the fallacy of this procedure if we re-examine the meaning of the word 'sense'. We have seen its ordinary meaning, of the routine logical operations necessary to describing a man putting on his hat and walking into the Strand. But we get further when we remember that hats and street are social products, and so are all the mental operations necessary for constructing and describing them. The human brain developed in a more or less organised human society. Language, and therefore thought itself, is a social product. So, in turn, are all the refinements of our feelings. The intellect is the product of feeling, but also the producer or shaper, of feeling. A mouse can feel afraid, but not in the way Macbeth and Hamlet are afraid. Language is essentially utilitarian, more the colleague of the intellect than of feeling. If we use it to express feeling, as in poetry, we must preserve it as an intermediary. A man, in short, cannot convey his feelings to another man without employing his mind in the business. Poetry thus must make sense, though sense is not its primary business. It is only in rare cases that language can excite emotion when no logical connection can be deciphered in it. There are some lines in Shakespeare, about suicide, which are in the highest degree striking without 'making sense':

It is great,
To do that deed which ends all other things,
That shackles accident and bolts up change;
That sleeps, and never plates more the dug,
The beggars' nurse, or bearer'.

But it is safest to take these lines as incorrect, through some error of the first printer. Such as experiment would not be in Shakespeare's style, which is immensely flexible, but always positive and definite,

In general the defect of surrealist experiments is that the feelings of one man are meaningless to another until they are passed through the rationalising mechanism of the mind; and then they acquire generality, because it is reason or sense that binds us together and provides us with common experience. All this underlies the paradox that we cannot understand any other mind in its individual combinations; but we can understand humanity as a whole because its experience exists in us all. Just as poetry without feeling is nonsense so is poetry that contains only feeling: It is sound and fury, signifying nothing.

Social Cement

Reason being the social cement, we may proceed to define 'sense' as that which tends towards a healthy relationship between individual and society, and a healthy growth of each. But if language is the product of reason, and poetry the most elaborate development of language, it follows that poetry must be organically linked with social progress. Modern experiments in 'nonsense' have obscured the real issue. The sense that poetry needs is not more grammatical sense, but social sense. Why, after all, does *The Lady of Shalott* bore us? Because such a languid day-dream could only interest someone could only interest someone like *The Lady of Shalott* herself, a young lady in a convent, perhaps. We, with wars, revolutions, discoveries, famines, stalking round us, cannot possibly work up any interest in her. Poetry must be the most vivid expression of the most profound feelings of its age, forced into the channels of the most rigorous though. Wordsworth told us long ago that a poet must be able to think as well as feel.

There are times when no great social issues are agitating the public mind. Then poetry will be more personal, and it will not reach the greatest heights. Shakespeare, Milton and Wordsworth, the three great English poets, lived in the three great periods of English history. None of them put any political programme into verse, except Wordsworth, who did it in old age in bad verse. Their business was to disentangle, and to intensify, the highest and strongest passion of their times. *Paradise Lost* is not about politics, but no one who had not lived through, and fought through a civil war, could have written it.

In our age, issues are sharper, more defined, and more overwhelming than ever before. A poet writes today for the Evolution—I use the word, in a general way, for the great social changes, that we all feel the necessity of. Otherwise, by and large, he writes nonsense. These great changes require the development of our highest feelings, and these feelings unlike the occasional passions stirred up by demagogues, can only be transferred from one man to another by means of poetry. This is, in the end, what Shelley said, and what Tennyson forgot. 'Poets are the trumpets that ring to battle, the unacknowledged legislators of the world'.

29

THOUGHTS ON THE FUTURE OF *GHAZAL*[1]

To begin with, the future of *ghazal*, like the future of all poetry, depends above all on the talent of its future practitioners. Pedantically speaking, there is nothing good or bad in any poetic form but the poet makes it so.

Leaving these truisms aside, for some insight into the future of this much-maligned and much-admired form of expression, it is best to look at its past. Not the distant past when its excellence was unquestioned, but the recent past when its raison d'être was first brought into question. This was in the mid-nineteenth century when, in Ghalib's phraseology, 'the last candle of freedom anguished by the ending of the convivial night flickered and died'; when the last battle for liberation was fought and lost.

A Scapegoat

In the breastbeating that followed, poetry which was then synonymous with the *ghazal*, was denounced as one of the factors responsible for this debacle. And the outcry was led by the then young or not so young, 'modernists' of the time, Altaf Hussain Hali and Mohammad Hussain Azad. Only a few decades earlier, music was similarly held responsible for the Iranian Nadir Shah's sack of Delhi—a slander that is alive to the present day even under such august auspices as the *son et lumiere* in the Red Fort.

While there is no denying that consciousness and social or political factors do interact, and literature, particularly poetry, is one of the prime mentors of human consciousness, it is equally undeniable that it is social and material factors which are primary determinants of consciousness in any given situation—and not the other way round.

The decadent literature of the later Mughal period was a product of a decadent feudal order and not its progenitor. Thus, when poets like Hali wrote, 'If all our poets migrated *en masse* we shall say in unison "good riddance",' these venerable gentlemen were talking through their turbans. Take one simple proof. None of the 'modernists' of this era were able to mirror the tragedy and heartbreak of their age in their British-sponsored poetic experiments with the same suggestive truthfulness as Ghalib's *ghazal*. All the same, most intellectuals of the time, including Ghalib himself, felt that *ghazal* was the last flicker of a dying candle. But no such thing happened. After a brief interlude of the highly moralistic, didactic, and pseudo-Western pedestrian exercises there followed, *ghazal* not only managed to survive (clandestinely for some time through the gramophone disc and the dancing girl), but even regained its ascendancy in the field of poetic through a whole crop of new talent: Asghar, Jigar, Firaq, Fani, Yas Yagana, and others. These were the gay twenties, the age of romantic aesthetes, political demagogues and the picaresque theatre.

New Denigrators

This interlude was also short-lived. The end of the decade ushered in the Great Depression, mass unemployment, communal riots, and a host of other ills. Like the crisis of the previous century, this era also produced its literary activists by 'reciprocal causation'. The realist 'progressives' on the one hand, the escapist subjectivists, on the other. 'To hell with the *ghazal*,' cried both for opposite reasons. With very few exceptions, theoreticians, in spite of their correct political and historical insight, had little grounding in their own classical literatures. In consequence, like their predecessors of the previous century, they also equated the *ghazal* with feudal decadence, romantic dalliance, and formalistic conceits. The subjectivists held, on the other hand, that *ghazal* was a relic of outdated, hackneyed, oriental tradition, a collection of tiresome clichés which allowed no room for experimentation in ultra-modern Western forms of diction nor provided a terminology for the exploration of subconscious cesspools. And once again, despite this outcry, *ghazal* not only managed to survive, but even lured into its parlour some of the best talent in both camps.

I am sorry to have dwelt so long on the past instead of talking about the future—the question I was supposed to answer. This is because literature, like history or time, is a continuum, and even its occasional mutations cannot be traced to a traditional causation. Before I come to the present or future, therefore, I would like to raise two basic issues.

(i) Why is it that whenever we are faced with a situation of social or political crisis or malaise, of all forms of writing the *ghazal* is generally singled out as the prime target of criticism?

(ii)   Why is it that after every onslaught this particular form re-emerges rejuvenated and refurbished?

Personality of the Age

(i) Of all forms of traditional expression, the *ghazal* is in some ways the most facile and the easiest to manipulate. Even a partial access to its vast storehouse of imagery, diction and phraseology can turn out perfectly acceptable imitations of the genuine article by judicious shoplifting of the required raw material. As a result, it attracts the largest number of spurious poets and engenders the bulk of spurious poetry. Certain obvious devices, the choice of lilting metre and rhyme, the clever turning of a phrase, etc., are enough to elicit a conditioned response from a *mushaira* audience or a radio-listener and even good poets cannot always resist these blandishments. At the same time, it has a fairly rigid verbal and formal framework which permits little deviation. And then it so easily lends itself to music, and music is so easily integrated into other media like the film or television. All these factors account for the *ghazal's* popularity among the literary masses and its unpopularity with the literary elite. It hobnobs with the former for the same reasons that it repels the latter—it transcends class barriers and, thus, comes to symbolise the 'poetic personality' of an age and is held accountable for all the failings of this age.

(ii) Why then can't we get rid of this *pir-i-tasmapa* (the legendary old man in 'Arabian Nights' who could not be shaken off if he climbed upon someone's shoulders) or Urdu poetry? And should we? Some of the reasons may be inferred from what has already been said above. First, its rhythm and formal pattern, the musicality of the metre, the novelty of metaphor and imagery, the spontaneity of rhyme, are all closely attuned to the conditioned reflexes of response—hence its unique 'communicability'.

Social Comment

Second, its rigidity of form is coupled with an equal if not greater freedom in the use of not only William Empson's seven but innumerable forms of 'ambiguity'. Because of its name ('whispering words of love' is one interpretation among others) and because of its essentially lyrical diction, the *ghazal* is largely regarded, if one may be permitted the use of a popular vulgarism, as 'love-poetry'— a concept that has sorely confused its Western translators. Since love is a physical passion, the love-object must be either masculine or feminine, and since in Persian verbs a common gender is used for both and in Urdu either a plural or a masculine gender is generally used these learned pundits have to do a great deal of head-scratching to choose 'he' or 'she' in translation and to decide on the sexual proclivities of the poet. That the 'beloved' in a *ghazal* verse may be neither he nor she, but an ideal or an institution or a way of life or it may be no beloved at all but a tyrannical prince, or a fickle patron, is just one of the many ambiguities employed by the *ghazal* writer to express not subjective feeling but social comment. *Ghazal* poetry does include a great deal of exquisite love poetry in the conventional sense, but this is only secondary to its primary function, or to the secret of its survival and popularity for more than eight hundred years. This secret is the same as the secret of all lasting poetry, namely, its continual adjustability to the demands for aesthetic articulation of contemporary experience.

Ghazal is able to do this, as hinted above, not by any innovation or modification of form but various manipulations of the meaning of meaning; i.e., endowing a word or sign with a number of concomitant references explicable only in a particular textual or social context. Thus, a mere turn of phrase can enliven even a beat-up cliché, and a worn-out metaphor of the classical past can be given a purely contemporary significance. Thus, Farhad of the Persian legend becomes the working-class of today, and Laila of the Arabian Desert the goddess of liberation. The *ghazal* is a chameleon, *mashuq-i-hazar sheva* in the Persian phrase, 'a beauty with a thousand wiles'. It continues to flourish because of the one quality which is necessary for the 'survival of the fittest'; adaptability to changing environments.

So Much Will Die

There is, however, one proviso. The *ghazal*, as already pointed out, draws its sustenance from the storehouse of classical tradition. It depends for effective communication upon the reader's or listener's emotive and cognitive linkage with this tradition. If, however, we forsake this cultural patrimony, and if the onslaught against our cultural identity by institutions like the English-medium school or the Western media, is allowed to succeed, *ghazal* poetry might wilt and die. But with it so much else we hold dear today will also die. This might well happen if the new class of Western-oriented literary wiseacres who are only semi-literate in their own literatures are finally allowed to take over.

NOTE

1. *Viewpoint*, Lahore, 7 September 1983.

Section V
SOCIAL

30

NO HOLIDAY FROM VIRTUE[1]

Sir Ganga Ram. His statue on the Mall is no longer there, but the hospital endowed by him still brings solace to multitudes of sick and ailing. It trains the best of our women doctors. His old school houses the Lahore College for Women. His building on the Mall is tenanted by some of our major business houses. The old office of his Trust provides shelter and care to scores of blind children. Horses and cattle drink at the water-troughs donated by him.

A foreign friend I was taking round the town was impressed by the magnitude of the dead man's philanthropy. He wanted to see and know more. And, unwisely, as I discovered too late, I took him to see the *Samadhi*, the last resting place of the near-forgotten benefactor. I had not seen the place for many years. I vaguely knew that many years ago some homeless refugees had wandered into, and settled in this vicinity, as they had wherever a roof or even a vacant open lot was to be found. I also know that many of these pockets of horror and want and misery still live with us. But we who live in the green and gold of the Civil Lines rarely see them. And when they thrust themselves on our sight we refuse to see. Even so, I was utterly unprepared for what we saw.

An infinity of squalid hovels, reeds and mud and gunny-bags struggled up to the square white courtyard of the mausoleum. Dogs nosed in the dirt. Evil smells from the putrefying banks of the old Ravi fought and blended with more evil odours from the huts. The silted up tank of the *Samadhi* was rank with scum and weeds. We entered the courtyard. At the door of the central stucco chamber, where the ashes of the dead man are buried, a man lay dying, covered in a threadbare quilt. An old woman sat by him, wearily warding off flies. The four hollow towers at the four corners of the courtyard low and completely unventilated, except for the opening arch, were alive with women and children. The interior of the burial-chamber was blacker than night with smoke and more populous than a rabbit warren. Reeds and gunny-bags honeycombed the floor to keep heaven knows how many households apart. And in the centre, over the ashes of the dead philanthropist, some housewife's cauldron boiled. A *pipal* tree growing in some crevice in the wall thrust its way out of the onion-shaped dome.

This really was a journey to the end of night. Strange and weird thoughts visit one here and even they are welcome to escape the speechless nightmare clutching at one's throat. The needs of the living, I thought to myself, must have precedence over reverence for the dead, even though it comes to this. They have sheltered here, homeless, nameless, disinherited, dehumanized, because no one else would give them shelter, except this dead philanthropist. His charity continues after death because for the likes of him there is no holiday from virtue-not even after death. But these are idle thoughts. Reverence for the dead and the needs of the living both have their demands on the community, and both demands must be met. To ignore the demands of the dead makes no difference to the dead. It only degrades the living. And this, in some ways, is even deadlier than ignoring the demands of the living.

NOTE

1. *Civil and Military Gazette*, 24 March 1961.

31

WHO WAS TABATA SHARRA?[1]

Who was Tabata Sharra? I came to know him first during my student days. Warriors, poet, dacoit and troubadour, he would split the skulls of his foes with the abandon of a werewolf and mourn over the body of a dead comrade with the love and tenderness of a woman. A bright speck of colour he was in the dusky annals of Pre-Islamic Arabia. It was a real delight, therefore, when I recently renewed my acquaintance with him through the courtesy of my friends in the *Dairi Maarafi Islamia*—The Urdu Encyclopaedia of Islam. I am referring, of course, to the article on the Arab poet in the fascicules of the Encyclopaedia, now under preparation. This project deserves to be better known than it is.

This project is, of course based on a European work of the same name. The attitude of the European nations towards Islam and the achievements of the Muslim peoples in the field of culture and science has passed through several stages during the last one thousand years. As a matter of fact, Islam remained an anathema for the West till almost the end of the eighteenth century. The purpose of every Islamic study, during this entire period, was to strengthen the age-old prejudices of the European mind.

Hardly any attempt was made to evaluate Islamic thought and its contribution to human knowledge even with approximate objectivity. In the eyes of most of the Western scholars, a Muslim was a blood-thirsty fanatic devoid of every virtue of character and intellect. Even a historian like Edward Gibbon was not free from these prejudices.

Professor Bevan, therefore, had to admit in the *Cambridge Medieval History* that 'those accounts of Mahomet and Islam which were published in Europe before the beginning of the nineteenth century are now to be regarded simply as literary curiosities.

The West & Islam

In the recent past, however, the attitude of most Western scholars towards Islam has considerably changed. There is now a greater regard for truth, and a greater understanding of the historical role of Islam. Considerable amount of Islamic literature has been rendered into Western languages and certainly the most convincing proof of their endeavours is provided by the *Encyclopaedia of Islam.*

The Encyclopaedia of Islam was first published in Leiden between 1908 and 1938. This monumental work, in four volumes, covers almost the entire field of Islamic thought and history. It contains biographical notes on eminent Muslims, and articles on every aspect of Muslim law, culture, science, art and literature. This *Encyclopaedia* has been produced under expert supervision and includes contributions from Western scholars of international repute.

Following the Turkish and Arabic examples, the University of the Punjab has taken upon itself the task of preparing the *Encyclopaedia of Islam* in Urdu. Although the Urdu Encyclopaedia is based on and closely follows the Leiden Encyclopaedia, it is by no means a translation of the English version. It includes many original contributions by prominent Muslim scholars, as also extensive additions and modifications by the editorial staff. Certain factual errors, found in the original book, have also been rectified

Variety

The fascicules under review discuss a large variety of subjects. There are three long articles on the *Tafseer* (commentary) of the Holy Quran. These articles are fairly exhaustive and deal with the origin, growth and the ever-widening scope of the *Tafseer* in the Arabic, Persian and Urdu languages. Various schools of thought, found among the commentators from the earliest to the present day, have also been briefly mentioned. Articles on *Taarikh* contain much useful information regarding the role of history in Islamic thought.

The problem of *Tauheed* has been very elaborately discussed. Although the concept of the oneness of God has not been treated historically and requires a more detailed discussion, very close attention has been paid *Ilme Tauheed*. The article discusses the origin, fundamental principles and the causes of the development of *Ilme Tauheed* in great detail.

There is a very interesting essay on *Takfeet* (inlay work). This art of decorating metal and wood pieces with inlay work has been among the most popular of the traditional crafts in Muslim countries, especially Iran and the Indo-Pakistan subcontinent. Thin pieces of gold, silver or other precious metals are embedded in copper, brass and other alloys and the motifs used are mostly floral.

The discussion on *Tanzeemaat* may prove to be very useful for the students of Turkish history. *Tanzeemaat* is the term used for constitutional reforms which were introduced by Turkish Sultans between 1839 and 1879. The dates and details of these *Tanzeemaat* are generally not found even in history books.

Articles on *Taubah*, *Tatar*, *Tabata Sharra*, *Tamium Dari*, *Tiflis* and *Tajik* are extremely interesting and contain much new information.

The author of the article on Taj Mahal has refuted Father Manrique's claim that the plan of this wonder of the East was prepared by Geronimo Veronis, a Venetian architect. He has conclusively proved that the plan for this monumental work was conceived by Ustad Isa of Shiraz and his associates attached to the court of the Emperor Shah Jahan.

It is obviously not possible, however, to do justice in a brief review to a work of such gigantic dimensions. It is about the most ambitious project currently in hand in the Urdu language and when complete, the love, labour and research invested in it will enrich not only the meagre store of our own language, but also the world treasure-house of Islamic learning.

This is mainly because Western Orientalists for all their scholarship are sometimes apt to flounder in their understanding and interpretation of Oriental texts and since countries of the East have not so far been in a position to match them in similar research, the fallacies in standard Western works have often been uncritically accepted.

The Urdu Encyclopaedia of Islam is perhaps among the first major attempt at comprehensive reappraisal of Western learning regarding Islam.

An Encyclopaedia has necessarily to serve both the scholar and the layman and not infrequently fails to please either. The layman might complain that it splits far too many hairs for his liking and a scholar might grouse that some hairs have not been split enough. In this regard the Urdu Encyclopaedia of Islam is perhaps slightly biased in favour of the scholars.

For one thing, the language of the text could perhaps be made simpler without much loss of stylistic dignity. For another, if the references interspersed in the text within innumerable brackets were relegated to the foot of each page as notes, the text would make for easier and continuous reading.

One should also like to suggest some uniformity in the use of either the Gregorian or the Hijri calendars in the determination of historical dates. As it is, sometimes one, sometimes the other and sometimes both have been used.

Similarly, Western names and words are rendered sometimes in Roman and sometimes in Urdu letters. Uniformity in this regard would also be desirable.

A work of this description demands an extensive secretariat and adequate resources and it is possible that there may be editorial difficulties owing to limitations of resources which stand in the way of absolute perfection. But then perhaps there is no such thing as absolute perfection.

NOTE

1. *Civil and Military Gazette*, 30 July 1961.

32

THE RIGHT TO OWN WOMEN

A section of our male population, so the rumour goes, is getting rather worked up regarding the new Ordinance on Family Laws. Or is being persuaded to get worked up. As a partisan of the male species, this strikes me as extremely unwise. In the world as it is today (including the women as they are) one could have hardly hoped for a more favourable dispensation.

We are living in 1961. In the world of today (or at least most of it) you can no longer own another country as a colony even if you have the force. You can no longer own slaves even if you have the money. You cannot even own an unreasonable amount of land even if you have the titles which your forefathers so thoughtfully obtained for you from the Raj. How much longer then could one hope to continue in the undisputed ownership of one's women? Sooner or later the challenge had to come to this unilateral right as it already has to so many others. That this challenge has come in so unbelievably mild and considerate a form should surely be a matter for thanks rather than indignation. After all what does this Ordinance demand of us men?

First: it does not curtail the right of a man to marry or not to marry (because it is men who marry women, not women who marry men). It merely demands that if a man does marry, the marriage should go on public record. This only means that after this law becomes effective, a man will no longer be able to pretend that he is not married to a particular woman when he is or to pretend that he is so married when he is not. This may cause some inconvenience to certain incorrigible philanderers and professional operators in the marriage market but it hardly affects the rest of us one way or the other.

Second: the new law does not rob a man of his right to marry a second, third or fourth time. It merely demands that before he does so he should either obtain the consent of his first wife or convince an impartial tribunal that he has good reasons for an additional female. This certainly would be inconvenient for those whose motives for second marriage will not bear public scrutiny. But if we refuse to accept this procedure, it will be a patent admission that not only a few but everyone who takes on a second wife does it for unspeakable reasons. This would be obviously against the interests of the Party; it would be wiser to sacrifice the convenience and pleasures of the few.

Third: the new law prescribes nothing to limit a man's right to divorce and change his wives at will. He can still discard a wife whenever he pleases. If he does not like her hairstyle or the way she makes curry. The law merely prescribes that if and when a man does pronounce divorce, a certain period of time should elapse before it becomes operative to give the man a chance to change his mind and to give his betters a chance to argue him back into conjugal amity. For the rash and choleric ones among us this provision should be a boon rather than a bane, (no nightmares of arranging temporary wedlock for a wife renounced in a fit of temper); for the rest a session with the elders should hardly be a major inconvenience.

This then is all there is to it—or almost all—and nothing drastic would appear to have happened—not to me. The protest if any, therefore, should lie with the other side and the agitation, if any, should appear among their ranks. But the women, let it thankfully be said, appear quite pleased with what they have got.

Yet something drastically important has really happened which is not exclusive to either men or women but concerns both. What has really happened is the acceptance of the principle that marriage of man-woman relationship is not merely a personal but also a social relationship, that the adjustment of these relations is not entirely a private but also a public concern. And the terms 'personal' and 'private' have for centuries meant to us exclusively male. In a way this principle is nothing new. In fact the very institution of marriage is based on its acceptance. What is new is the acceptance that these relationships and their adjustments are not static but dynamic. They must be governed not by the attitudes and proclivities of a particular section of the community no matter how strongly and fanatically advocated but by the temporal demands of the stage of social evolution that a community has reached. Thus at one time both men and women were bought and sold with communal sanction. Then only women. And later even though the bond of slavery would no longer command social sanction, the bond of wedlock was presumed to confer on man almost similar unilateral rights with regard to possession or disposal of his women. The Family Laws Ordinance accepts that even this disguised form of woman-ownership is, in principle, even though not yet entirely in practice, henceforth no longer legally or socially tenable, that the conjugal relationship will henceforth be subject to the same social dynamic which operates in the realm of other laws.

The resentment of the diehard section of woman-owners, therefore, is not entirely misplaced.

There is one point of detail, however, already pointed out by some women's organizations which does seem to merit further consideration—the chairmanship of the proposed Arbitration tribunals. There appears to be much weight in the plea that this office should not be entrusted to the chairmen of Union Councils. Suppose the poor man is contemplating second marriage himself, or his son is straining at the conjugal leash, or his niece is having trouble with her in-laws. The law does not appear to provide that in such an eventuality, the chairman can or should vacate his chair in favour of a more disinterested party. When the relevant rules and regulations come to be formulated this question may well be given some thought. The custody of children in broken up families deserves even more urgent thought. For some unknown reason it appears to have received none.

33

GENTLEMEN VS. PLAYERS

The woman in the fairy tale laughed and wept by turns when she saw the charming Prince. 'I laugh,' she said, 'to see once again a human face so fair. I weep because in a short while my ogre will come and gobble you up.'

There must be many among us, I am sure, who contemplate the institution of official film awards with much the same mixture of delight and apprehension.

There is cause for delight because the State has at last recognised the film as an art form and this might in time induce the community to view it in the same light. There is cause for delight that film-makers and film-workers whom fortune and the judges favour will henceforth be entitled to the same public esteem as their honoured contemporaries in the orthodox arts.

A respectable citizen may thus come to feel that putting his money into film-making will not necessarily mortgage his chances of salvation in this world and the next, nor shaking hands with a film star make him lose caste with his *biradri*. Film-work thus has now some promise of being regarded as a vocation rather than as a term of abuse. Film-players, or at least some of them, may join the ranks of gentlemen.

All this is not only to the good but is absolutely essential if the film in Pakistan is ever to establish itself either as art or as industry. Artistic standards are in the final analysis a matter of social responsibility and social responsibility is inconceivable without social acceptance.

This, however, is only half the picture. The other half is apprehension and distress. This half stems not from the awards as such, but from the mode and timing of their institution. If the first batch of awards had been scheduled for distribution a year or even six months after the date of their announcement, producers, artists and technicians might perhaps have done something to deserve them. It would have been fatuous to hope for a crop of masterpieces even then, but anyone who had or thought he had something in him could at least have tried.

As it is, however, the work which will come up for judgment was done without the remotest association with any idea of prestige. None of the producers, directors, artists, and technicians concerned had really cast himself in the role of a competitor for the dignity of a Presidential award. He can justly plead, therefore, that the test has been sprung on him unawares: he could have shown up much better if someone had warned him in time.

This, however, is only a minor consideration. The major consideration is the risk of stamping sub-standard, inartistic, slipshod performances with the seal of State approval.

The judges might argue, of course, that they were merely making the best of the many bad jobs inflicted on them, that after sitting through an interminable series of banalities they could not very well declare that they had nothing to show for their pains. Some awards, alas, had to be given.

It is extremely, doubtful, however, whether any award-winner will agree that his newfound virtue was mothered by necessity. No one can hope to convince the producer or director of a jubilee hit that his box-office success was in reality a heap of unmitigated rubbish. It would be even more difficult to convince a person honoured during the coming Festival that the greatness thrust upon him merely elevated him to the rank of the one-eyed in a realm of the blind.

Self-criticism demands even a higher and more developed sense of aesthetic understanding and discrimination than the criticism of others and this is certainly not the weakness of the general run of our film workers. There is, therefore, a real danger that the first batch of awards, if injudiciously and indiscriminately given, might encourage rather than discourage mediocrity. It might stabilise the extremely depressed artistic standards now prevailing, instead of setting the sights for higher targets.

Let us not exaggerate, however, either the delight or the apprehension.

The State awards will undoubtedly help to meet one vital need of the profession of film-making—the need for respectability and social acceptance.

There are, however, even more grievous lacks that no awards can meet—lack of finance, lack of talent, lack of technical training and know-how. And, in a way, even these are related to the basic need for dignity and respectability. What is to be done regarding all these deficiencies?

Let us examine for a moment the situation with regard to the other arts. Perhaps the only arts we have come to recognise as respectable since the coming of Independence are painting and the allied plastic arts. This is so primarily because in both East and West Pakistan, the fine arts, as they are called, have been accepted as an academic discipline and have been integrated, at least on a limited scale, with the public educational programme. They have, thus, automatically transcended all social prejudices.

In consequence the study of painting or sculpture for any boy or girl interested in doing so is considered neither more nor less desirable than, let us say, the study of history or philosophy. In fact, for young girls a smattering of art has already become something of a social attainment. Music has not become respectable yet but it is well on the way to respectability for an entirely different reason. The reason in this case is the sheer eminence of individual talent, like the talent of Roshan Ara Begum. This talent, however, has been nurtured in the closed circle of the ancient *gharanas* to which an average amateur, whatever his potential talent, has no access.

As a result, while a potential painter has some opportunity and the scope of his opportunity is daily expanding, both to discover and to develop his talent, such opportunity is as yet hardly available to the potential composer or musician unless he manages to arrange his paternity in the right class. This talent, therefore, will never come to the surface until the family institution of the *gharanas* is replaced by public academies.

The film in Pakistan needs both these sanctions—the sanction of public discipline as well as the sanction of individual merit. The two are interdependent. If training for the film is made a component of the national technical training programme which is in the process of taking shape today, the film workers of tomorrow will, by and large, be young men and women whose vocation was determined by free choice based on innate aptitude and talent, not a last resort dictated by the tyranny of social rejection.

Film studios then will take their place beside other cultural and industrial enterprises of the country instead of serving as dumps for social waste-products. Facilities for high-grade training are, therefore, one obvious priority. The talent thus attracted, however, and the training thus acquired or imparted can find expression only through the medium of actual film making and it is doubtful whether such expression will ever find adequate scope in the purely commercial field.

The second priority, therefore, is financial patronage for amateur and experimental ventures. Such patronage can, of course, be institutionalized through reputable cultural organizations at present devoted to the other arts. It is only then that delight at the present developments will in some measure become unconfined.

What about the apprehension? It is obviously too late now to do anything about the awards already decided upon, but their memory will soon fade if more exacting standards are set and observed when the day comes round next year. The broad criterion should be that a piece of work, if it is to merit an award, must be entitled to some respect not only in our own but in the eyes of the entire film world. And to set correct comparative standards it may be necessary to invite both judges and entries, from other countries. The task is not only to make gentlemen out of players but also to teach players how to play.

Section VI
POLITICAL

34

LIKE A VESTURE SHALT THOU CHANGE THEM[1]

In a few days from now the footlights will be on again to illumine another act of the abysmal tragi-comedy that goes by the name of West Punjab politics. As the curtain drops on each miserable scene, the audience is reminded of the great things this stage had once promised them, of the heroes that peopled it once, and the great spectacles that have once trailed across its boards. There is no other province in India or Pakistan that has sacrificed more for the cause of national liberation in the past than the Punjab has, and none that shoulders greater and heavier responsibilities today to maintain us in freedom. Nowhere else did the Indian Muslim League win bigger victories against bigger odds than it did in the Punjab, and no other people in India or Pakistan paid for these victories, in blood and honour and happiness in the same heavy measure as the people of the Punjab paid. When liberation came it was the Punjab that clasped to its warm but hungry bosom the gigantic mass of destitute and miserable humanity represented by the refugees. It was the Punjab again along with the NWFP that was called upon to share with the *Azad* warriors the dire and prolonged travail of the Kashmir struggle. And our bill of national duties is as full and crowded today as it was yesterday. In the rehabilitation of the refugees, in defence, and food and commerce and industry, in the political and organizational tasks that await us in the coming days to win Kashmir, the role ordained for the West Punjab continues to be vital and overwhelmingly pregnant. In view of it all, the people rightly expected that their national leadership in the Province, their national legislature and the national Party would conduct themselves in a manner merited by our past and demanded by our present. Not only have these expectations not been fulfilled but the people charged with opening up the path of fulfilment have instead converted themselves into mountainous heaps of junk to clutter it up. Every one agrees that the junk must be cleared but hardly any one has the courage to set about it or even to declare frankly and unequivocally that the time has come to do so of that this is the way to do it. This timidity is understandable. It is not very pleasant to part with the comfort of cherished illusions or to denude pet words and slogans of their insubstantial charm. These columns are no exception. We too have done no more than to lay down pious exhortations for the leaders—and the Party to follow, or to express pious hopes that things would straighten themselves out somehow and one should not despair of a solution within the present political framework. It is high time, however, that we all pulled our heads out of the sand. Let us admit that if West Punjab is ever to be rescued from the present political quagmire, the scheming hands of our present claimants to leadership—the Provincial Premier and the Provincial President—are not the hands to achieve it. Whether they both squeeze themselves into the Ministerial closet or remain apart, whether one remains glued to his gilded *gaddi* or the other ousts him, whether one continues to afflict the Provincial administration with his leadership and the other the Provincial Party, our political bark will never sail down the current of progress; it will continue to toss and turn in the whirlpool that has caught it and rot itself with motion. Let us also admit that the majority of our MLAs are no more than a bunk of political cretins who largely belong to the same social and political species as the unlamented Unionists, and who managed to get themselves elected to the peoples' House by the simple act of tacking on the popular League label to their coat tails. Let us also admit that the minority of our MLAs, whose level of intelligence approximates to normality, have since the partition paid little thought to the troubles and affliction of their electors but have displayed a great amount of alacrity in hanging on to the tail of every prospective winner in the Ministerial steeple-chase. And let us admit furthermore that the Muslim League Party as reconstituted today is a very different kettle of fish from the one that stormed the Unionist barricades. Three years ago a position in the Muslim League ranks connoted allegiance to a cause; it meant sacrifice and abnegation. Today it means power and office—a shop or a factory or a seat in the District Board, a licence to bully the local authority or a job for a worthless nephew. This is unpleasant talk, we know, and we have also heard the cliché concerning dirty linen. But it is much more sensible to wash the linen, however, unseemly the sight, than to continue to stink. This briefly then is the situation. We have a brace of leaders committed to nothing but their own ambition, who have all along behaved as cut-purses of the power and the rule and who are capable of guiding our people to no other destination except the broad gate and the great fire. Can they deny that they have both forced the provincial administration and the Provincial Party into political harlotry; that, for factional ends they have encouraged, initiated or condoned the grossest dishonesties in public affairs; that under their twin care the fair vesture of freedom has been greased and soiled beyond all recognition. Then we have a Legislature whose members no longer represent either the people, or the programme, or the principles, that won them their seats; we have legislators whose parliamentary and legislative decisions are governed by one overriding consideration, namely, who throws the bigger coin into the hat that they are perpetually passing round. Last, we have a Party whose rank and file is as honest and sound as it is possible for any body of men in these days to be, but whose leadership has been largely filched by intriguing self-promoters. Let us, therefore, admit that there is no short-cut to political health in the Punjab, if the scalpel no more than grazes her political skin; that if we want to a change not merely one Premier, one Minister, one MLA or one League functionary but the whole caboodle. How can this be done? It can be done very simply by referring the political future of the Province, back to the common man once more. In 1945 he judged the Unionists who professed to represent him and found them wanting; let him judge those who claim to represent him now. And let no man be excluded, for reasons of means and substance from the exercise of his unfettered opinion, because political equality is the least that freedom presumes. In other words, let us have new elections on the basis of adult franchise. We can imagine the hysterical flutter that this suggestion will cause in certain dovecots. But what is the alternative, we ask? Should we allow the whole Province to go to the devil merely because constitutional niceties demand that a handful of people should be kept where they are, even though we are all convinced that their political souls have travelled long beyond the possibility of salvation? Or should we abolish democracy altogether and allow ourselves to be governed by a self-appointed bureaucracy neither answerable to the public, nor amenable to its discipline? 'But how can we have new elections before the constitution has been framed,' someone might exclaim, 'and how can the Constituent Assembly change the old basis of franchise in such haste, and in any case how can you conduct the elections in times of emergency like the present?' The answer depends entirely on how much importance we attach to the Punjab, and not to Punjab alone for what happens in Kashmir and the rest of Pakistan is closely associated with our future. If it did the Constituent Assembly no harm to make a sufficiently drastic change in the interim.

NOTE

1. 23 January 1949.

35

DISGRACE

We have learnt with horror and surprise that a political detenu, who has recently undergone a serious eye operation, is receiving medical attention in the Mayo Hospital handcuffed to his bed. The detenu in question is Mirza Mohammad Ibrahim, the labour leader. Mirza Mohammad Ibrahim is the President of the Pakistan Trade Union Federation; he is the acknowledged leader of a large section of organized labour in Western Pakistan: he is also, if we are not mistaken, a member of the Provincial Muslim League Council. All these considerations are important but we can forget them in considering the case. Let us also forget the offences, however, heinous, that Mr Ibrahim is alleged to have committed. We need not pay an iota of attention to his political convictions, and to the class or section or party that he represents. It does not matter one brass farthing what his activities are or have been or are likely to be. We are primarily concerned with one basic consideration, namely that a citizen of Pakistan is being treated by the agents of the State in a manner that smacks of sadism and bestiality. We hold that any agent of the State who behaves in a manner that is calculated to bring the good name of the State into disrepute deserves public censure and official condemnation. We hold that the authorities who ordered a sick man to be handcuffed to his bed have behaved in this disgraceful fashion. We hold that any police or executive functionary who considers that he is serving Pakistan by aping Hitler's Belsen Guards, anyone who thinks that he is securing the interests of the State by indulging in unnecessary brutalities, is no friend of Pakistan. He must be made to undergo either elementary political education to learn the meaning of freedom or elementary moral discipline to understand the meaning of humanity. Whoever is responsible for the civilized phenomenon we are discussing should probably do both. It should have been obvious to him that even a homicidal maniac could not do much harm with both his eyes bandaged and a policeman outside his door. It should have been equally obvious to him that in a free country that boasts of being civilized, even a felon is entitled to a certain amount of decency and consideration as a fellow national and a fellow human being, let alone an important political worker whose guilt is as yet unestablished by any court of law. We may or may not be interested in the individual now being subjected to this unnecessary suffering but the principle of the case effects us all. Should we permit the police brutalities of the British days to continue and allow Pakistan to be bracketed with the other semi-fascist backwoods of medieval terror or must we insist on humane and civilized standards of public and official conduct to stand ahead of the enlightened world. We have no doubt regarding the answer that our people will give. A free people are also a proud people and will not easily suffer insults and indignities from petty tyrants.

36

STALIN'S PEACE OFFER[1]

Once again undeterred by the failure of his last year's effort, Marshal Stalin has taken the initiative in throwing a peace feeler to America and the other Western Powers. In reply to four questions put to him by an American news agency, the Soviet leader gave categorical answers, which can be used as a basis for an East-West peace conference if the Anglo-American bloc so desires. Marshal Stalin directly linked the Soviet traffic restrictions with the attempt to form western Germany into a separate state and said that the Soviet Authorities would lift the Berlin restrictions if America, Britain and France desist from their plans in the Western zone. He further expressed the willingness of the Soviet Government to make, jointly with America, an antiwar declaration, to be followed by a peace pact and gradual disarmament. Marshal Stalin also expressed his preparedness to meet President Truman to discuss these matters. These statements may prove momentous, not because they represent anything new in Soviet policy, but because this reiteration of the Soviet stand paves the way for an early and amicable settlement of the differences which exist between the two sides. If the West accepts, what amounts to an invitation to peace, it is possible that the danger of the third war will be averted for a long time to come. This can happen if the politicians of the West give up their theory that a world war is inevitable, simply because capitalism and socialism cannot exist side by side. This peculiar theory, which has no basis in fact, has gained more and more adherents with every failure of the former Allies to agree on interpretation of their wartime pacts. Nevertheless, it is difficult to understand why the co-existence in peace of two systems, which could ally against a third to fight a total war in such close alliance, should be considered impossible. It is clearly necessary for both sides to do all they can to restore mankind's faith in the possibility of peace, for without this no joint declaration and no treaties will have any meaning. Once it is generally accepted that peace is not only desirable but possible, and that believers in the two systems need not fly at each other's throats, then the next steps can be contemplated. For this important task, Marshal Stalin has set the ball rolling by his resent statement. If the powers of the West co-operate, war may cease to be the vital danger it is today.

NOTE

1. *Pakistan Times*, 6 December 1949.

37

GHOSTS OF YESTERDAY

The Governor-General of Pakistan has recently been pleased to grant an interview to Malik Sir Khizar Hayat Tiwana. It is not known why the Head of the State was persuaded to receive the person most hated by the people of Pakistan, nor do we know what was discussed between the Quaid-i-Azam's successor and the agent of those who sought to thwart the Quaid's mission of securing an independent State for our people. We would like to believe that the meeting had no bearing on any matter of public concern, but if Khwaja Nazimuddin and Khizar Hayat Tiwana had met merely on the basis of past acquaintanceship to converse on the weather or *shikar*, why was the Court Circular of Pakistan blackened with a name that is synonymous with wilful national betrayal? Even if some measure of personal friendship had ever existed between the two, we have no doubt that Khwaja Nazimuddin, who has direct knowledge of the role played by Khizar Hayat, would forego the doubtful pleasure of renewing it in order to respect the sentiments of Pakistan's people. May be the interview was officially arranged, in which case the people of Pakistan, and especially of the West Punjab, have a right to ask the Central Government why a man who dare not show his face in the streets of Lahore and who is compelled to remain incognito while travelling anywhere in Pakistan, should have been honoured in this way? On the other hand if the interview was allowed on Tiwana's request, what has he to say to the Governor-General either on his own behalf or on behalf of his foreign masters? Again, if the meeting was arranged by the increasing number of his friends at the Centre, what was their particular object? Did they want him to give technical advice with regard to the working of the Safety Acts and Ordinances?

Those who may seek to minimise this issue should release that interviews by the Head of the State have a special significance which cannot be ignored. Just as a Vidkun Quisling or a John Amery could never be darkened by the figure of a Khizar Hayat. It is not our intention to discuss disrespectfully any action of the Head of the State. But the Governor-General is a symbol of the present Government and, therefore, his smallest action is rightly assumed to express official policy. It is against this new trend in the Central Government's policies of making alliances with elements despised by our people that we wish to raise our voice. By himself, Khizar Hayat deserves to be completely ignored and his name would find prominence in our columns only if he were tried by a national tribunal for his many crimes against the people. But he too is a symbol—of slavery to foreign interests, of gross betrayal and of deliberate help to forces that even today are working against our country. In itself even the grant of an interview has a limited importance, but there are other indications also to show that the Unionists and their ilk are being patronised by those in power.

This policy of joining hands with known traitors must be resisted, for in the long run it can only work as a wedge between the national leadership and the people. We are not unmindful of the virtues of forgiveness, and we would not object to our national leadership's alliance with any section of Pakistanis, who were honest in their past political differences with the overwhelming majority of our people, and who were now sincerely prepared to work for public good; but the line must be drawn when persons who knowingly worked as enemy agents try to re-enter the fold of politics by the backdoor. The Tiwanas are really no longer a danger, no matter how much their faithful friends may try to help them. The men who tried to stab us in the back at a time of the greatest danger, will never be regarded by the people with anything but well-deserved hatred. The danger is not that any of them will rise to positions of influence among the people, but that they will drag the present national leadership down to the depths of their own degradation.

We appeal to the Muslim Leaguers in the Centre to ponder over the implications of a growing association with persons who were and are regarded as public enemies. They can bring with them only their own utter demoralisation and an abject fear of any contact with the people. Their past guilt is well established, their present bankruptcy is fully known; allowing them to share power placed in the hands of the Muslim League leadership by a trusting people can only cause grave disaffection. The Central leadership should go to the people with the full confidence that they will support every policy formulated to further their welfare and strengthen the country. The present period of national reconstruction requires as much enthusiastic public cooperation as was necessary to achieve the right to establish a State of our own. Let there be no backsliding, for it can only lead to stagnation and general frustration. Bold planning, idealism, hard work and respect for the people's rights and wishes are essential to create the dizzy, dazzling structure of a great and prosperous Pakistan, the dreams of which cemented the unity of our people and saw them marching on the road to success. In this task, these ghosts of yesterday have no place and any attempt to make them join the ranks of those who seeks to lead us in the battles of today and tomorrow will only cause confusion and chaos.

38

BORROWED FEET

A controversy has spurned up in the local Press regarding the incumbent of the public post that has recently been invested with supreme executive and constitutional authority in the Province pending the restitution of a democratic and representative Government. We have deliberately kept this red herring in cold storage because we feel that any discussion, at this stage, regarding the personality of the Provincial Governor will only serve to confuse the real political issues that confront the West Punjab public today, and any praise or criticism that takes the person of the Governor for its subject will merely distract attention from the basic public demands that should be put forward and the crucial conditions that should be fulfilled to secure the future of democracy. These issues, we hold, relate not to the personality of the Governor but to the nature of electoral colleges and constituencies, to the allocation of party tickets, to the conditions of civil liberty and the duration of Governor's rule. The second reason of this controversy is that, to our mind, all autocratic regimes are unacceptable whoever holds the reins of power, and the nature of an administration under 92-A does not depend on the nationality of the administrator, nor is it likely to undergo any radical transformation if his nationality were changed. We consider that if at any time abnormal and extraordinary conditions, such as those prevailing in our Province today, under the suspension of a democratic constitutional Government necessary, the suspension should be the briefest possible and whoever is made the custodian of public rights for the duration should be made to restore these rights to where they belong at the earliest possible opportunity. It would be wrong to give the people the impression, therefore, that the fundamental thing is not the restoration of their suspended rights and the rehabilitation of democratic Government, but the habits and proclivities of the custodian and the caretaker. We hold with no 92-A type of Governor, black, white, brown, or blue, except for the minimum period that is absolutely essential and unavoidable. Having said all that, however, we do maintain, as we always have, that the employment of any foreign national in any post that carries with it important executive and administrative authority is not fully compatible with the dignity of any sovereign state. We maintain today, as we have always maintained, that in Pakistan the continuance in executive office, not only of the British Governor of the West Punjab, but of all British officers except those employed in purely technical capacities, is both unnecessary and undesirable. The present controversy in the local Press, regarding the West Punjab Governor has unfortunately became so coloured by personal and factional considerations that even this cardinal issue has been eclipsed. We agree with a section of the Press which holds that the Governor's post in the West Punjab should be immediately nationalised but we feel that to confine one's advocacy of nationalisation to one particular post, however important, is a superficial narrowing down of the problem. As for those who openly preach that that no Pakistani is good enough to govern his own land as well as a Britisher, we can only sympathise with them for the unfortunate affliction that has deprived them of the blessings of the unlamented British Raj. We do not consider it a matter of shame if we employ a whole army of foreign experts to set up for us, research laboratories, technical schools, and industrial training centres; we are prepared to welcome every foreigner whose assistance and advice in many fields, scientific industrial, or cultural we can utilise with benefit. But we do consider it a matter for deep national humiliation that, we cannot even run our own Government except with foreign human material. Any one who advocates the continued utilisation of such material in the structure of our national state, seconds the age-old Churchillian thesis that we are really unfit to govern, that we did not really achieve freedom but freedom was thrust upon us. We can think of no other argument to support continued patronage of any foreign national, whose loyalties belong elsewhere, in the humblest executive post, let alone the post of a virtually autocratic satrap in a Province. It may be said that such patronage is but an expression of friendship and goodwill towards a sister member of the Commonwealth. The argument would be cogent indeed if we were also some times asked to supply a Speaker for the House of Commons or for a financial expert to control the economy of Australia. Surely we can also boast of some Pakistanis who would do credit to the highest office under any Government but no other of the Commonwealth has so far even considered this type of import. It can also be said that but for the presence of British Governors, British Police and British Army and Civilian officers, we might make a hash of our administration owing to our inexperience. The answer to this one is simple. If we cannot learn the art of administration except by making a hash of it in the first instance, then let us make a hash of it by all means. We shall never learn otherwise. It is time we accepted the elementary dictum that no one can learn to walk on borrowed feet, and the sooner we start using our won feet the lesser the chances of our tripping at every step, when our borrowed feet rejoin the body where they actually belong.

39

INDONESIA WEEK

The West Punjab Democratic Youth League deserves to be congratulated on its decision to organise an 'Indonesia Week' with the purpose of explaining the issues involved in the Indonesian situation, mobilising public opinion and enlisting help in favour of the Republic. It is important for our people to realise that despite the two World Wars fought in the name of democracy and freedom, these two essentials to human happiness and progress are still absent from many parts of the world. Many powerful nations, paying formal homage to democracy and freedom, seem to be determined to ensure that there shall be no extension of either, if it is going to infringe on their special privilege, provides a classic example of what Mr Winston Churchill meant when, as Great Britain's Prime Minister, he said that the Atlantic Charter would not apply to any Eastern country. It also illustrates how the functioning of the United Nations can be deliberately retarded and blatant aggression allowed to cloak itself in hypocritical words, when the majority group wishes to favour a sister imperialism. Remembering the agony of our own political bondage, Pakistan's sympathy is naturally with the Indonesians. Apart from sentiment, engendered among other things by ties of religion and colour, the worsening world situation should compel us to look beyond our frontiers and investigate the causes of this perennial international tension, so that we can throw our weight on the side of justice, righteousness and peace. It is proper that the lead in encouraging our people to look beyond the horizon should be taken by the country's youth; it is their privilege to blend idealism and enthusiasm with realistic objectivity—a combination which the short sighted and narrow-minded profession politicians might well emulate.

40

PILGRIMAGE TO WASHINGTON

Two propaganda machines, both ranking among the world's largest and most powerful are now busy producing, publishing and disseminating a mass of propaganda in order to present Mr Nehru's four-week visit to America as an event of great international significance. Perhaps neither Indian nor American evaluations of the significance of this much-advertised tour of India's Premier may be regarded as being completely erroneous. This view, however, is subject to one important qualification, namely, that the likely consequences of a possible Indo-American accord, which may understandably be far-reaching insofar as they affect either one or both of the two parties have been so magnified as to suggest a serious impact on other nations' behaviours and policies. Neither the exuberance of the words nor the vague terminology in which laudatory remarks about Mr Nehru's leadership and the democracy that he represents have been couched hide the plain fact that the men who matter in America today view India as the natural leader of Asia—a place which during the Second World War was assigned by America to Kuomintang China and this decision naturally involves that India will be built up as the bastion for the defence of the West's commercial, economic, political and strategic interests in Asia. If this 'leadership' is not a purely academic or moral nature, it is also obvious that India will be provided with the resources and the wherewithal to make its political and economic position strong vis-à-vis other Asian countries. Inspired reports appearing in influential sections of the world, particularly American and Indian Press, have indicated that in the matter of the implementation of President Truman's programme for 'aid' to the under-developed countries as well in vital issues affecting the West's political strategy in Asia, India will be given a position which will accord well with its role of 'leadership'. Whether or not Asian countries, especially India's neighbours, and the movements for the social and democratic emancipation of the Asian peoples will succumb to the pressure and interference which will inevitably result from the proposed combination of American and the Republic-to-be of India is a different matter.

Mr Nehru's visit to Washington has provided an occasion to the protagonists of an Indo-American partnership to wax eloquent in praise of India's cultural heritage, political institutions and the political elements who now govern that country with the alleged intention of leading the masses forward to happiness and contentment. The vast masses of the American people, who today know as little about the India of Mr Nehru as they knew about the China of Mr Chiang in the period following Pearl Harbour, are being told that to back the present Indian regime is the best and the surest way of rendering fraternal assistance to Asia's starving multitudes. What the common people in America have been told is that India is a new sovereign nation which is led by an enlightened, democratically-minded and progressive set of people, that the present state of democratic liberties in India does not leave much to be desired, that the Congress party rule is responsible and responsive, that the present socio-economic structure is being modified to ensure the greatest good of the greatest number and that the present pattern of Indian nationalism is one which is ideally suited to the development of all cultures, languages and minorities. What the Americans have not been told is that India is being made to suffer the mono-party dictatorship of the Congress, which, because of its open subservience to the interests of the moneyed classes, is being rapidly alienated from the people and is fast undergoing the same process of degeneration and disintegration which was manifest in the affairs of China's Kuomintang from 1927 onwards. What the Americans have not been told is that the Indian ruling classes are retaining in its entirety the present semi-colonial and semi-feudal structure of society in order to perpetuate exploitation, are imprisoning thousands of political workers for the sin of ventilating popular grievances, and are compromising with the dark forces of social reaction with a view to imposing a Fascist regime on the people and denying cultural and linguistic freedom to the Indian minorities.

Mr Nehru's address to the American Congress, provided one is able to discern the writing between the lines, gives a clear enough indication of the why and wherefore of his pilgrimage to Washington, that is, of what he is going to ask for in America and what he is offering in return. In the first place, it is common knowledge that America, faced as it is with an economic crisis at home and a political crisis abroad, is not going to waste its resources on any country which cannot be relied upon to produce the desired results primarily in the direction of its international alignments and in the field of attracting American investments. Mr Nehru knew clearly that without a clear, unambiguous statement on these two matters all his praises of 'this great democracy' and the abundant talk of India's 'goodwill' towards America will not cut much ice. Consequently, in his address to the US Congress he controverted his earlier thesis that the aim of the Indian foreign policy was to steer clear of the Big Power conflict by declaring that 'where freedom is endangered, or justice threatened, or where aggression takes place, we cannot be and shall not be neutral.' It should be borne in mind that these phrases were used in the full knowledge that the audience was American and that it gave its own particular meanings to terms like 'freedom', 'justice' and 'aggression'. The abandonment of the myth of Indian neutrality now makes it possible for India openly to assume commitments in respect of Western, especially American, interests in the backward countries of Asia.

Mr Nehru's remarks that India would gladly welcome mechanical and technological aid 'on terms which are of mutual benefit' does not rule out the possibility of the terms being for the most part in favour of one party. Chiang Kai-shek has never abandoned the pretence that the terms on which he received American aid favoured China as well as America. The possibilities of a loan and of substantial technological assistance can only be considered bright when India agrees to open its doors more widely for the penetration of US capital into Indian economy. The logic of currency devaluation, the downward tendency of the Indian stock market and the general decline in Indian industrial production strongly favours the adoption of this course by India.

41

THE SERVANTS OF THE PEOPLE

Activity on the Ministerial front in West Punjab continues with unabated vigour. There has been another demand by the 'opposition' group (if our readers will pardon this abuse of a respectable term) for a quicker showdown, another evasive manoeuvre by the Ministerial group and the latest gossip is that the Centre intends to make another effort to play the referee and somehow call it quits. We need hardly offer an apology, therefore, to revert to the theme of our political ills that we began discussing under another heading some days ago. We promised to review the conduct of the two political factions in the Province during and after the recent meeting of the Muslim League Assembly Party. Why was this meeting called? This is the first question that is likely to suggest itself to any disinterested observer who has watched the profound and undisturbed slumbers of the Party during the long summer days and the longer winter nights. No new public question of outstanding importance had arisen to justify this hasty gathering of the clans, no new tragedy had befallen, no new blessing descended from the skies. We certainly have problems relating to a slack and inefficient leadership and administration, there is the scarcity of food and the enormous rise in prices, but these have been there all the time and were as acute before Messrs Noon and Daultana promised to join the Mamdot Cabinet a few weeks ago and were so unceremoniously jilted by the Khan. The legislators who called the meeting were also good enough to express their solicitude for Kashmir but here again it is difficult to think of any novel aspect of the situation that could have suddenly dawned on their consciousness when the fighting was about to end. Why then was this meeting called? Since its object was neither a Christmas carousal nor a political revolution, the meeting was obviously meant as it turned out to be no more than another stratagem for the long-coveted prize of Party leadership. There is nothing wrong either with the desire or with the effort to change an incompetent or undesirable leader. But there is an honest and straight-forward way of doing things and there are also ways that are crooked and dishonest. If the people who called the meeting had no other object in view except to express their lack of confidence in the Premier, the honest and straightforward course for them was to give notice of a straight no-confidence motion in the first place. Why did they wrap up their real intentions in all sorts of innocuous-looking resolutions? Because, you simpleton', We can hear a master strategist reply, 'it is unwise to expose your hand before you are sure of your cards. Votes are tricky things and our MLAs are more slippery than the slipperiest eel. It would have been silly to commit yourself to a trial of strength before you had obtained the thumb-impressions of all your potential partisans to proclaim their allegiance.' The whole show, therefore began with a trickery. The meeting was called on false pretences and the leaders who called it displayed some dexterity in political manoeuvre but hardly exhibited either political courage or democratic decency. This is fact number one. When the Party actually met however, it was the turn of the West Punjab Premier to flout all cannons of democratic decency by his flat refusal to acknowledge the factual if not the formal verdict of the Party he is supposed to lead. It has not been contested that forty-two members of the party did sign a document expressing their lack of confidence in the Premier. It has also not been contested that a large number of members insisted that the Premier should put his leadership to the test of the vote there and then or as soon after it as possible. It is also not denied that many hard things were said regarding the working of the present Cabinet and the title and ability of the Khan of Mamdot to lead the Party were seriously brought into question. If the Khan had, as he claims he has, the majority behind him the honest and straightforward course for him was to face the no confidence motion like a man. Nay, in view of the nature and the volume of adverse criticism he should have insisted on a vote of confidence to justify his continuance in office even though no formal no confidence motion was moved. If some paltry constitutional consideration stood in the way of this proper and manly course, he should at least have fixed the earliest possible date to vindicate his honour. Instead of this he allowed the shafts of bitter criticism to rain on his impervious skin and then slunk away from the fight hugging his Premiership to his bosom. This inglorious exit was followed by an inane statement by the Party Secretary that the Khan still commanded a majority and the meeting to consider the no-confidence motion would be called in 'due course'. Why did the Khan need a 'due course' if he already commanded a majority. 'Because, you simpleton' the master strategist from the other side answers, 'It is unwise to expose your bag as long as there is a chance of adding the two birds in the bush to the one bird in hand'. The show, therefore, ended with a trickery similar to the one with which it began. The Premier displayed a dexterity in manoeuvre equalling that of his opponents and a lack of courage and seemliness also matching theirs. This is fact number two. Since the inconclusive ending of this meeting the two parties have persisted in the same tactics; there is extreme haste for the next meeting on one side and extreme tardiness on the other side. One group is anxious that the meeting should be held before its majority melts away, the other is keen that it should not be held until it does. Thus 'the servants of the people' who have no other care in the world except to serve, continue to strive as desperately as they can for mastery over the people. One of is the Premier of the Province, the other its President. The tussle is far from ended and we shall continue with an analysis of the post-Christmas developments.

42

SINDH HARI REPORT

Popular resentment in Sindh at the Government's refusal to publish the minute of dissent appended to the Haris Committee Report is entirely justified. The dissenting note, however unpalatable it might be to the big landowners, is really a part of the Report and its arbitrary suppression can only be regarded as highly improper. Since it is widely known that the unpublished Minority Report had strongly urged the desirability of introducing radical changes in the existing Tenancy Laws, the Government decisions acquires a partisan character highly unworthy of a Muslim League Ministry. The plea that the third Member, who happens to be a senior Civil Servant had in his report gone beyond the Committee's terms of reference is a silly bureaucratic argument which provides no excuse for the unprecedented Government action. We hope the Sindh Ministry will have the sense to retrace its step, for the report relates to one of the most important problems in the country, still awaiting solution by the various Muslim League Governments.

CHRONOLOGY

Name	Faiz Ahmed Khan
Literary Name	Faiz Ahmed Faiz
Date of Birth	13 February 1911
Place of Birth	Kala Qadir Town, District Sialkot
Father	Khan Bahadur Sultan Mohammad Khan
Mother	Sultan Fatima

Early Education

1915	Began his education by memorizing Holy Quran at the age of four years
1916	He entered Moulvi Ibrahim Sialkoti's famous school for education—Arabic, Persian and Urdu
1921	He got admission to Class IV in Scotch Mission High School, Sialkot and passed with distinction

Secondary Education

1927	Passed Matriculation in first division from the Punjab University
1929	Passed intermediate in first division from Murray College, Sialkot

High Education

1931	Passed BA (Honours) in Arabic from the Government College, Lahore
1932	Passed MA (English Literature) with distinction from the Government College, Lahore
1933	Passed his MA in Arabic in the first division, from Oriental College, Lahore.
Teachers	Shamsul Ulema Meer Syed Hasan (Arabic), Yusuf Saleem Chishti (Urdu)
Syllabus Teachers	Ahmad Shah Bukhari, Sufi Tabassum, Maulvi Mohammad Shafi
Literary Teachers	Dr Taseer, Maulana Salik, Maulana Chiragh Hasan Hasrat, Pundit Hari Chand Akhtar

Service and Other Engagements

1935	Lecturer in English at MAO College, Amritsar
1936	Took full part in the establishment of Progressive Writers Association
1940	Appointed English teacher in Hailey College of Commerce, Lahore
1942	Joined the Army as Captain in 1942 and worked in the department of Public Relations in Delhi
1943	Was promoted to the rank of Major
1944	Was promoted to the rank of Lt. Colonel.
1947	Resigned from the Army and returned to Lahore
1947–1951	Labour Advisory Committee, Government of the Punjab
1951	Vice President, Pakistan Trade Union Federation
1948–1970	Member, Executive Council, World Peace Council; President APP Trust
1959	Appointed as Secretary, Pakistan Arts Council and worked in that capacity till 1962
1964	Principal, Haji Abdullah Haroon College, Karachi
1964–1972	Vice President, Pakistan Arts Council, Karachi
1974–1977	Advisor, Cultural Affairs, Ministry of Education, Government of Pakistan
1958	Founder Member, Afro-Asian Literary Association

Editorship and Journalism

1938–39	Editor of monthly *Adab-e-Latif*, Lahore
1947–58	Chief editor of daily *Pakistan Times*, Lahore; daily *Imroze*, Lahore and weekly *Lail-o-Nihar*, Lahore
1978–84	Chief editor of Afro-Asian literary quarterly *Lotus*, Beirut

Detention

1951	Arrested in Rawalpindi Conspiracy Case under Pakistan Safety Act on 9 March
1955	Released on 6 April
1958	Again arrested under Safety Act and was released in April 1959

Marriage

1941	Married to British born Miss Alys George. Sheikh Abdullah performed the Nikah rites
1942	First daughter Salima was born
1945	Second daughter Moneeza was born

Honours

1946	The British government conferred on him the title of MBE
1962	the Soviet government gave him the world-famous Lenin Peace prize. The views expressed by Faiz on this occasion demonstrated his humanism, fearlessness his love for speaking truth, frankness and his love for freedom of expression

Books

Collection of Poems

1941	*Naqsh-e-Faryadi*
1952	*Dast-e-Saba*
1956	*Zindan Nama*
1965	*Dast-e-Teh Sang*
1971	*Sar-e-Wadi Seena*
1978	*Sham Shehar Yaran*
1981	*Mere Dil, Mere Musafir*
1997	*Nuskha Haiya Wafa*

Collection of Prose Writing

1962	*Meezan* (essays in literary criticism)
1971	*Saleebain mere dareeche main* (letters)
	Muta-e-Lah-o-Qalam
	Pakistan Times Ke Idarye
1981	*Mah-o-Saal; Ashnai* (Travelogue)
1973	*Safar Nama Cuba*

Death

1984	On 19 November in Lahore